On the Trail of
Richard III

On the Trail of
Richard III

KRISTIE DEAN

AMBERLEY

This book is dedicated to Jon and my family for their love and support.

First published 2015
This edition published 2016

Amberley Publishing
The Hill, Stroud
Gloucestershire, GL5 4EP

www.amberley-books.com

British Library Cataloguing in Publication Data.
A catalogue record for this book is available from the British
Library.

ISBN 978 1 4456 5597 8 (paperback)
ISBN 978 1 4456 3662 7 (ebook)

Typeset in 11pt on 15pt Sabon.
Typesetting and Origination by Amberley Publishing.
Printed in the UK.

Contents

Contents

Acknowledgments

I would like to thank the following people for their contributions towards helping make this book a reality:

St Mary the Virgin and All Saints, Fotheringhay: Brian Rogers, Vicar.

Ludlow Castle: Sonja Belchere, Custodian.

Wijk bij Duurstede, Utrecht: Esmee Foppen, Kasteel Duurstede; Ron Helsloot, Head of Educational Department, Dom Cathedral.

The Palace of Placentia: Jonathan Partington, Greenwich Heritage Centre.

Lambeth Palace: Amy Wilson, Events and Tours Manager.

Middleham: Debbie Allen, Museum of Yorkshire Dales National Park Authority.

Church of St Mary and St Alkelda: Trevor Peacock, Church Warden.

Palace of Sheen/Shene: Bev Kerr, Council for British Archaeology.

Pontefract Castle: Ian Downes, Senior Heritage Officer.

York Minster: Sarah Menys, Administration Assistant, York Minster Historic Collections.

York Guildhall: Dean Leighton-Eshelby, Civic Officer; Fiona Young, Visitors Centre Co-ordinator.

Cawood Castle: Natalie Earl, Media Assistant, the Landmark Trust; Linda Shortt.

Abbey of Stratford Langthorne: Revd Stennett Kirby, West Ham Parish Church; Nicolas Weedon, HMDW Architects.

Margate: Robin Colyer, Local Historian.

Norwich Halls: Sharon Page, Communications Officer, Norwich City Council; Shaun Canon, The Halls Manager.

Norwich Bishop's Palace: Coralie Nichols, PA to the Lord Bishop of Norwich and the Archdeacon of Norwich; the Very Revd Jane Hedges.

Norwich: Frank Meeres, Norwich Records Office; Jonathan Draper, Senior Archivist, Norwich Records Office.

Castle Rising: Lord Howard; Matt Smith, Castle Rising History Group.

Sudeley Castle: Sian Jocelyn, Visitor Services Manager.

King's Lynn: Alison Gifford, Visit Norfolk; Hannah Verge, Archivist, Norfolk Record Office.

Low Countries: Hans van Felius, Senior Archivist at the Noord-Hollands Archief, Haarlem, the Netherlands; Peter van Druenen, local historian and author.

Sandal Castle: Ian Downes, Senior Heritage Officer; Wendy Jewitt, Library Area Supervisor, Wakefield Council.

Coventry: Rob Orland, local historian.

St Mary's Guildhall, Coventry: Marcus Lynch, General Manager.

Tewkesbury Cathedral: Patrick Webley, Honorary Abbey Archivist.

Calais: Office de Tourisme Intercommunal Calais Côte d'Opale; Dominique Darré.

St Omer, France: Laura Lévêque, Régisseur des œuvres des musées de Saint-Omer.

St Mary's Barnard Castle: Revd Alec Harding; Kim Harding.

Palace of Westminster: Anooshka Rawden, Collections Manager, Society of Antiquaries, London; Virginia Smithson, Department of Britain, Europe and Prehistory, The British Museum; Tracey West, Commercial Visitors Services Team Leader, Houses of Parliament.

Northampton: Suzie Lennox, Customer Access Supervisor for Northamptonshire County Council's Record Office.

St Alban's Cathedral: David Kelsall, Archivist, St Alban's Cathedral Archive; Jane Kelsall, author of *Humphrey, Duke of Gloucester, 1391–1447*.

Reading: Angela Houghton, Collection Systems Curator, Reading Museum and Town Hall.

Nottingham Castle: Gordon A. B. Young, City Archaeologist, Nottingham; Marie McLardy, Heritage Site Services Co-ordinator.

Gainsborough Old Hall: Jane Fennell; Victoria Mason Hines, Site Co-ordinator; Madeleine Hawkins, Business Support Assistant.

Lincoln: James Stevenson, Collections Access Officer, Lincolnshire Archives; Angie Clay, Site Co-ordinator, Lincoln Castle.

Leicester: Dr Alan Brine, Head of Archives and Resource Management, De Montfort University; Frances Lund, Assistant Archivist, Archives and Special Collections, De Montfort University.

Leicester Cathedral: Liz Hudson, Director of Communications, Diocese of Leicester.

Leicester, St Mary de Castro: Terry Doughty.

Leicester, King Richard Visitor Centre: Iain Gordon, Visitor Centre Director; Sarinda Bains, Marketing Officer, Leicester City Council; Emma Lay, Marketing and Events Manager.

Fastolf Place, London and Magdalen College, Oxford: Dr Robin Darwall-Smith, Archivist at Magdalen College.

Woodstock Manor: Karen Wiseman, Head of Education, Blenheim Palace.

Gloucester: Lesley Downing, Archive Assistant, Worcestershire Archive and Archaeology Service; David Evans, Deputy Head, King's School; Christopher Jeens, Archivist, Gloucester Cathedral Library; Teresa Jones, Senior Archive Assistant, Worcestershire Archive and Archaeology Service; Sarah Aitken, Gloucestershire Archives.

Salisbury: Valerie Goodrich, Salisbury Museum; Louise Tunnard, Marketing & Admin Officer, Salisbury Museum.

Exeter: Josephine Halloran, Heritage Assistant, Devon Heritage Centre.

Cambridge: Dr Patricia McGuire, Archivist, King's College.

Scarborough: Simon Roe, Site Manager, Scarborough Castle; Jake Tatman, Historic Properties Steward.

Kenilworth Castle: Holly Woodward, Property Manager at Kenilworth Castle; G. D. Symes, Town Clerk.

Bosworth Battlefield: Richard Mackinder, Bosworth Fieldwork Team; JoeAnn Ricca, President, Richard III Foundation.
Richard III Society Library (American Branch): Susan Higginbotham, Librarian and Author/Historian.

Special thanks goes to my husband, Jonathan, for managing to keep our household together while I spent an enormous amount of time engrossed in the fifteenth century, and to the rest of my family, friends and co-workers who indulged my forays into the medieval world. I would especially like to thank my parents and in-laws for always being supportive, even when it meant time out of their already busy schedules. I would also like to take this time to acknowledge Sharon Bennett Connolly and Anne Marie Bouchard, co-administrators of my Facebook group, Richard III and His World, for their time and support. Thanks as well to my travelling companions, Autumn Speegle and Valerie Brook, for allowing Richard III to dictate our travel itineraries, not only once, but time and again.

I would also like to thank Amy Licence, Susan Higginbotham, Wendy Dunn, Natalie Grueninger, Sarah Morris, and Kathryn Warner for being willing to answer all sorts of publishing queries. Many thanks to Rachel Madison, Michelle Hubbard, Daniel Newman, Heather Sullivan, Dawn Poore, Meagan Butler, Lisa O'Donnell, John Smith, Mark Garner, Katherine Trott and Angie Parker for their encouragement. I would also like to thank the team at Amberley for their support, especially my editors Nicola Gale, Emily Brewer and Christian Duck, and also Sarah Greenwood and Amy Greaves.

Introduction

Richard III has always fascinated me. In fact, the fascination has been with me for so long that I cannot pinpoint an exact date when it began. I do remember writing an impassioned short story about Richard III in a Western Civilisations course at university. A combined obsession with two historical figures from two different dynasties, Richard III and Anne Boleyn, led me to pursue a career in the study of history. Receiving my master's degree in History in 2004, I left the world of public relations and began teaching my passion to others, both at secondary and at community college level.

In 2012, my passion was fired anew when the body of Richard III was located under a car park in Leicester. As with everything else associated with Richard, the find elicited controversy. Factions developed even within the society established in his name. There were those who refused, and still refuse, to believe that the remains are Richard's, despite DNA evidence. Even some noted historians have cast doubt on the conclusions of the find.

The belief that Richard's body was tossed into the river was also a difficult one to overcome, even though there was no contemporary source that mentioned the event. For others, the problem became where to bury Richard. Although other locations, such as Westminster Abbey and St George's Chapel at Windsor, were suggested, the main debate seemed to be between those who wanted him buried at York and those who wanted him buried at Leicester. A lawsuit to have Richard reinterred at York was brought by the Plantagenet Alliance, a group of people claiming relationship to the king.

Ultimately, the Alliance lost the lawsuit and plans began to reinter the king at Leicester Cathedral, which is the nearest consecrated ground to the place where Richard's remains were discovered. The next controversial decision was that of how to rebury a Roman Catholic king in an Anglican church. Others began to argue over the design of the tomb. Nothing associated with Richard seems to be without controversy, and this is perhaps what makes him so intriguing to so many people.

Richard III is perhaps the most controversial king not just in England but throughout Europe. His very name can polarise historical meetings, turning the tamest historian into a veritable tiger protecting his or her cub. In his lifetime, Richard seemed to be a walking contradiction, loyal to his brother but seen as a murderer of innocents in the death of his two young nephews. During the reign of the Tudor monarchs, both Shakespeare and More added to this perception, with Shakespeare turning his fictional Richard into an evil, hunchbacked man capable of murdering not only his nephews in order to claim the crown, but also his wife in order to marry his niece. Even though Shakespeare was writing a play, many later confused the work of dramatic fiction with reality and passed it on as such.

During the twentieth century, Richard's tarnished reputation received a helping hand. In 1924, the Richard III Society was formed, dedicated to the arduous task of ensuring that Richard received a balanced assessment in history and promoting scholarship into the time period. Other organisations, such as the Richard III Foundation, sprung up with similar goals. Primary sources were re-examined, and other plausible explanations for events surrounding the reign of Richard III were sought.

On 22 August 1485, the field of Bosworth saw the death of more than just a king; it saw the death of a long-reigning dynasty, as well as the end of era. Many historians date the ending of the medieval period at the beginning of the Tudor reign, making Richard III both the last medieval and the last Plantagenet king of England.

Introduction

For the past thirteen years, I have travelled to the United Kingdom to visit historic sites – many of them associated with the Plantagenets. In the process, I have amassed a tremendous amount of historic research. There is something about standing in a castle or church and knowing the history of Richard's connection to it that brings him alive in one's mind. It is as tantalisingly close to time travel as one can get, and I wanted to help bring this feeling alive for others.

At every location, I would think, 'I should write a history travel guide'. After years of thinking about it, I decided the time had come to pick up the pen and get to it. It was not hard to decide about whom I was going to write. Richard III was top choice, and it seemed like an especially good time to write the book as interest in Richard was high. More people had begun to want to search out locations that Richard had visited, so I was surprised to find that no comprehensive guide existed. This book has been written to help both the armchair traveller and the person who is able to visit the locations first hand. It is designed to bring each location alive, not only to help the reader and the visitor use it to place Richard in each location with historical context but also to shed a bit of light on the history of the location itself. Additionally, it is my hope that this guide will serve as a resource for future generations in discovering what sites were extant when Richard's body was found. One of the main purposes of the book is to show Richard in a new light – to illuminate his character through the places and events that shaped him into the man he became.

During the research for this book, I sifted through many primary and secondary documents related to Richard and found, to my amazement, that many locations had lost sight of their connection to Richard. Some early histories of locations glossed over Richard as if he did not even exist, choosing to skip from Edward IV straight to Henry VII. Not every location that I found made it in to the book, as some were mere one-night stays with little connection to Richard. Some were included despite the fact that there is no extant site, because these were important in Richard's history. A few locations, such as the King Richard III Visitor Centre, made it into the book even though Richard never visited, because they focus on him.

As we learn more about Richard and Bosworth, some accepted ideas may need to be tossed out and new ones examined. I have included the latest information possible regarding Bosworth, but with each new discovery the current scholarship changes. Hopefully, soon we will have a better understanding of where the battle occurred. Several people, as well as new organisations such as the Bosworth Battlefield Heritage Society, are leading the way and trying to raise awareness of how much work still needs to be done.

Because of the nature of this book, I have chosen not to use footnotes or endnotes. This does not indicate a lack of research. With two exceptions, I have travelled to each location in the book, and I have talked with local historians, archivists and authors to gather the in-depth knowledge to write a book of this scope. I have also read extensively, spending most of my days engrossed in the fifteenth century both in primary sources and books about Richard and in books about the time period itself. When possible, I have located early histories of each location to flesh out the history of the place even before Richard arrived.

As with all things Richard, there are many contested topics. When faced with a conflict, I have chosen to go with what I feel the primary documents support. Several historians dispute with each other on the accepted scholarship, and even primary sources contradict each other. For example, when discussing Richard's youth, historians disagree on the dates he spent under the care of Richard, Earl of Warwick. I have chosen to use the accepted view of current historians who feel that Richard would have been with Warwick from around 1465.

As the fate of the princes in the Tower has been a subject of much speculation in many books through the years, most people have already come to a decision about the princes. I have chosen not to delve into that controversy as it is beyond the scope of this book.

One theory fairly recent to scholarship is that Richard may not have immediately set sail with Edward IV to the Low Countries. Based on evidence, it appears that Richard stayed behind for a few weeks, perhaps trying to raise men to help Edward. While researching the history of King's Lynn, I came across a reference about the *Corporation's Hall Book II* entry on Edward's visit. Richard was not mentioned in the entry, leading me to believe that he was not initially with Edward during his flight from England. This theory is supported by the short article 'Richard was Late', written by Livia Visser-Fuchs, as well as Josephine Wilkinson in her book *Richard: The Young King to Be*.

How to Use This Guidebook

The book has been arranged in a loose chronological framework of seven categories: Early Life, The King's Brother, Edward's Right Hand, Lord of the North, The King's Uncle, King of the Realm, and Richard's Final Days. With few exceptions, each location is introduced only once, even though there are several places that Richard visited numerous times. I have tried to include the location in the category where it first appears so that it fits into a chronology. Once the location is introduced, every association it has with Richard and the York family is explored. London was the biggest exception. I included locations in London throughout the book as Richard visited there so often during his lifetime. Leicester was another location that was hard to place. Even though Richard visited it more than once, I felt it really belonged in Richard's Final Days.

Each entry is meant to be able to stand alone as its own guide, as well as being part of the greater whole. Readers can read the various sections as they travel without losing the benefit of the entire book. This means that at certain times, historical facts are repeated across sections if they relate to more than one location. In some instances, Richard visited several locations within one city during different visits. When this has happened, I have grouped the city together as a whole, with each location receiving its own subsection. As an example, Richard visited York several times throughout his life. I have chosen to place York in the chronology at the first point

Richard visited it, which means that his entire history with the city is explored then.

I have included locations that no longer have any visible remains as well as locations that are now privately owned, in addition to those that are easily accessible. As one of the purposes of the book is to explore how Richard's world shaped him into the man he became, it seemed imperative to include as many locations as possible that had a hand in influencing his story.

However, there are a few sites that I have not included because all we have in regards to the location is the knowledge that Richard was in the general area. These locations, while excellent tourist attractions, did not offer much for someone interested in Richard. I also have not included a few sites that Richard did visit because his visit there was of such short duration. These sites, including Berkhamsted, Minster Lovell and the Angel Inn at Grantham, are worthy of a visit, but did not make it into the book. Despite recent speculation that Richard might have been born at Berkhamsted, most historians agree that he was likely born at Fotheringhay.

Much of Richard's early years are shrouded in the mists of time, so I have chosen to only include sites that historians are fairly certain he would have visited or those that have been found in the primary sources. On one occasion, I have included a castle with important ties to the York family, but no obvious visit by Richard. When a location's association with Richard seems to be tenuous, I have made that clear.

Contact information is given at the end of each section so that readers can easily locate current opening times and prices. The postcode of each extant location is given as well.

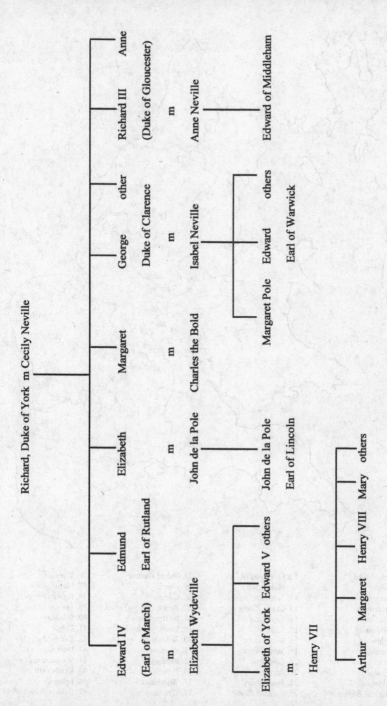

Richard, Duke of York m Cecily Neville

Edward IV (Earl of March) m Elizabeth Wydeville

Edmund Earl of Rutland

Elizabeth m John de la Pole → John de la Pole Earl of Lincoln

Margaret m Charles the Bold

George Duke of Clarence m Isabel Neville

other

Richard III (Duke of Gloucester) m Anne Neville

Anne

Margaret Pole → Edward Earl of Warwick, others

Edward Earl of Warwick

Edward of Middleham

Elizabeth of York m Henry VII

Edward V others

Arthur Margaret Henry VIII Mary others

York family tree.

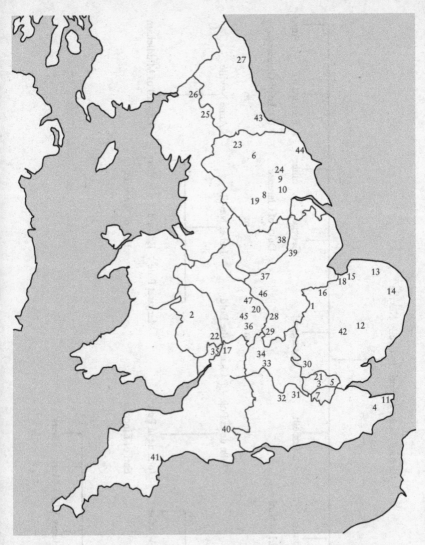

Map Key:
1. Fotheringhay
2. Ludlow
3. London
4. Canterbury
5. Greenwich
6. Middleham
7. Richmond
8. Pontefract
9. York
10. Cawood
11. Margate
12. Bury St Edmunds
13. Our Lady of
    Walsingham
14. Norwich
15. Castle Rising
16. Crowland
17. Sudeley
18. King's Lynn
19. Sandal Castle
20. Coventry
21. Barnet
22. Tewkesbury
23. Barnard Castle
24. Sheriff Hutton
25. Penrith
26. Carlisle
27. Berwick-upon-Tweed
28. Northampton
29. Stony Stratford
30. St Albans
31. Windsor
32. Reading
33. Oxford
34. Woodstock
35. Gloucester
36. Warwick
37. Nottingham
38. Gainsborough
39. Lincoln
40. Salisbury
41. Exeter
42. Cambridge
43. Durham
44. Scarborough
45. Kenilworth
46. Leicester
47. Bosworth Battlefield

Part I

Early Life

Richard was born into a country that was on the brink of civil war. His family were destined to be key players in the conflict that would divide the country into the factions of Lancaster and York. This division would find its way even into his own family. While we do not know very much about Richard's earliest years, most historians agree that he was born at Fotheringhay Castle.

Fotheringhay, Northamptonshire

All that is left of this once impressive castle is a grassy mound by the river and a few fragments of masonry from the keep. Standing here, it is hard to picture the busy, bustling place this fortress once was. It is almost as if the execution of Mary, Queen of Scots, held in the Great Hall of Fotheringhay in February 1587 left an indelible mark of sadness on the area.

The original motte-and-bailey castle is thought to have been built by the Norman Earl of Northampton and Huntingdon, Simon de Senlis, around AD 1100. It subsequently passed to Scottish hands through the marriage of his widow, Maud, to King David of Scotland. By the time the castle came to Marie de St Pol in the fourteenth century, it was walled, moated and built of stone. After her death, the castle reverted to the crown, and Edward III granted it to his son. Edmund, the 1st Duke of York and Richard's great-grandfather, enlarged the castle in the shape of a fetterlock during his tenure as owner. In the fifteenth century, the castle served as an administrative centre for the dukes of York.

Birthplace of a King

Richard was born on 2 October 1452 in the keep at Fotheringhay. The eleventh child of his parents – Richard, Duke of York, and Cecily Neville, the Rose of Raby – no one expected him to become king. In a poem about the children of the Duke of York, the 'Clare Roll' simply stated that 'Richard liveth yet'. Earlier biographers of Richard took this to mean that he was a sickly child, but that is only one possible interpretation of the meaning of the poem. As Richard was the seventh son, but only the fourth one to survive, it might be the poet was pessimistic about his chances. In any event, this formidable castle on the banks of the River Nene was where Richard spent his formative years.

Richard was born into a world fraught with peril. The Lancastrian Henry VI was an ineffectual king whose weakness allowed competing factions to grow at court. Prior to Richard's birth, his father had gone to London with more than 5,000 men to make an appeal to the king. He was upset, in part because of his exclusion from the king's council and because of accusations of treason. A direct appeal to the king seemed to be his only hope. In addition to this, Henry VI did not have an heir, and York felt he should be heir presumptive. This situation was difficult, and was made harder as each side grew more suspicious of the other.

Part of the problem was that York had a claim to the throne that was as strong, if not stronger, than the claim of the king. Henry VI was descended from Edward III's third son, John of Gaunt, but York was a descendant of Edward III's second son (through the female line) and also Edward III's fourth son. For a time, York was able to work within the government, but the ascent of Somerset in the king's favour showed York that he would not be able to institute reform. In 1452, York refused to go to a council meeting and headed instead to London, trying to raise forces. Unfortunately for him, he was not supported, and he had to apologise to the king.

For a short time, he stayed out of the public eye, but this temporary solution would not last for long.

Richard's constant companions in his early years would have been his two siblings closest in age – his sister Margaret, and his brother George. Their parents would have been in and out of Fotheringhay as Cecily often travelled with her husband. There was probably a flurry of excitement every time they visited the castle.

The Castle

The view from the mound is impressive, with the spires of the collegiate church of St Mary the Virgin and All Saints rising in the distance. The River Nene winds around the mound and disappears into the distance on its way to the Wash. Visitors today will often find canal boats docked on the sleepy river beside the castle site. During Richard's time, the river would have been humming with activity. On Richard and Edward's visit in 1469 the view would have been one of constant commotion, as people scurried about in order to greet the king.

A moat surrounded the castle and the entrance would have been through a gatehouse. The great stone keep would have sat atop the mound surrounded by a wall, and would have been accessible through steps leading from the inner bailey to the top. During the time of Marie de St Pol, the castle was said to have a large hall, two chambers, two chapels, a kitchen, a bake house and a porter's lodge. When Richard lived there, the windows might have been ornamented by a falcon enclosed in a fetterlock, which was an emblem for the House of York.

It is hard to picture the great keep today, as nothing remains. Sitting atop the mound and using your imagination, you can picture the activity below as people wandered in and out of the lodgings, kitchen and chapel.

Even though Richard's elder brothers had already left home before he was born, it is likely that Richard probably saw his brothers here, at least on great occasions such as Christmas. It is easy to imagine the great hall packed with people enjoying Christmas festivities and a young Richard enthralled by his older brothers.

In 1469, Richard and Edward returned to Fotheringhay on their way north to deal with the rebels. In the early part of the year, a small uprising led by a man calling himself Robin of Redesdale had been quashed by John Neville. However, another group rose up quickly. Again, the rebellion was put down, but almost immediately, Robin of Redesdale resurfaced in Lancashire. The king was on a pilgrimage to the shrine of St Edmund. After leaving there, his party stopped at Norwich, where the king sent letters to his supporters telling them to assemble their forces. He then went on to Walsingham to visit the Shrine of Our Lady before finally coming to Fotheringhay.

In 1482 Edward, Richard and Alexander, Duke of Albany, met at Fotheringhay to discuss terms of England's support for Albany's seizure of the Scottish throne. Albany would be recognised by England as the lawful King of Scotland in exchange for certain land concessions to the English.

Visiting the Castle Site Today

My favourite place at the castle site is atop the mound on a bright day. Even though the castle no longer exists, the countryside is beautiful and peaceful. Sitting there, I like to take in the panoramic view and imagine a young Richard playing beside the river.

To get to the site of the castle, you will need to walk down a winding country lane. There is a sign that points the way. Near the river where the slabs of masonry remain, there is a memorial to Richard III erected by the Richard III Society. Next to this memorial is another for Mary, Queen of Scots. These fragments of masonry are enclosed by a fence. There is no admission fee, and a panel board on the site gives you an idea of what the castle might have looked like in its heyday. Fotheringhay Castle postcode: PE8 5HZ.

Church of St Mary the Virgin and All Saints, Fotheringhay

Rising up out of the countryside, the octagonal lantern tower of the Church of St Mary the Virgin and All Saints can be seen from quite a distance on the approach to Fotheringhay. The church, built in the Perpendicular style, is even more impressive up close. Originally a collegiate church, it was founded in the fifteenth century by Edward, Duke of York. He established the college in 1411 beside the original parish church, which was later included in the design for the college.

The college was sizeable, with a master, twelve chaplains, eight clerks and thirteen choristers, and was founded for the purpose of praying for the royal family.

Unfortunately for Edward, his death on the bloody field of Agincourt prevented him from seeing his idea come to fruition. Part of the building appears to have been finished, though, and Edward was buried there. His nephew, Richard, Duke of York, fulfilled his wishes and signed a contract with the freemason William Horwood to complete the church. After Richard's death at Wakefield, it would be some years before work would begin again.

Once he felt his reign was secure, Edward IV refounded the college and granted it a new charter. Under Henry VIII, the college surrendered its liberties, and under Edward VI it was granted to the Duke of Northumberland, John Dudley. Historians disagree as to whether or not Dudley completely removed the roof from the choir and demolished some of the buildings. Regardless, the church did fall into ruin and many of the buildings surrounding the church were destroyed.

The close proximity of the church to the castle makes it likely that Richard III visited here as a child. It is known for certain that he visited the church on at least one momentous occasion. The reinterment of his father and brother would have been a proud moment for the House of York.

In July 1476, the bodies of the Duke of York and Edmund of Rutland were placed in the hearse or hearses built in the priory of St John at Pontefract. According to Anne Sutton and Livia Visser-Fuchs in their work *The Reburial of Richard Duke of York, 21–30 July 1476*, the coffin of the Duke of York, covered with his heraldic symbols, was placed in the centre of the hearse. A lifelike effigy was placed within the hearse, dressed in dark blue, with a cap of purple. An angel was behind him holding a crown of gold behind his head. These trappings, reserved for royalty, were most likely used to strengthen the claim of the dynasty of the House of York. The crown behind his head probably symbolised that he was a king uncrowned – a king by right.

The bishops of Durham, Hereford, Chester and Bangor, as well as other abbots and priors, were present for the exhumation. The next morning, after a requiem Mass, the coffins were placed in an elaborate funeral carriage. Richard, as chief mourner, would have ridden directly behind the carriage as it made its way towards Fotheringhay. He and the other mourners would have been dressed in mourning habit. It was a grand procession, attended by several of the leading nobles of the realm.

At each stop along the way, religious ceremonies were held as the bodies lay in the church. According to Sutton and Visser-Fuchs, a new hearse awaited at every church. After requiem Mass, the old structure with its valuable, decorative features, such as candles and valances, was left at the church as alms. Sutton and Visser-Fuchs believe that the hearse used for the ceremony at Fotheringhay was the same one as that made for the obit of 1463. If so, it was elaborately decorated with fifty-one wax images of kings and 420 wax angels. The hearse was sprinkled with silver roses, and escutcheons of arms covered the hearse and the valance. Edward IV's emblem of the sun adorned the structure.

On 29 July, the procession arrived at Fotheringhay, where it was met at the cemetery by the king, who was dressed in royal mourning colour of dark blue. Carried by twelve men, the coffin and effigy were taken into the church and placed in the elaborate hearse. Edmund's coffin was carried to its waiting hearse in the Lady Chapel. The king and other nobles, including Clarence and Gloucester, accompanied the bodies into the church. After the religious service, the king and queen, through their agents, gave an offering of yards of cloth of gold, which was laid in the shape of the cross over the body.

The next day was the official funeral and reburial. An elaborate ceremony was held, including three services led by the Bishop of Lincoln. After Mass and the celebration of the achievements of the Duke of York, the bodies were reburied. Following the service, alms were distributed to the poor.

After the ceremonies, a large feast was held both outside and inside the castle. To seat everyone, tents and tables had to be constructed. We know that items had to be brought from various places, as there are records of men being paid for carting them. The feast was enormous, and included such things as ale and wine, fish, rabbits, partridges, pheasants, herons, chickens and honey, as well as many other dishes.

One omission from the record of the reburial is Richard's mother, Cecily Neville. While she is not mentioned in the sources, this does not necessarily mean she was not there. Perhaps her role in the ceremony was just to watch. After all, she was not a dowager queen, so her role in the ceremonies would have been murky as the duke was being buried as king by right.

It is not known what the duke's tomb looked like. The original tombs were destroyed and no existing sources contain a description. Leland described the tomb of York's uncle, Edward, as one on which 'lyith a flat marbil stone with an image flatt yn brasse'. As Edward IV was implying that his father was 'king by right', he probably commissioned a much more elaborate tomb, fit for a king.

When Elizabeth I visited Fotheringhay, she was appalled by how decrepit her ancestors' tombs were, so she commissioned new tombs for them. Legend has it that when Cecily Neville's body was unearthed, a ribbon with a papal indulgence was found tied around her neck and the ink was fresh as if it had been written the day before. The tombs are decorated with the York badge of a falcon and fetterlock.

Visiting the Church Today

There are several exhibits related to Richard and the Yorks within the church. The York Window was erected by the Richard III society and features shields to commemorate the family. On my visit in 2014, there were also panels which told the story of the castle, the church and the Yorks. Make sure you see the copy of the 1434 contract for the building of the church. It was copied by William Dugdale in 1669 from the original.

It is believed that Edward IV gave the church the elaborately decorated pulpit. The pulpit has now been painted to resemble how it might have appeared in the fifteenth century. The thoroughly modern stairs leading up to it are obviously not part of the original. Before leaving the area, make sure you walk outside to the east side of the church. Here you can see evidence of the arches where the choir of the collegiate church was separated from the parish nave. Church postcode: PE8 5HZ.

Ludlow, Shropshire

The Castle

Another of the Duke of York's homes was to be found in Shropshire in England. Ludlow Castle was both a stronghold and a much-loved family home. It was here that the Duke of York set up a separate household for his older sons, Edward, Earl of March, and Edmund, Earl of Rutland. Although we know little of Richard's movements during his early years, in all likelihood he would have visited some of his father's family estates, and Ludlow would have been one of the most grand.

Observing the castle from the banks of the shimmering waters of the River Teme, it appears a stony edifice amid a green morass of trees and vines. Its appearance is both imposing and breathtaking. John Leland, writing in the sixteenth century, said, 'The town of Ludlo is very propre, welle walled and gated, and standeth every way eminent from a bottom.'

One of the events at Ludlow that affected Richard happened when he was very young. A council was called to meet in Coventry in June 1459 and his father and associates were not invited. This raised red flags of alarm for the Duke of York and his friends. Mustering a force at Ludlow, the duke at first wanted to maintain a defensive position in hope that he would get an audience with the king. With few troops against an overwhelmingly large number of royalists, the outcome appeared bleak. After the desertion of the Calais garrison over to the royal side, all hope was lost. The Duke of York fled to Ireland with his second son, and Edward was sent with Warwick and the others to Calais. The rout at Ludford Bridge was an early setback for the House of York.

Duchess Cecily is thought to have remained behind at the castle with her younger children. During the sack of the town and castle by royalist forces, she would have been protected. Despite reports that she was mistreated, it is unlikely given her status. A romantic myth has taken root about the 'rout of Ludford' where Cecily is portrayed as heroically protecting her young sons at the town's market cross. It is doubtful that she would have left the relative safety of the castle to venture out among soldiers who might not have recognised her. At any event, she was taken and placed in custody. Fabyan says that the king despoiled the town and castle and sent the Duchess of York and her children to her sister, the Duchess of Buckingham.

Visiting the Castle Today

Although a ruin, enough buildings remain at Ludlow to get an idea of the stateliness and sheer size of the castle. Visitors enter the castle through the outer gatehouse, which was likely the main entrance from the town. The porter's lodge and stables were all built after 1500 and would not have existed during Richard's time.

Standing with your back to the gatehouse and looking across the outer bailey, you can see the remains of St Peter's Chapel on the far left. This chapel was built by Roger Mortimer in the fourteenth century. Renovations occurred throughout the following centuries, but traces of the original chapel can still be detected. Close by is Mortimer's Tower, which was constructed in the thirteenth century. According to the castle's guidebook, tradition holds that Richard, Duke of York, and his eldest sons escaped the Lancastrian forces via this tower.

Now, standing with your back to St Peter's Chapel, face the keep. This Norman keep was originally a gatehouse, and it was added to in several stages. This tall tower with its four square turrets is accessible today through the inner bailey. Legend has it that a lion was kept in the bottom of the keep and served as the castle's executioner. While the atmosphere of the lower part of the keep is ominous, this legend is one that seems to have no basis in fact.

Enter through the arched doorway to the right of the keep. The buildings directly in front of you make up the North Range. The Great Hall's entrance would likely have been reached by a grand staircase leading to the richly ornamented pointed archway. As you enter the room, its width and length give credence to its former grandeur. It is easy to picture the York family here, with Richard of York and Cecily on the dais at the upper end of the hall. The room held no fireplace in that day, but would have had an open hearth to provide heat for the inhabitants. The solar wing and the chamber block are on either side of the hall. Here the family would have had their apartments.

Leaving the hall, you come back out into the inner bailey. One interesting feature here is the round chapel. The Chapel of St Mary

Magdalene was an important part of the castle. Round naves were built to imitate the church of the Holy Sepulchre in Jerusalem. Richard likely spent time here during his visit to Ludlow. Step inside the chapel to see the ruined, but still well-ornamented, decorations.

For more information on visiting the castle, see the castle website at www.ludlowcastle.com. For drivers, take advantage of the city's park-and-ride scheme. For more information, visit www.travelshropshire.co.uk/bus/park-and-ride/ludlow-park-and-ride.aspx. The postcode for the park and ride is SY8 1ES. Ludlow Castle's postcode is SY8 1AY.

The Parish Church of St Laurence, Ludlow

Built on one of the highest elevations in the town, the parish church of St Laurence was formed in the shape of a cross. Most of what you see today as you stand outside the church dates from the fifteenth century, but there was worship here for centuries before that. Some parts of the building date from the twelfth century.

Richard would have seen the church of St Laurence on his visit to the town. An impressive sight, the building might have caught the attention of a young boy excited to be visiting his elder brothers. Sometimes referred to as the 'Cathedral of the Marches', this church has been witness to significant events during its history, including the sack of the town by Lancastrian forces after the escape of the Duke of York and his sons from Ludlow. The church is impressive, with Perpendicular architecture and decorative bosses. The nave is divided from the side aisles by pointed arches, but in Richard's time it would have held many side chantries. The roof would also have been brightly painted.

Today, the church boasts beautiful nineteenth-century stained-glass windows. For our purpose, there are three interesting panels in the West Window. See if you can pick out the images of Richard, Duke of York, Edward IV, and his son, Edward V.

Carved angels overlook the chancel, enlarged in the fifteenth century. In the west end of the chancel, look up to see if you can find the bosses of the falcon and fetterlock and the white rose of York. Take time to admire the misericords under the choir stalls. Some of them are unusual, while others are simply comical. The elaborately carved bench ends in the chancel stalls are worth a second look as well.

One of the oldest items in the church is the font. It is believed to be at least 1,000 years old, and would have been here during the York family's tenancy at Ludlow. For the armchair traveller, the church provides a pictorial tour on its website, www.stlaurences. org.uk/history-and-virtual-tour/a-virtual-tour-st-laurences. Parish church of St Laurence postcode: SY8 1AN.

My Favourite Places

I have two favourite places at Ludlow. First, I love the view of the castle and surrounding countryside afforded from the top of the keep. A panoramic plethora of sights awaits the person with enough stamina to make it to the top. From here you can see down into the ruined areas of the Great Hall or turn and see the spire of St Laurence in the distance. If you look down, you can also see the river as it cuts its way toward Dinham Bridge.

My second favourite place in Ludlow is the Breadwalk. To reach the Breadwalk, turn right out of the castle, go down the hill and cross Dinham Bridge. At the end of the bridge, turn left and stay to the signposted path. The walk leads you along the riverbank and offers great views of the castle. If you bring a picnic lunch, you can eat at one of the benches that line the path. At the other end of the walk, you will cross Ludford Bridge. This picturesque walk allows you to get an idea of the scope of the landscape.

Fastolf Place, London

After his father had escaped to Ireland, Richard and his remaining family were kept in custody by his mother's sister and her husband. Once released from this custody, they came to London, where they stayed at Fastolf Place. Located in Southwark, it had been one of the homes of the soldier John Fastolf. Acquitting himself admirably during the Hundred Years War, Fastolf had amassed a considerable fortune. Before his death, he spent massive amounts of money renovating his homes here and at Caister Castle.

John Paston offered the town house to Cecily and her three

youngest children. After several days, Cecily left to go and meet her husband, who was returning from Ireland and wanted her with him. Edward, Earl of March, kept the children company, visiting every day.

Little information survives to show us how the home looked, although some of the layout can be deduced from expenditures. In a home of this size there would have been a hall, likely done in plaster. Based on homes surviving from the same time period, there likely would have been a buttery and a cellar nearby. In *Great Houses, Moats and Mills on the South Bank of the Thames*, Christopher Phillpotts says that the home included the lord's chamber, complete with a 'Round Tabull', a lord's closet and other chambers. As Richard and George were still young, they probably raced through the galleries or spent time staring through the glazed windows at the bridge across the moat.

Nothing remains of this home today. An excavation occurred in the 1990s, but it turned up very little. Giant buildings dominate its location today, making a visit to the actual site impossible. It is possible to get near to the site, however. Walk down Tooley Street to where Bermondsey Street branches off to the right. Fastolf's property was on the left near where More London Estates stands now.

Utrecht, the Netherlands

After Cecily's loss of her husband and son Edmund, and the Yorks' disastrous defeat at Wakefield, Cecily was consumed with worry for her two youngest sons. Since they were potential heirs to the throne, they had become political targets. According to the *Great Chronicle of London*, she sent George and Richard abroad to the Low Countries. We do not know where the boys landed, but they eventually ended up near Utrecht.

Burgundy, under Philip the Good, was known for its magnificent court. Philip instituted the Order of the Golden Fleece, so the court was seen as a centre of chivalry. Due to the politics of the time, taking the two boys into his own court did not appeal to the duke. He sent them instead into the care of his illegitimate son, Bishop

David. As Utrecht was considered an independent principality, this was not in Philip's duchy. This way, he avoided antagonising either the Lancastrians or the Yorks.

The politics between Bishop David and the people of Utrecht were tense. For this reason, he often resided outside the city at his castle at Wijk bij Duurstede. He was in the process of renovating and adding to the castle, creating a grand and impressive showcase surrounded by a moat and accessible only by drawbridge.

There is some confusion as to exactly where Richard and George passed their time while in Utrecht. Was Bishop David at Wijk bij Duurstede during the renovations? Livia Visser-Fuchs, in her article 'Richard in Holland', translated a letter from Bishop David to Edward IV, where David says that he and his subjects had given hospitality to Edward's 'famous brothers, and moreover to merchants, subjects of your royal majesty, who betook themselves to our city of Utrecht and elsewhere in our lands …' While this could be read to say the boys were in Utrecht and other areas, it also could be the merchants who were in the city and elsewhere. The murkiness of the record makes it unclear. With no further evidence that the boys were elsewhere, it appears likely that they would have stayed with Bishop David at his principal residence of Kasteel Duurstede.

The castle was large, with a rectangular courtyard and towers at each end. The old keep was incorporated into the new building. Much of the castle is gone, but the Burgundian tower and the donjon have been restored. The former opulence of the castle is obvious, even today.

Visiting Today

The castle is open Thursdays through Sundays from 10 a.m. until 6 p.m. It is also possible to rent the location for business meetings and weddings. The castle is open to visitors on the second Saturday in September and for several festivals. Check out the castle's webpage at www.kasteelduurstede.nl/ before visiting. An internet browser with a translate feature can help translate the page.

Part II

The King's Brother

After Edward claimed the crown in March 1461, the boys' futures began to shift and take a different shape. While they had been treated courteously before, they had been shipped to the least embarrassing place for Duke Philip. After the York victory on the blood-soaked field of Towton, Richard and George would become more than the sons of a duke. They were now king's brothers and would need to be treated as such.

Nicholas O'Flanagan, the Bishop of Elphin, wrote to Francesco Coppino, the Bishop of Terni, about this change in the boys' fortunes:

> It is reported among the English lords that the Duke of Burgundy is treating the brothers of the king with respect. This pleases them wonderfully, and they believe that there will be great friendship between the duke and the English ...

O'Flanagan even spoke of a possible marriage between one of the brothers and Mary of Burgundy, Philip's granddaughter. While this marriage never came to pass, the duke did send for the boys and treated them well.

Sluis (Sluys), the Netherlands

On their way to meet the duke, the boys first went to Sluis. Situated on the Zwin River, Sluis had experienced rapid growth as a port of Bruges and was an important trading town. It owed its growth to the silting up of the Zwin River. Successive ports had been built to help with trade as the previous port silted up. In order to protect the area, Philip the Bold of Burgundy had reinforced the city with strong walls, canals and high entry gates.

A prosperous town, Sluis would have been bustling with activity. Wealthy merchants and nobles would have lived in richly decorated houses. As young boys, Richard and George would have been fascinated by the bustle of cargo being unloaded from ships and sent on its way to Bruges. While in Sluis, they probably caught a glimpse of the town's belfry and its city walls.

Most likely they were honoured by a reception once they came to the town.

Visiting Sluis Today

A picturesque town with a medieval belfry and surviving town walls, Sluis is proud of its medieval heritage. It is also a thriving shopping town with a large selection of restaurants.

Although we do not know exactly where Richard and George stayed while they were here, Livia Visser-Fuchs has suggested that they stayed at an inn called Teste D'Or. Unfortunately, the inn is no longer extant. However, you can still visit the belfry and the town walls, which were standing when Richard and George visited the city.

City Walls

Visitors today cannot see the entirety of the city walls as a large part was destroyed along with the castle in the nineteenth century. However, three of the town's gates, the Westpoort, the Oostpoort and the Zuidpoort, all built prior to Richard and George's visit, still remain. As prominent guests, the boys and their retinue would have been met at one of the city gates and escorted to their residence.

The Sluis Belfry

A visitor's first stop should be the town belfry, which was built at the end of the fourteenth century. The tower has four turrets, which, according to the museum, were graced with banners bearing the arms of Burgundy, Flanders, the duke and the town. While it is the medieval building, the belfry did not escape the ravages of war and fire, but it has been restored to its original grandeur. It hosts an art exhibition as well as two historical exhibitions. A climb to the top of the tower affords beautiful views of the area. For more information on visiting the belfry, see the website at www.vvvzeeland.nl/en/vakantie/museums/23866/museum-het-belfort/west-zeeuws-vlaanderen/sluis. Postcode: 4524 CD.

The easiest way to visit Sluis is by car. There is ample parking available near the town centre. Alternatively you could catch a bus from Bruges.

Richard and George's time in Sluis was short. Master Antonio, physician to Francesco Coppino, was asked to go to meet them and accompany them to Bruges.

Bruges (Brugge), Belgium

In the earlier medieval period, Bruges had been a commercial port, thriving with trade and with access to the latest goods. During the twelfth century the city's direct link with the sea began to silt up, but fortunately a new waterway was found. In the early fifteenth century the dukes of Burgundy made Bruges a residence. Once the ducal court was established here the city became known as a place of culture, with artists such as Jan van Eyck and Hans Memling working and living there. People from all over the western world could be found in the city centre trading in the marketplace.

Frustratingly, we do not know where Richard and George stayed while in Bruges. It is doubtful that they stayed in the ducal palace, as one source says that the duke visited them at their residence. They may have stayed at one of the inns in the town or at the home of one of the rich merchants or nobles. However, we do know that the boys were fêted by the nobility. Livia Visser-Fuchs' translation of the town records states that the boys were given a banquet in their honour, with the duke, the ladies of the city and the nobles present. This banquet would have occurred at the Stadhuis.

Stadhuis

The city hall in Bruges is one of the oldest in Belgium. For almost 640 years, Bruges has been governed from this magnificent hall built in 1376. Today the exquisitely decorated gothic hall contains nineteenth-century paintings that depict historic moments and figures in Bruges' history. Standing in the back of the hall, try to picture the historic scene. The Duke of Burgundy would have been seated on a dais at the head of the room, with Richard and George seated beside him. It was their first state occasion as the brothers of a king and likely would have been overwhelming. Their fortunes had shifted over time, taking them from embarrassing exiles to honoured guests. The room would have been filled with noise and laughter as servants bustled about bringing food and drink to the crowd.

Originally the room was divided into two rooms, a vestibule and the aldermen's hall. Above and to the left where the minstrels' balcony is now is the demarcation line between the two rooms. The banquet would have taken place in the aldermen's hall.

Look up to see the ornamented vaulting. In medieval times, the vaulting would have been as richly decorated as it is now, with bright colours and scenes. Intricately woven Flemish tapestries likely hung on the walls, adding a sense of grandeur to the hall.

The room adjoining the hall was a smaller hall, which today serves as a museum. Several artefacts, including Carolingian coins, tell the story of the region over several hundred years.

Visiting the Stadhuis Today

The Stadhuis is open seven days a week. At the time of writing, the opening hours were from 9:30 a.m. until 5 p.m. It is best to double check the website at bezoekers.brugge.be/en/stadhuis-city-hall before visiting. I would not recommend driving in Bruges. There is abundant parking right outside the city centre, and most of the medieval sites are within walking distance.

Basilica of the Holy Blood

There are no records of Richard and George visiting the Basilica of the Holy Blood, but its proximity to the Stadhuis, as well as its religious relics, makes it likely that they did visit. Even if they did not, they would have seen it as they went to the banquet at the Stadhuis.

Tradition states that Joseph of Arimathea wiped some blood from the body of Christ and kept the cloth. This cloth was later brought back to Bruges by one of the returning Crusaders, probably Count Thierry of Alsace. This blood became the church's main relic.

There are two chapels in the Basilica. The lower chapel is the older crypt of Saint Basil and is Romanesque. Built in the mid-twelfth century, this chapel is not as elaborately decorated as the Gothic chapel above. Rebuilt in the fifteenth century and restored yet again in the nineteenth century, the Gothic chapel is filled with riotous colours and murals adorning the walls. Every colour of the rainbow seems to be represented within the room. The highlight of a visit is when the vial containing the blood is brought out of its golden reliquary for pilgrims and visitors to touch and pray over.

Since at least the thirteenth century, a procession takes place annually where the holy blood is taken out and paraded through the city. Richard and George would have missed the procession by a matter of weeks.

Visiting the Basilica Today

The square that both the Stadhuis and the Basilica of the Holy Blood are in is called the Burg. The opulence that surrounds this square shows how wealthy the merchants and nobles of the city were in medieval times. The Basilica of the Holy Blood is located in the right corner. In Richard's time, the façade would not have looked like it does now, as it was built in 1533 and reconstructed in the nineteenth century. Check the website to determine times that the chapel is open, and if you are interested, in times that you may touch the vial of blood. www.holyblood.com/.

One of the main buildings of the Burg, St Donatius church, which would have been one of the buildings in this square, is now lost to history. Richard and George would have seen this impressive church while visiting the Stadhuis.

The Market Square

If you want to feel like you have stepped back in time, a visit to the Market Square is a must. The vividly coloured guild houses, the towering belfry and the crowd of people all give the impression that you have momentarily swept through the veil of time and are in medieval Bruges. The Government Palace, finished now in Gothic Revival, was originally where the boats would unload their goods. Many of the restaurants along the square were once guild houses, whose members profited from the trade that passed through this city.

The Belfry

The belfry has dominated the city since the thirteenth century. Standing eighty-three metres tall, the belfry towers over the other buildings. While the octagonal tower was not added until after Richard's and George's visit, the building still would have been impressive. At that time, the belfry would have been topped by a large square tower with four round turrets. Flemish cloth was sold in the halls surrounding the belfry, and it would have been a busy place.

Visiting the Belfry Today

If you want to get a panoramic view of the city, climb the 366 stairs to the top of the belfry. From here you can see most of the city. The climb is broken into intervals, and you will also get to see the treasury room, where the town charters were kept, as well as the victory bell. Perhaps the bells will chime as you ascend. Most of the tunes the bells play are current popular songs and not medieval tunes.

For information about visiting times, see bezoekers.brugge.be/en/belfort-belfry.

Gruuthuse Museum

During Richard's second time of exile, this time with his brother Edward, he was a guest of Louis Gruuthuse. Gruuthuse was the governor of Holland and Zeeland. Richard and Edward had been his guests in his home in The Hague. On their way to meet with the Duke of Burgundy, they stopped for a time at another of

Gruuthuse's homes, this time in Bruges. Gruuthuse had two homes near Bruges, but his main residence was in the city. I think it is more likely that he would have brought Richard and Edward here than to his other residence.

Gruuthuse's main residence while in Bruges bordered the canals and was near the church of Our Lady. A large courtyard led to exquisitely detailed buildings. The home was large as Louis had added a south wing on to the already palatial building.

Visiting Bruges Today

Unfortunately, the Gruuthuse Museum (also known as Gruuthusemuseum) is undergoing massive renovations and will be closed until at least 2017. I was fortunate enough to visit on the last day before it closed. The museum does not focus on the family, but on a collection of fine lace, tapestries, and objects. Upon its reopening, it will focus more on the history of Bruges.

As you tour the building, keep in mind that Richard and Edward would not have seen the chapel that allowed Louis and his family to observe services in the church of Our Lady without ever leaving their home as it was not built until later. For more information about the status of the museum, visit bezoekers.brugge.be/en/gruuthusemuseum. Gruuthuse was buried in the church of Our Lady, but it is not possible to visit his tomb.

Bruges has much to offer a Richard enthusiast as it is a city that celebrates its medieval heritage. From the canals to the bridges to the museums, it would be easy to spend days in Bruges without more than scratching its medieval surface. Make sure you visit the church of Our Lady, which is right next door to the Gruuthuse Museum.

Travelling to Bruges is easy. Trains run from Brussels several times an hour. For information, see www.belgianrail.be/. Parking in Bruges is also easy. You do not want to drive into the medieval heart of the city, but overnight parking is available in the large multistorey car parks nearby. For more information, see www.car-parking.eu/belgium/bruges.

Calais, France

Richard's First Visit to Calais

After Edward had soundly defeated the Lancastrians, Richard and George began their trip back to England. Accompanied by a retinue of courtiers and soldiers from the Burgundian court, they journeyed towards Calais. As they trudged through the muddy marshland that surrounded much of the city, a defensive fortress towered before them. The city was in the shape of a rectangle and was surrounded by a high brick wall. Around the wall was a deep double moat. Approaching from the south, the land they crossed could be flooded by the town for further protection.

They would probably have entered through the Bolougne Gate, one of the town's four gates. While no records remain of where they stayed while in Calais, they most likely stayed at the castle. The castle had been in a ruined state in the early part of the 1440s, but its great hall and chamber had recently been rebuilt. The castle lay in the north-west corner of the town, and as they made their way towards it along the narrow streets and through the market squares, they would have seen rich merchants' houses, each with a roof of tile or slate.

Soon, the great circular keep of the castle loomed before them, its bailey surrounded by six circular towers. As they crossed the bridge over the moat separating the castle from the town, they faced the gatehouse. Once inside the inner bailey, they would have been faced with an unusual sight. Another moat separated the keep from the bailey. It is easy to picture the boys having a meal either in the great hall or in their chambers, struggling to stay awake as the exhaustion from the past few weeks caught up with them.

Calais and the English

By the sixteenth century, Calais, the last English outpost, was all that remained of the large English empire on the Continent. When Richard and George visited, the highly fortified town was a large trading centre for the English. Wealthy merchants coexisted with the Calais garrison on crowded, narrow streets.

Edward and Calais

Although this was Richard's first visit to Calais, it was not his family's first connection with the town. Edward had fled here with the Nevilles after the disastrous rout of Ludford Bridge. Having been attainted by the king, Edward and the Nevilles were exiles. Welcomed in Calais, they made it their base of operations for the next few months.

Being ensconced in Calais did not necessarily mean the men were entirely safe, however. Somerset had started towards Calais with the king's letters patent to claim the captaincy of Calais. Instead, he was met with gunshots from the town and from Rysbank Tower. Landing further down the coast, Somerset made his way to Guines Castle, where, according to Cora Scofield, he won over the garrison with promise of payment. Unable to keep ships from trading with Calais and other men from joining the Yorkist earls, Somerset faced an enormous task.

After the Yorks managed to seize Sandwich, Somerset's cause seemed lost. In Sandwich, the Lord Rivers, Duchess Jacquetta and Anthony Woodville were captured and brought back to Calais. A tense confrontation ensued between the Yorkist earls and the Woodvilles, and Rivers was accused of being a 'knave's son' who had made himself by marriage.

Several months passed before Somerset struck. He and his soldiers marched towards Calais. Near Newnham Bridge along the Boulogne road they were met by soldiers from Calais, who killed many of Somerset's men, forcing a retreat.

Soon afterwards, the rebels issued a manifesto stating that they wished the king no harm; they merely wanted to fix the problems within the country. The earls soon left Calais to press their cause in England.

The Duke of Clarence and Calais

Years after his first visit to Calais, the Duke of Clarence would once again visit the town. This time, he was allied with the Earl of Warwick in a conspiracy against his brother, Edward. Whether driven by greed, jealousy, or some other reason, the duke had gone against his brother's direct command and was planning to marry Warwick's daughter, Isabel.

On 11 July 1469, Isabel and George were married by Isabel's uncle, the Archbishop of York, in a public ceremony. The ceremony likely occurred in St Mary's church, as the men wanted the marriage to be as public as possible. In *Calais: An English Town in France, 1347–1558*, Susan Rose states that despite claims the wedding was held in the castle, it would not have been as there was no suitable place for a wedding that large within the castle precincts. According to Scofield, the ceremony was a well-attended affair with five Knights of the Garter and other lords and ladies present. The marriage between Isabel and Clarence was in open defiance of the king's orders.

Having had so much success with his first manifesto issued from Calais, Warwick tried the gambit again. This time the letter he sent was co-signed by Clarence, stating that there were people within the realm that were influencing the king and excluding those of his blood from having a say. To remedy this, they planned to petition the king and asked for supporters to meet them in Canterbury. Soon afterwards, the men left Calais, bound for Canterbury. The next time they tried to flee to the safety of Calais, as Isabel's labour pains were intensifying, the garrison turned them away and she lost her baby. Given his parents' precarious position, his small body may have been tossed into the raging sea instead of receiving a proper burial.

Calais in 1475

Richard, Edward and George all travelled to Calais with their men in 1475. England had allied with Burgundy in a planned invasion of France. According to Edward's biographer, Charles Ross, the king was attended by all five dukes, the marquis, three of seven earls and a large retinue. Clarence and Richard both commanded large groups of men. The final place of assembly of the men was at Calais. The ultimate outcome of the invasion was the Treaty of Picquigny. Richard, having prepared for war, was unhappy with the treaty.

Visiting Calais Today

Sadly, there is nothing left of the castle or much of the medieval town of Calais. After the Second World War the town was essentially destroyed. The castle, with the arms of St George painted on the gun ports' shutters, is gone. Most of the town's brick walls are also gone, although portions were incorporated into the citadel.

St Mary's church, now known as Église de Notre Dame, where George and Isabel likely married, is still standing, although it is undergoing renovations. At the time of my visit it was closed, but the plans suggested it would reopen by the time of publication. Upon completion of the renovations the church will be open in July and August from 2 p.m. until 5 p.m.

Arriving in Calais from England is easy. Trains run often from London St Pancras International to Calais Frethun. Be aware that Calais Frethun does not have a cash machine, so you need to have exchanged pounds for euros before your trip. For more information on arriving by train, see www.eurostar.com. Alternatively, you can catch a ferry to Calais, either as a foot passenger or with your car. DFDS Seaways and P&O Ferries both operate a service from Dover to Calais. See their websites at www.dfdsseaways.co.uk/ and www.poferries.com/. Additionally, you could drive to Dover and travel via the Eurotunnel. For more information, see www.eurotunnel.com/uk/.

Canterbury Cathedral, Kent

Upon returning from exile, Richard and George were fêted and treated as befitted their new role as princes of the realm. It must have been a heady time after the early years of grief and stress. One of their first stops on their way to reunite with their family was at Canterbury.

Few cathedrals in England can claim to be as intimately tied to the history of the country as Canterbury Cathedral. Christians have worshipped in Canterbury for more than a millennium. As early as the sixth century, St Augustine came to Canterbury on a mission to reinstate the Christian faith in the land. In the tenth century, the Benedictine monastery was founded at Christ Church. After a fire destroyed the earlier monastery, Lanfranc, Archbishop of Canterbury in the eleventh century, rebuilt it in a majestic style. In 1072, the office of Archbishop of Canterbury was confirmed as the chief bishop in England. This meant that whoever was

Archbishop of Canterbury would be the most powerful prelate in the country.

The cathedral was a place of pilgrimage to the shrines of several saints, including St Dunstan and St Anselm, but it is best known for the shrine of its most famous archbishop, Thomas á Becket. Richard would have been familiar with the story of the esteemed archbishop, who had once been a close companion to Henry II. After becoming archbishop, Thomas, to Henry's surprise and horror, began to ardently defend the Church's rights. The relationship turned into a series of heated confrontations, once causing Thomas to leave England for exile in France. Henry supposedly exclaimed, 'Who will rid me of this turbulent priest?' Four knights decided to assist Henry with his request. The murder of Archbishop Becket was a particularly heinous one as it occurred within the church in the north-west transept. Miracles began to occur at Becket's tomb and he was declared a saint soon after his death. His shrine became an important pilgrim spot.

Canterbury under Lancastrian Rule

In 1451, Henry VI visited Canterbury. While here, he held his council in the prior's chapel. The council probably spent much of its time discussing the increasingly bad situation in France. His queen, Margaret of Anjou, came to Canterbury on pilgrimage in October 1454. She was met at the entrance to the church by the prior and convent dressed in their green copes. The next day she attended Mass and visited the shrine of St Thomas. She also heard Mass with music while in the crypt of the church.

Henry VI also came to Canterbury on pilgrimage in August 1460, following the Battle of Northampton. Effectively a prisoner of the Yorks, he was accompanied by several bishops, but also Edward, Earl of March, as well as Richard, Earl of Warwick, and Richard, Earl of Salisbury. He was received by the Archbishop of Canterbury and the Bishop of Ely, as well as the prior and the monks, again wearing their green copes.

On 8 August, the king was part of a procession to the shrine. As he was in Canterbury until 18 August, Henry was also present for the vigil of the Assumption of the Blessed Mary. He was at the first vespers, uncrowned, as well as High Mass and second vespers.

Return of the Yorkists

According to Meriel Connor's translation of *John Stone's Chronicle*, it was on the twenty-sixth day of June in 1460 that Edward, Earl of March, Richard, Earl of Salisbury, and Richard, Earl of Warwick came to Canterbury upon return from Calais. After a brief time in Calais, the Yorkist earls claimed that they were going to help protect the country by removing the king's ministers. Archbishop Bourchier had met the earls in Sandwich and offered them his episcopal protection. By the time they reached the outskirts of Canterbury they had with them 'a great company of people'.

Outside of Canterbury, the earls were confronted by Robert Horne, John Scott and John Fogge, who had been sent by Henry VI. After a discussion, the men reached an agreement and then went to the shrine of St Thomas. The agreement was good news for the Yorkists, as all three men joined their cause. Afterwards, they made their way towards London and then on to Northampton.

The Yorks and Canterbury

After Edward IV had taken the throne from Henry VI, Richard and George headed back to England from the Low Countries. As mentioned above, one of their first stops in England on their way to London was at Canterbury. Arriving on a Saturday during the vigil of the Holy Trinity, George and Richard were received by the prior and the monks in green copes at the doors of the church. That evening, the boys were present at vespers. The next day George and Richard were in the procession for High Mass and at second vespers.

While in Canterbury, the boys would likely have been lodged in either the Archbishop's Palace or the prior's lodging. The home of the archbishop was grand and was expensive to finish. Archbishop Boniface is said to have remarked that even though his predecessors had built the majority of the building, he should be considered the founder as he had to settle all the debts. Second only in size to the Great Hall at Westminster, the archbishop's hall was often used to entertain royalty, the nobility and foreign guests. At some point in the next few years, Richard and George are also believed to have come under the care of the Archbishop of Canterbury, Thomas Bourchier. If they were under the Archbishop's care for a time, they probably spent most of their time at Lambeth Palace as opposed to Canterbury.

Thomas Bourchier brought Richard and George with him to Canterbury in August 1463. On this visit both of the dukes were in procession and at High Mass. George had a sword carried before him in procession to underscore his significance as the heir to the throne.

In 1465, Edward visited Canterbury again. He was received by the archbishop, the prior, and the convent, dressed in green copes. Elizabeth, by now Queen of England, arrived later and was received by the archbishop, the prior, and the convent, this time dressed in white copes. Instead of the customary response of *Summe Trinitati*, the monks greeted Elizabeth with the response of *Audi Filia*, which includes the phrase, 'the king has greatly desired your beauty'. The next day, Edward and Elizabeth were in the procession. This time the monks were wearing their red copes. After vespers, the royal couple visited nearby St Augustine's.

While at Canterbury, Edward and Elizabeth received the good news that Henry VI had been captured. In celebration, Edward and Elizabeth attended a service and afterwards took part in a procession to the shrine of St Thomas.

Later, in 1468, Edward, George and Richard accompanied their sister to Canterbury as she made her way towards Margate, where she would leave England and head to the Low Countries to marry Charles, the Duke of Burgundy. Other barons, earls, and knights were with them, including Anthony Woodville, who would continue on the journey with Margaret until after she married Charles. The group attended the first Mass of St John and the High Mass. After nones, they rode out towards Thanet and on to Margate. This must have been both a sombre and joyous occasion. Margaret was fulfilling her familial duty in marrying for England's interests and for the furthering of the House of York. However, they all knew this might be the last time they would see each other. Margaret, George, and Richard were close, having been raised together. However, the fact that the king left the party once but rode out again to meet them speaks of his love for his younger sister. This time in Canterbury is especially poignant as it would mark one of the last times that these four York siblings would be together in harmony.

Family Feud and Canterbury

Once George had made up his mind to ally with Richard, Earl of Warwick, he spent a few days in the prior's lodging at Canterbury. His mother, Cecily, travelled with him to Sandwich, his port of departure. Some historians suggest that she was siding with George against Edward, while others suggest that she wanted to talk George out of his rash decision to try to wrest the throne from his brother by ruling through him or by removing him completely. Whatever the case, it is impossible to know Cecily's thoughts on the issue. She stayed with a small household at the prior's lodging for a few days before heading back to her home at Berkhamsted.

After his marriage to Isabel, George, accompanied by Warwick, came to Canterbury to gather support. Eventually he would find his way back into his brother's fold, partly due to the influence of his sister and mother. Most of his motivation probably stemmed from his realisation that he would not have a place in the new government Warwick was trying to form. With Warwick's other daughter, Anne, married to the Lancastrian heir Edward, George probably saw all chance of gaining the throne slipping through his fingers.

Following the Lancastrian defeats at Barnet and Tewkesbury, Edward, along with Richard and George, came to Canterbury on the feast of St Augustine the Apostle. With them was a large contingent of armed men, as Edward was concerned about possible rebellions. Edward would visit again in September with Elizabeth to receive an indulgence.

Richard and Canterbury

As King of England, Richard visited Canterbury in the November of 1484 for slightly more than a week. As king, he would definitely have stayed in the Archbishop's Palace and not the prior's lodgings. Anne was likely with him, as she spent much of her time at her husband's side. The illness that would kill her in 1485 had not seriously weakened her by this time. Anne Crawford points out in her book *The Yorkists* that Anne did not fall seriously sick until after the Christmas of 1484. She was with Richard at Christmas and so was probably with him in November as well.

While at Canterbury, Richard and Anne would visit the shrine of St Thomas. Having done this before, Richard would be familiar with the process. There were four principal places for the pilgrim to visit, each with its own custodian. According to Meriel Connor in her introduction to *John Stone's Chronicle*, the route for the pilgrims was first to visit the martyrdom by the passage beneath the steps which rose from the nave to the monks' choir. In the martyrdom was an altar dedicated to the Virgin. On this altar, sometimes called the Altar of the Sword's Point, was displayed the sword that had been broken in half as it was used to smash Becket's head during his assassination.

After leaving the martyrdom, Richard and Anne would have moved past the original site of the tomb and the altar of the Virgin Mary in the undercroft. The original tomb was also a spot for pilgrim donations and prayers.

Finally, as they reached the Trinity chapel, they would have seen the shrine. Anne and Richard would have climbed the flight of stairs to the elevated shrine on their knees, as most pilgrims did. The bottom of the shrine was made of stone and contained recesses where pilgrims could rest injured or diseased parts of their body to get as close as possible to the saint's healing powers. Above the stone was a box suspended by a rope and pulley for raising and lowering it. According to one description, the raising of the canopy caused the silver bells attached to the canopy to ring out with a beautiful tune. When the box was raised, the reliquary containing the relics would appear. The shrine was covered with gold plates, with a gold wire netting over it encrusted with jewels, of which one of the largest had been given to the shrine by the King of France. At the Dissolution, it was said that more than twenty wagons were needed to carry away the treasures contained at the shrine.

Polydore Vergil describes the shrine of St Thomas as surpassing all belief:

> The magnificence of the tomb of St. Thomas the Martyr, Archbishop of Canterbury, is that which surpasses all belief. This, notwithstanding its great size, is entirely covered over with plates of pure gold; but the gold is scarcely visible from the variety of precious stones with which it is studded, such as sapphires, diamonds, rubies, balas rubies, and emeralds; and on every side that the eye turns, something more beautiful than the other

appears. And these beauties of nature are enhanced by human skill, for the gold is carved and engraved in beautiful designs, both large and small, and agates, Jaspers and cornelians set in relievo, some of the cameos being of such a size, that I do not dare to mention it: but everything is left far behind by a ruby, not larger than a man's thumbnail, which is set to the right of the altar. The church is rather dark, and particularly so where the shrine is placed, and when we went to see it the sun was nearly gone down, and the weather was cloudy; yet I saw that ruby as well as if I had it in my hand; they say that it was the gift of a king of France.

The ruby that Vergil mentions was also described by the Burgundian ambassador as being half as large as an egg. In Queen Mary's time, it was described as a diamond. Vergil may have mistaken the brilliant shine of the diamond as a ruby in the gloom of the church.

After visiting the shrine, they would have visited the reliquary that Erasmus says contained the 'perforated skull of the martyr' with its forehead left bare. Kneeling in front of the reliquary, Richard and Anne would have been offered the skull to kiss.

While at the shrine, Richard probably thought of the troubles he was enduring during his reign. Fresh in his mind would have been the upcoming execution of William Collingbourne, a man from Wiltshire who had written a derisive lyric regarding Richard and pinned it to the door of St Paul's Cathedral. The lyrics 'the Catte, the Ratte and Lovell our dogge rulyth all Englande under a hogge' referenced Richard (the hog), Sir William Catesby (the cat), Sir Richard Ratcliffe (the rat) and Viscount Francis Lovell (the dog). These men had been placed in positions of power by Richard upon his taking the throne, which bred resentment among some members of the nobility. All three men were loyal to Richard, standing by him throughout his reign and fighting with him at Bosworth. Catesby was executed following the battle, Ratcliffe died during the fight and Lovell escaped, his fate unknown. At the time of the poem, they were among Richard's most trusted friends.

Collingbourne had not just penned a line of poetry, he had been trying to incite a rebellion and bring Henry Tudor to England. Richard was incensed and determined to make an example of

Collingbourne, so in December 1484, he had Collingbourne hanged, drawn and quartered.

Visiting Canterbury Today

While you will not see the lines of dirty, bedraggled pilgrims on their way to the shrine of St Thomas, you will see hordes of tourists making their way into the cathedral church. The admission fee into Canterbury is steep, but it is well worth the cost and the fees go to help preserve the building for future generations.

The first part of the cathedral that a visitor sees is the Christ Church Gateway. This elaborate, embellished gate was built in the sixteenth century, so Richard would never have seen it. It is well worth a look, however, as it is beautifully carved. It also demonstrates the grandeur of the buildings associated with the cathedral, and earlier gateways would have been just as elaborate. Stepping into the precincts, one of the first things that strikes a visitor is the great Bell Harry Tower. This tower replaced the original Romanesque tower but wasn't finished until 1498. Although Richard would have seen the work in progress, he would never have seen the cathedral with the massive tower fully completed. There is much to see within the walls of Canterbury's cathedral, but our tour will focus on those related to Richard.

Upon entering the church the first thing that strikes one is the sheer soaring heights of the nave. Supported by clusters of columns tapering into delicate rib vaulting, the ceiling seems to float in the air. Beautiful stained-glass windows near the ceiling allow light to flood in the room, augmenting the light from the larger windows below. It is easy to imagine a young Richard stopping to look up at the magnificent ceiling. From here, walk to the flight of steps leading to the ornately decorated stone screen which divides the nave from the choir. The effigies of the six kings who adorn the screen, including Henry IV, Henry V and Henry VI, rest on pedestals under intricately carved canopies. The screen used to include statues of Christ and his apostles, but sadly these were destroyed in the early seventeenth century. It is likely the statues Richard would have seen would have been painted with bright colours.

Stand facing the screen and then look to your left. The large stained-glass window contains images of Edward IV and his family and was commissioned by the king. Sadly, the images in the window were destroyed by a puritan, Richard Culmer, and had to be recreated. Some early sources say the head of Edward IV was part of the original window. However, the panels in the window would have been arranged differently during Richard's last visit.

Continue on down the steps under the window until you are standing in the martyrdom. This would have been one of the first areas a pilgrim would approach. Thomas á Becket was killed here by four knights in the service of Henry I. The doorway to the cloisters is said to have been the doorway the men burst through to kill the archbishop. If you look at the floor you will see the name Thomas cut into the stone. Follow in Richard's footsteps as you enter into the crypt with its Romanesque features, including massive, extravagantly decorated columns with their carved capitals. A good example of a medieval wall painting still exists here as well. Richard and Anne would probably have passed right by these features, as they were used to them, and would have headed straight to the former tomb of St Thomas. If you walk past the Chapel of the Holy Innocents the next large area you come to is the site where St Thomas's body was entombed from 1170 to 1220.

Leave the crypt and work your way back to the choir. This gem of architecture was rebuilt and enlarged after a fire destroyed the original building. The vaulted stone ceiling rests on clusters of slender shafts of Purbeck marble, which alternate with shafts of Caen stone, engendering a delightful contrast. Look for the Chair of St Augustine, which stands at the top of the steps that lead from the altar to the Trinity chapel. The chair is only used as part of the triple enthronement of archbishops of Canterbury. Richard would have seen the same chair you see today.

As you leave the choir, exit to the south aisle and work your way up towards where the Trinity chapel once stood. A candle marks the area where St Thomas's shrine once rested in the now demolished Trinity chapel. Richard and Anne would have spent time here in front of the shrine as the custodian showed them the treasures attached to it. After leaving the shrine, they would have gone to the Corona, where you should head now. The Corona is where the cathedral believes the skull of St Thomas was kept. Today the area serves as the Chapel of the Saints and Martyrs of Our Own Time.

Leaving the Corona, continue onward until you reach the tomb of Henry IV and his wife, Joan of Navarre, which is directly across from his chantry. You can walk up steps to a raised platform to get a look at the effigies of Henry and Joan. Henry IV is the king that deposed his cousin, Richard II, took the throne and so began the royal Lancastrian line.

Continue walking down the aisle until you see the tomb of Archbishop Bourchier. Richard would never have seen this tomb as he predeceased the archbishop. A loyal adherent of Edward IV, Bourchier was instrumental in securing the release of Edward's son, Richard of Shrewsbury, from sanctuary. He crowned Richard III, but failed to attend the coronation feast afterwards. He kept his feelings about Richard to himself, so we do not know whether or not he supported Richard's usurpation of the throne. He crowned Henry VII and, shortly before his death, performed the wedding ceremonies for Henry and Elizabeth of York.

Head on towards the cloisters. The vault tracery of the cloisters is richly decorated by heraldic devices and grotesques. See if you can find any coats of arms that you recognise before you make your way into the chapter house. The chapter house is the largest in England and the roof is a beautiful example of a barrel vault. As a passage from the Archbishop's Palace connected to the Great Cloisters, Richard possibly saw the room on at least one of his visits. As can be seen from his building works, Richard liked well-lit rooms and the large windows of the chapter house probably appealed to him.

Sadly, the Archbishop's Palace with its magnificent great hall no longer exists. Even the ruined archway that remains is from a later time. Palace Street, near where the grand palace once stood, is named in its honour. Despite this, it is worth taking time to explore the grounds of the cathedral to get an idea of how the buildings would have looked in Richard's time.

If you are only in Canterbury for a day and are driving, one of the three park and rides around the town is a good option. It is hard to find parking in the city centre. If you are visiting by train, Southeastern Railway has trains that make the journey from London in under an hour. See the webpage at www.southeasternrailway. co.uk/. High-speed trains can also be found on National Rail. For more information, see www.nationalrail.co.uk/. For information on visiting Canterbury Cathedral, call +44 (0) 1227 762862, or visit the cathedral web page at www.canterbury-cathedral.org/visit/information/. Canterbury Cathedral postcode: CT1 2EH.

The Palace of Placentia, Greenwich, Kent

After returning from the safety of the Low Countries and spending time with their mother, the boys were brought to their brother at Greenwich, with several celebrations along the way. Little is known of their movements in their early years as the king's brothers, but the king did provide for their households through the Great Wardrobe.

Most likely the boys and Margaret stayed largely at Greenwich, as much of the goods for them went there. A pleasant palace on the banks of the Thames, Greenwich had been built by Humphrey, uncle to Henry VI. Here, Humphrey had built a stone and timber manor house, complete with a limestone tower and a park of 200 acres. The palace, which included several gardens and courtyards, extended from the banks of the Thames to the foot of the hill, where he built his stone tower. Humphrey and his wife were given a licence to crenellate both their home and the tower. The home, later taken over by Margaret of Anjou after Humphrey's death, was named Placentia or Pleasaunce.

The king and queen each had a ward in the house. In the queen's ward, there was a chamber, a parlour and a gallery, which overlooked the garden. Under the reign of Henry VI, a brick wall was built between the home and the Thames.

Edward IV enlarged the home in the first few years of his reign and stocked the park with deer, making it a beautiful residence. He would later grant the palace to his wife, Elizabeth. While here at Greenwich, the boys probably had tutors to help educate them in a manner befitting a prince.

The first Christmas after being crowned king, Edward came to Greenwich for his celebrations. It is probable that George and Richard spent time with him here. Perhaps they held their father's first year's mind here – a requiem Mass held on or near the deceased's date of death or burial. It is tempting to picture Richard,

George and Edward remembering their father together before the brothers' bonds would be broken by Clarence's perfidy.

In 1480, when Margaret visited England, the palace was magnificently decorated. Tapestries of the story of Paris and Helen were hung within the rooms, which had been fitted for Margaret. She had a feather bed with a valence of velvet. Pieces of woven wool tapestry covered the tables, with each pane containing an image of 'roses, sunnes, and crowns'. A white rose *en soleil* was one of Edward IV's badges, most likely because of the parhelion that occurred at the Battle of Mortimer's Cross.

This visit from Margaret must have been bittersweet, as the brother she was closest to in age, George, had already been executed. There had been talk of marrying her stepdaughter, Mary, to George prior to Mary's marriage to Maximillian. Despite his repeated betrayals of Edward, Margaret appears to have favoured George. It must have been hard for her to be in England with her family without him. It would have also been a happy time, a chance to see her two remaining brothers and meet her nieces and nephews. For Richard, it would have been a happy occasion, as he and his sister seemed to have a good relationship.

Another family event that took place at Greenwich was a tournament held in honour of the marriage of Richard, the young Duke of York, and the heiress Anne Mowbray. There is no evidence that Richard took part in this tournament, but he would have been in attendance.

Visiting Greenwich Today

Sadly, nothing remains of the former palace of Placentia. During the reign of Henry VII the house was rebuilt in red brick and enlarged. The palace was the birthplace of Henry VIII and his daughters, Mary and Elizabeth. It was here, in May of 1536, that Queen Anne Boleyn was arrested and taken to the Tower. After the Stuart reigns and the English Civil War, the castle fell into a serious state of disrepair, and the Royal Naval College was built on the location. Humphrey's Palace of Placentia stood where the west wing of the Royal Naval College, currently housing the University of Greenwich, now stands.

The best way to arrive at Greenwich is by river, as that is

how Richard would have reached the palace. Take a boat from Westminster Pier, and as you travel the Thames, imagine Baynard's Castle, Cecily Neville's home, and catch a glimpse of the Tower of London. Of course, the river's depth has changed over the years. The boat ride is not a long one, but it gives a better idea of the layout of London and what the countryside would have looked like.

If you prefer to visit from London via rail, take the Docklands Light Railway (DLR) to Cutty Sark for Maritime Greenwich. Tower Gateway is a good place to catch the DLR. Check Transport for London's site for rail updates and times. Greenwich Postcode is SE10 9NN.

My Favourite Place in Greenwich

I love to climb the hill to where the Royal Observatory now stands, as the views are incredible. On a clear day, you can see the buildings in London. It is also the location where Humphrey's tower, later called Greenwich Castle, once stood. It is easy to imagine Richard climbing the hill as a young boy, exploring as boys often want to do. He would have seen an entirely different view than the one we see today. But pause for a moment. You are standing where he would have stood, with only the thin veil of time between you. It is a heady sensation.

Lambeth Palace, London

While Richard and George were still young they may have been placed in the care of Archbishop Thomas Bourchier. The *Calendar of the Patent Rolls* records a grant given to the 'king's kinsmen ... because in time past at the king's request he supported the king's brothers the dukes of Clarence and Gloucester for a long time at great charges ...' If so, the boys would have spent time at Lambeth Palace.

For almost 800 years, Lambeth Palace has been the London home of the Archbishop of Canterbury. Situated on the south bank of the Thames, its close proximity to Westminster and to the king made it an ideal location for the archbishops.

Lambeth Palace was built in the thirteenth century. By the time

Archbishop Bourchier lived here, the house would have become even more palatial, as each successive archbishop added his own touches to it. The grounds of the palace were huge, allowing the boys a good place to walk and ride.

Bourchier was a kinsmen of the boys, but he had managed to walk a fine line between the Yorkist and Lancastrian factions for years, acting as a mediator between the two groups. He agreed with the Yorkists on many levels, but he was also loyal to the king. It was probably for his long loyalty to the best interests of both sides that Edward continued to trust him. It was not until the Duke of York had been killed at Wakefield and the queen's forces menaced London that Bourchier became an unwavering supporter of the House of York.

He gave his loyalty to Edward and agreed that he should be king. It was Thomas who placed the crown on Edward's head, and Edward seems to have trusted him. During the Readeption of Henry VI, Bourchier worked to restore Edward to the throne.

Richard, George and Thomas would recognise little of Lambeth Palace today. Much of the palace has been torn down, renovated, and rebuilt. Even Morton's Tower, the large red-bricked gatehouse, which is the entrance to Lambeth Palace today, was built in the last decade of the fifteenth century.

Chichele's Tower

Richard would have recognised Chichele's Tower, which was begun by Archbishop Chichele in 1434. It was not as large in Richard's time, as the two top floors were added in the early part of the sixteenth century. Approaching the tower from the Thames, Richard would have seen the statue of St Thomas Becket which had been placed in a niche after the tower's completion in 1435.

Standing inside the tower, it is easy to see where it was built against the entrance to the chapel. Fortuitously, the entrance arch to the chapel has been preserved. Three black round pillars of Purbeck marble hold up each side of the arch, with two slender pillars in the centre. Trefoil cut-outs are on each side, giving the door a unique shape. While Richard would not have known the arms above the door, as they are those of a later archbishop, he would recognise the ceiling with its carved heads.

Chapel

Even though the chapel is one of the oldest surviving parts of the palace, it has changed since Richard's time. As the chapel was largely destroyed by bombs during the Second World War, scorch marks still scar its floor. There are a few bits in the chapel that Richard would have recognised. Look in the choir stalls to see preserved medieval tile that Richard would have walked on. The layout of the chapel is close to what Richard would have seen as well.

George and Richard would have been in this room during church services on the days that they were at the palace. The smell of burning candles, the voice of the priest and the small bowed heads of Richard and George are easily imagined in the ambience of the chapel.

The Atrium

While Richard and George would not have seen the atrium the way it appears now, they would have seen it in its original state. This area makes up the Ewer Court, a courtyard that was here in medieval times. Looking at the entrance to the crypt, it is easy to see some of the renovations that have been done through the years, including bricked-in arches and doors. Perhaps the two boys spent some time walking in this courtyard as they explored the grounds of the palace.

The Crypt

This is the oldest part of the palace. Built in the twelfth century, this crypt has stood the test of time and escaped massive renovation work, mainly due to the fact it was susceptible to flooding. This meant that it was predominantly used as a storehouse, so Richard and George would most likely never have seen it.

Visiting the Palace Today

The palace is usually open to visitors only through a pre-booked guided tour. Dates and prices for the tours can be found on the Ticketmaster website at www.ticketmaster.co.uk/Lambeth-Palace-Tours-tickets/artist/1663351. On certain days of the year, the palace is open to all visitors. For more information on open days, call +44 (0) 207 898 1200 or see Lambeth Palace's website at

www.archbishopofcanterbury.org/pages/visit-lambeth-palace.html.
Lambeth Palace postcode: SE1 7JU.

Middleham Castle, North Yorkshire

Rising up out of the dales, Middleham Castle is every bit the fortress
it appears. The large, impregnable walls still look formidable, even
in a ruinous state. In 1823, English geographer E. W. Brayley said,
'As it is, majestic in decay, Middleham Castle, as an object, is the
noblest work of man in the County of Man.' You will find the castle
is as striking today as it was then.

The first stronghold at Middleham was a motte-and-bailey castle
likely built in the eleventh century. Its position can still be seen
from the present location of the castle. After the new stone castle
was built, the old site was deserted. The new site was not in a
highly defensible position; however, evidence remains to show that
protective fortifications were built, including a moat around the
castle, as well as an outer courtyard.

Through the years, the castle passed from Alan the Red, a
Norman who came over with William the Conqueror, to his
brother, finally falling into the hands of the Nevilles through the
marriage of Robert de Neville to Mary, daughter and heiress of
Ralph FitzRanulph. The Neville family would expend money to
enlarge and enrich Middleham during their time as its owners. The
castle would eventually pass to Richard after the death of the Earl
of Warwick.

Perhaps no other place held more meaning for Richard than the
imposing stone walls of Middleham Castle. So many significant
events in his life took place within the keep of this impressive
edifice – events that would change Richard as well as the country.
From his days in the earl's household to his days as King of
England, Middleham would hold both happy and depressing
memories.

The Gatehouse
Despite centuries of decay, the gatehouse is still imposing. It stands
three storeys high, with an arched stone entry. This was not the

original entrance to the building, but was a fifteenth-century addition, and would have been the entrance that Richard would have used to reach the inner courtyard. Look up at the gatehouse and find the turrets. While there is little evidence that sculpted stone figures of armed men would have adorned the battlements, these men can be seen on other Neville properties, such as Raby Castle, and it is likely they would have graced Middleham's battlements as well. Channels in the gatehouse show evidence of a portcullis, which would have offered extra protection.

Arriving at Middleham, Richard would have observed a very different town than the quiet town we see today; there had been a settlement there since Roman times. By the time Richard arrived, it was a bustling market town and important centre for the Earl of Warwick. It is easy to imagine Richard passing through the town and spotting the formidable towers for the first time, easy to picture his pride in his surroundings – pride that he was placed in the household of the greatest lord in the land to begin his training. Maybe he looked up at the turrets of the gatehouse as he entered into the castle through the north entrance. Whatever his thoughts, he had been placed in the care of the Earl of Warwick, and he would come to love this retreat from court.

Richard entered into the household of the Earl of Warwick to complete his education, and it is likely that he spent some of his time at Middleham. Paul Murray Kendall has Richard entering into the earl's household as early as 1461, but as David Baldwin points out, references to Richard during this time period place him in other locations. Very little is known about Richard's education, which probably resembled that of most nobles at the time, but it is known he spent time with the Countess of Warwick and her two daughters, Isabel and Anne. Isabel was nearer to Richard's age, but Richard would have been acquainted with both of the girls, and perhaps a friendship was formed at this time that would later foster a caring marriage between Richard and Anne.

Middleham is also the most likely place for Richard to have established friendships with the nobles who would eventually die fighting with him in battle. Another friendship that Richard presumably fostered at Middleham was with Francis Lovell, who proved time and again to be intensely loyal to Richard. It is conceivable that the two of them became close during their time at Middleham and other Warwick holdings, even though there is dispute as to whether Lovell and Richard were in his household during the same years. It seems likely they did meet while in the earl's care given their lifelong friendship.

Standing inside the inner courtyard, you will see a wooden staircase leading up to the keep. In the fifteenth century, this would have been a massive stone staircase. Walking towards the keep, you can just make out some remnants of the stone stairway. The twelfth-century keep dominates the area today, just as it would have in Richard's time.

The Great Hall and Privy Chamber

When Richard came back north after the death of Warwick, he made Middleham his principal residence. From here, he would have administered justice in the area. By entering into a mutually advantageous marriage with Anne Neville, he was able to secure the loyalties of people in the North previously loyal to the Neville family. But he also generated loyalty in his even-handed treatment of the people, and he would keep this northern support for the years of his reign.

All that is left of the Great Hall where Richard would have conducted much of the business of the North, entertained guests and held court is a shell. If you pause long enough, in your mind's eye you can recreate the scene. Hear the laughter and the thump of dishes being placed before Richard and his guests, and see the servants scurrying to and fro attending to everyone. It would have been a lavish scene, as Richard spent heavily on feasting. One of the guests he entertained here as king was a German nobleman named Nicholas von Poppelau. The king made a good impression on Poppelau, who described Richard as having a 'great heart'.

Richard's council would have met in the Great Hall and administered justice for the area. As Paul Murray Kendall points out in his book *The Yorkist Age*, 'Richard of Gloucester's council at Middleham became such an effective instrument of justice in the 1470s that after Richard became king, he created the Council of the North, which the Tudors continued.'

One of the earliest problems Richard would have to deal with during his tenure in the North was the Bastard of Fauconberg. Thomas Neville, an illegitimate son of Lord Fauconberg, and the Earl of Kent, William Neville, had led an uprising against Edward IV. Neville had been pardoned and sent north with Richard into Yorkshire; however, he returned south without permission and was arrested. Richard dealt swiftly with him, having him executed at Middleham.

From the hall, there would have been access to the great chamber and the privy chamber. These rooms would have also been well used by Richard during his tenure at the castle, and were equipped with a fireplace and access to latrines in the tower. A chapel lies to the east wall of the keep. Little remains, but if you take a closer look, you can make out the tracery windows in the walls. With the destruction of time it is harder to picture, but try to imagine the household meeting in the chapel to observe morning prayers. Take the stairway to the viewing platform for views of the site of the original motte-and-bailey castle, as well as the panoramic view of Wensleydale.

The South Range

The two-storey south range of the castle had towers located at the south-east and south-west corners. This range held several rooms at the first-floor level, with the one at the east end having a fireplace and south-facing windows. Two more chambers were in the west end of the range, with very similar layouts. These rooms were large and were described in the 1538 survey as a lady chamber with a gallery to the presence chamber.

The south-west tower is also known as the 'Prince's Tower' because legend has it that Richard's only legitimate son, Edward of Middleham, was born here. This is certainly plausible, because the 1538 survey names a room next to the tower in the west range a 'nursee'. In the nursery, Edward's wet nurse, Isabel Burgh, and his governess, Anne Idley, would have played an important role in his young life.

At Middleham, Edward would have spent his days playing in the courtyard, watching mummeries in the Great Hall, and spending time with his parents when they were at the keep. It was also here he would die. The *Croyland Chronicle* said that he was 'seized with an illness of but short duration …' His death left Richard bereft of his son and heir at a critical time in his reign. After Edward's death in 1484, Middleham would cease to be one of Richard's favourite residences. The memories that he had enjoyed would now be tinged with pain.

Edward IV at Middleham

Richard was not the only York brother to stay at Middleham. Edward IV also spent time there. His first visit in 1461 after the Battle of Towton was voluntary, but another visit in 1469 was not. After tensions between them had breached their relationship, the Earl of Warwick took Edward prisoner and held him captive at Middleham for a short time. Edward was able to outmanoeuvre Warwick in this game of political chess and soon was back in charge of his country.

Visiting the Castle Today

Middleham Castle is managed by English Heritage. The castle has a small gift shop where there are a surprising number of interesting books for purchase. There is also a fascinating and controversial statue of Richard III in the bailey. Take some time to look at all the symbolism on the figure.

Be aware that there is no car park on site, but there is room for parking on the street. For opening times and other visitor information, please visit the castle website at www.english-heritage. org.uk/daysout/properties/middleham-castle/ or contact the castle directly on +44 (0) 1969 62389. Middleham Castle postcode: DL8 4QG.

The Church of St Mary and St Alkelda, Middleham

In 1477 Richard secured a licence from Edward IV to erect a college at the church of Middleham, which had served the parish since the thirteenth century. It appears Richard's plans for the parish church of the town he seemed to favour as home were grand ones. In July 1478 Richard set forth statutes as to how the college was to be governed. The college was to have a dean, six priests, four clerks and six choristers. There was to be divine service daily, in which they were to pray for the good estate of the king, the queen, Cecily,

Richard, Anne, Edward, and for the souls of his father, brothers, sisters and all Christians.

Richard had strict guidelines for setting up the collegiate church, which was to be named the College of the Duke Richard of Gloucester. The dean and priests were to be residents of the college. According to Reverend William Atthill, each priest was to have his own stall, named after a saint. 'Our Lady's stall', located on the right side of the choir, was assigned to Dean William Beverley. Other saints included St George, St Catherine, St Ninian, St Cuthbert, St Anthony and St Barbara.

Richard endowed the college with one acre of meadow, lying near the Yore, and the advowson of the parish of Middleham. Later he granted them ten further acres. Most likely as king he had ideas to further endow the college, but his defeat at Bosworth by Henry VII put an end to those plans.

Visiting the Church Today

Nestled in Wensleydale, the parish church of Middleham is located within easy walking distance of the castle. An interesting juxtaposition of old and new greet you as you enter the building. The south porch you are standing on is nineteenth century, but the doorway in front of you is thirteenth century. This combination of old and new is repeated throughout the building.

The church not only acknowledges but celebrates its association with Richard III. Inside the church is a replica of the Middleham Jewel, which was found nearby. Richard's emblem of a boar can be found under the stained-glass window that honours him. The window features St Richard of Chichester in one panel and St Anne in another. At the base of the window are Richard, Anne and Edward. This window is not from Richard's time but was placed here in the 1930s. In addition to the plaster impressions of the Great Seal of Richard III, there is an emblem of a white rose.

The church is open to visitors. For more information on visiting, see the church's website, www.jervaulxchurches.co.uk/middleham/st_mary_akelda.html. The church of St Mary and St Alkelda postcode: DL8 4PQ.

Palace of Sheen (Shene, Schenes), Surrey

Sheen, in Surrey, was in the hands of the crown as early as the reign of Edward I. Royalty appeared to have enjoyed the place, as both Edward I and Edward II stayed here. It was here on 21 June 1377 that Edward III breathed his last. His grandson, Richard II, loved Sheen and visited often with his wife, Anne. After Anne died at Sheen, Richard II was stricken with grief and demolished the building. Rebuilding was begun under Henry V and by the time of Edward IV, the palace was once again large and impressive.

A description of expenditures in *The History of the King's Works* paints a picture of Sheen at the turn of the fourteenth century. There was an apartment block containing nine chambers, a chamber by the garden with eight fireplaces and a 'great house' in the cloister, equipped with four latrines and four fireplaces. A hall had been brought from Wimbledon and re-erected.

Years after the destruction of the building by Richard II, Henry V began a rebuilding project. The new palace would be built on a grander scale of freestone, ragstone, timber and brick. Elaborate stonework and woodwork decorated the building. Two large stone towers stood tall on the east side of the palace on the building known as Byfleet. A large brick wall enclosed the garden.

It is known that Richard was at Sheen in February of 1472, in the company of Edward, Elizabeth and George. After the death of Prince Edward, the Lancastrian heir, at Tewkesbury, his wife, Anne Neville, was left a widow. George was married to Isabel Neville and hoped to gain control of the entire fortune. Towards this end, he had taken his sister-in-law into his custody. Richard decided to marry Anne, which made George furious. As Edward tried to intervene, George said that Richard could marry his sister-in-law but would not be able to share in the inheritance. His opinion on the matter was of little consequence. Richard and Anne did marry, receiving a papal dispensation in April of 1472.

Another event involving the York family is said to have taken place at Sheen during Easter of 1465. Queen Elizabeth's brother, Anthony Woodville, was accompanying her from the chapel when he was surrounded by the queen's ladies, who, as he knelt in front of the queen, fastened a band of gold to his knee. They also attached a letter to his cap requesting the king allow a tournament. Woodville was enamoured of the idea and supposedly wrote to the Bastard of Burgundy immediately, requesting that he be part of the tournament. While some historians dispute this version, saying this happened at the marriage of Margaret to the Duke of Burgundy, it is an interesting story as it demonstrates the chivalry of the time.

After Elizabeth Woodville died in 1492, the palace would say its final goodbye to her. As her funeral barge floated to her final resting place at Windsor, her body would have passed the palace where she had spent so many happy times.

Visiting the Palace Site Today

As with Greenwich, nothing remains of the palace at Sheen. In December of 1497, a great fire broke out at the palace and it was destroyed. Henry VII rebuilt the palace on a grand scale, keeping largely to the same area occupied by Sheen. The Southwest London Archaeology Unit believes that Henry's palace was also moated and built on the same ground plan as Sheen. All that is left of the Tudor palace of Richmond is the main gateway and portions of a block.

To get to Richmond from London it is best to travel by tube. Take the District line to Richmond. To visualise the area the former palace occupied will require imagination. Make your way to Richmond Green. Meander down Old Palace Lane to the river. You are standing where the palace once met the river. Travelling from London by boat, Richard would have seen the palace in all its glory. With enough imagination, so can you. Old Palace Lane postcode: TW9 1PD.

Pontefract, West Yorkshire

Given to the de Lacy family by William the Conqueror, the land on which Pontefract Castle would rest was a natural location for a stronghold. By 1087 there was already a motte-and-bailey castle on the spot, and in 1090, Robert de Lacy founded the Priory of St John of Pontefract. It would have been a busy town filled with people, especially as Pontefract had a weekly market and an annual fair.

The Castle

Built on a rock high above the town, it is believed that the general plan of the castle included a main ward with two wards to the south, which formed a double enclosure. The wall that separated the barbicans was five feet thick. In addition to the south and middle gates which led into the main gate, there were also west and east gate entrances. The castle yard was surrounded by a high curtain wall with at least seven strong towers. The towers would have included the King's Tower, the Queen's Tower, Gascoigne's Tower, the Round Tower and others. The keep's wall was twenty feet, six inches thick.

Inside the castle, near the gatehouse, stood a chapel dedicated to St Clement. Originally Saxon, the chapel was renovated by the Normans and served as a collegiate church until the sixteenth century. The round tower, sixty-four feet in diameter, stood on what was the artificial motte. It stood high above the other towers and was similar in appearance to Clifford's Tower in York. The inner bailey consisted of more than two acres and was an irregular oval shape. The castle was formidable, and it was considered one of the largest and strongest in England.

A tower known as Swillington Tower used to stand in the west front of the castle. As late as the 1870s, a portion of the basement remained. Richard Holmes, writing in 1878, said the tower was forty-six feet square, and ten feet, six inches thick. Thomas of Lancaster is said to have been held in the tower before his execution at Pontefract by Edward II, but this is unlikely as the tower was probably built after his death.

John of Gaunt, married to the Duke of Lancaster's daughter Blanche, inherited the castle after the deaths of the Duke and his other daughter Maud. Gaunt then enlarged the castle. It was here that Gaunt's nephew Richard II died, presumably in Gascoigne's Tower, after the usurpation of his throne. Whether he was murdered or died a natural death is a subject of debate.

In 1460 the Earl of Salisbury, Richard Neville, was brought to Pontefract after the Battle of Wakefield. On 30 December he was killed at the castle. Richard, Duke of York, and Edmund, Earl of Rutland, along with Salisbury's son, Thomas Neville, all died at the Battle of Wakefield.

It was in the Priory of St John at Pontefract that the bodies of the brother and father of Richard III had been buried following the disastrous defeat at Wakefield. They were later exhumed to be reinterred at Fotheringhay. Richard, as the chief mourner, would have escorted the bodies to Fotheringhay, where a large funeral took place.

In his role as steward of the duchy of Lancaster in the North, Richard's official residence was at Pontefract Castle. He would have delegated many of his duties, but he would have needed to visit to oversee works done in his name. This means that Richard was at Pontefract on more than one occasion.

Richard also made use of Pontefract as a prison. After the death of Edward IV, Richard hurried to meet King Edward V, who was being escorted from Ludlow to London. The young king was in the care of his maternal uncle, Anthony Woodville, his half-brother, Richard Grey, and his chamberlain, Thomas Vaughn. After meeting the men on the road to London, Richard arrested Woodville, Grey and Vaughn, sending Vaughn to Pontefract. He accused the men of conspiring against the king, as well as planning violence against Richard. The men were later executed at Pontefract. Shakespeare immortalised the scene in his work *Richard III* by having Woodville say,

> O Pomfret, Pomfret! O thou bloody prison,
> Fatal and ominous to noble peers!
> Within the guilty closure of thy walls
> Richard the second here was hack'd to death;
> And, for more slander to thy dismal seat,
> We give thee up our guiltless blood to drink.

In the second year of his reign, Richard issued a charter reasserting the ancient rights of the burgesses in Pontefract. He incorporated the borough at this time as well. Richard was at Pontefract several times during his short reign, spending more than forty days at this huge fortress. It was here that Richard prepared before heading off to face down a rebellion following Buckingham's defection.

In 1484, Richard wrote to his mother from Pontefract. The surviving letter conveys the depth of feeling Richard had for Cecily.

Madam, I recommend myself to you as heartily as is possible to me; beseeching you in my most humble and affectionate manner of your daily blessing to my especial comfort and defence in my need. And, Madam, I heartily beseech you that I may often hear from you to my comfort. And such news as there is here my servant Thomas Bryan, this bearer, shall show you; to whom may it please you to give credence ... And I pray God send you the accomplishment of your noble desires. Written at Pontefract, the 3rd day of June, with the hand of Your most humble son, Ricardus Rex.

Richard's letter to Cecily shows that they were still in contact during his reign, although it does not give us a glimpse into Cecily's mindset during this time. Was she angry with Richard? Was she happy that he was on the throne?

Visiting Pontefract Today

As with many sites associated with Richard III, Pontefract is a ruin. However, enough of the castle grounds remain to give you an idea of its magnificence as the main residence of the lords of the Honour of Pontefract. Standing at the top of the keep's ruins, you can picture the corbelled turrets that would have topped the quatrefoil keep. The remains today are trefoil, but it is likely that the keep was made along the same lines as Clifford's Tower in York.

Walk towards the area where the King's Tower and Queen's Tower would have been. The Great Hall is believed to have joined the two towers, linking both sets of royal apartments to each other. Here is where Richard would have passed most of his time. The area is lovely today, but there are few remains to see. However, you can walk the area where the towers and Great Hall would have been and imagine the elegant sandstone towers with their parapets.

It is likely that an extensive garden would have existed within the inner bailey, as most castles of that time period contained one. Richard probably walked within the garden to clear his mind. The castle's guidebook suggests that the garden would have been located near the revetment, or retaining wall, because a rare example of medieval garden seating, a stone bench, had been built into the wall.

Information boards are placed throughout the castle ruins. You can easily spend an hour or two at the castle if you visit every area. Admittance to the castle is free. For more information on opening times, visit the castle's website at www.experiencewakefield.co.uk/ thedms.aspx?dms=3&feature=1&venue=2190562. Postcode for Pontefract Castle: WF8 1QH.

Priory of St John at Pontefract

The Cluniac Priory of St John the Evangelist was founded in 1090 by Robert de Lacy. The priory buildings were destroyed in the battles between Stephen and Matilda, but were rebuilt. After his execution, the body of Thomas of Lancaster was buried near the altar of the priory church. After miracles were reported, a chantry chapel was built for Thomas's memory. Once word of the miracles got out, his chantry chapel became more of a shrine.

Keeping with the custom of the time, the Priory of St John would have been richly decorated. Remnants of its colourful medieval tile feature intricate patterns. As wealthy patrons both visited and were buried here, the church would have been opulently decorated with elegant tracery and brightly coloured wall paintings in order to impress. Its stained-glass windows would have flooded the nave of the church with light. In addition to its cloisters, the priory contained a chapter house as well as other monastic buildings.

Richard's father and his brother, Edmund, had been buried here after their deaths at Wakefield. During Edward IV's reign, the bodies were dug up and transported to Fotheringhay for grand reburial. Richard, as chief mourner, would have been present in Pontefract during this time.

Visiting the Priory Site Today

Nothing but a big field where the priory was located survives today. To find the field, with its informative panel, walk to Ferrybridge Road and Box Lane. The panel on Box Lane shows the layout of the priory. The priory is only a short walk from the castle.

Explore the field to get an idea of the size of the church and chapter house. There are several paths leading to different areas of the grounds.

York, Yorkshire

York has been a city since Roman times, when it was called *Eboracum*. After the Romans left, it eventually became an Anglo-Saxon town. By 867 the Vikings had conquered and taken over the town, and it later became part of the Danelaw. After the arrival of William the Conqueror, the city fell into the hands of the Normans, and William quickly had two castles built to fortify the rebellious city. Under King John, York became a self-governing city with the right to elect its own mayor. By Richard's time, the city had fallen into an economic decline.

Richard's earliest association with York would have been in relation to his father's death. While he would not have seen it, Richard would have undoubtedly heard about his father's death outside of Sandal Castle and the subsequent hanging of his bloody head on the pike above Micklegate Bar. One can only imagine the young Richard grieving for his father as he visualised this gruesome scene. It is ironic that a city with such a terrible association for him would come to be one of the places where he held the most support. He would visit the city many times over the course of his life, so there are several places in York that have associations with him.

Richard's affection for the city is shown by the numerous times he interceded for its citizens. He supported them in disputes with powerful nobles, as well as with Edward IV when the king threatened to revoke the city's liberties. The citizens of York welcomed the fact that Richard did not try to interfere with its mayoral elections and a mutual appreciation developed between the future king and York. York's affection for Richard is best shown by an entry in its public records following his death, 'King Richard ... piteously slain and murdered, to the great heaviness of this city.'

The York Richard would have known would have been a gritty, smelly place bustling with scores of people going about their daily work. Nestled between the rivers Foss and Ouse, the town was the city of the North. Timber-framed buildings crowded the narrow lanes of the city and animals roamed in yards. Parish churches with their soaring steeples looked over their flocks. Large stone walls had already been standing for centuries, surrounding the city to protect it from invaders, with main gates placed strategically in four places. Small houses and stores lined each bridge across the rivers.

Micklegate Bar

Micklegate Bar still stands in York today, as it has for more than 800 years. During that time, the city's main gatehouse stood witness to a number of events, and played host to several severed heads. A square tower with an arch and turrets, it is an imposing site today even without its barbican, which was removed before 1816. Its three-storey gatehouse sits high above the street, offering a good vantage point to watch for approaching visitors. Micklegate means 'great street', and even though it has changed since Richard's time, it still lives up to its name. One of York's earlier historians, Francis Drake, said that the bar also had a portcullis and a double wooden gate in medieval times, but these had been torn down.

Richard would have passed through the gate almost every time he visited the city. Upon his visit in 1476, the council decided that he would be presented with six swans and six pikes when he reached the city. In 1483, he was presented with bread and wine. As monarch, he would have been met and welcomed outside the city by the mayor and city fathers. When Richard visited York in August after being crowned king, he was met at Brekles Mills and escorted to the city through Micklegate in a lavish procession. The mayor and aldermen were garbed in scarlet, while the chamberlains were robed in red. After a series of elaborate pageants, the mayor presented King Richard and Queen Anne with gifts of marks and gold.

Visiting Micklegate Bar Today

Micklegate Bar's museum is run by the York Archaeological Trust. Today it contains the Henry VII Experience. The museum's information panels do a good job of explaining the history of York under Henry VII. For the more macabre, a replica of the Duke of York's head hangs on a spike in the museum.

Visitors can buy a reduced ticket to see both the Richard III Experience and the Henry VII Experience. For more information on visiting the Henry VII Experience, see the website at richardiiiexperience.com/visiting/. Phone ahead for further information to +44 (0) 1904 615505.

Walmgate Bar

Walmgate Bar was on the principal road from Hull and it makes sense that this would be the gate through which Edward IV would have entered upon his return from exile in March of 1471. After leaving Kingston-upon-Hull, where he had been denied entry, he made straight for York. Edward, Richard and the others with them were in a desperate situation. They were in hostile territory, with only a letter signed by Henry Percy to assist them in winning over the people.

Three miles outside of York, Edward's party was met by the city's recorder, who told the king that it was not safe for Edward to enter York. Edward and Richard persisted, and the group was met again outside of the city gates and asked to leave. Edward had left his troops outside the walls and had brought with him fifteen or sixteen people. Promising that he had only come to claim his inheritance as the Duke of York and not to claim the crown, he asked for their assistance in reclaiming his inheritance.

According to Polydore Vergil, Edward gave many speeches and flattered the citizens until they began to soften towards him. The Warkworth chronicler goes so far as to say that he cheered for Henry, saying 'A! Kynge Henry! A! Kynge and Prynce Edwarde!' and wore Prince Edward's symbol of a white ostrich feather in his hat. Having won over the citizens, Edward, Richard and the rest of the small group were allowed entrance into the city through Walmgate Bar. Richard's men, as well as the rest of the soldiers, remained outside.

The bar was damaged during the last siege of York in 1644 when it suffered artillery hits. The scars from those hits can still be seen today, despite repair work in 1648. The archway of the outer gate is Gothic and is the oldest part of the structure. If Richard were to see the gate today, the only part he would not recognise would be the timber building on the inside. Walmgate is the only gate in York to retain its barbican, which was completed in the fourteenth century. Its wooden gates are from the fifteenth century. The gate also retains its portcullis and it gives a better picture of what a complete gate would have looked like in the fifteenth century. Walmgate had an added fortification of a moat that passed under the barbican.

Above the gatehouse, there are two crenellated turrets, which offered a great vantage point where one could watch for any threats. People lived in the gatehouse up until the twentieth century. In the sixteenth century, the Elizabethan timber-framed building was added. Like Micklegate Bar, Walmgate also had its share of heads placed on spikes.

Visiting Walmgate Bar Today

Unlike Micklegate, there is no museum above Walmgate Bar. But this gem of medieval architecture is still well worth a visit. Visitors can walk along the walls to see what the battlements were like. You can also spend time walking around the barbican, looking for scarring from the artillery shells. I like to walk right outside the bar and look at it, blocking out the modern sounds of car horns and people talking on their mobiles. I imagine the fear and courage that both Richard and Edward IV felt on that day long ago in March, with a cold wind whipping across the Yorkshire dales, both men knowing that if they failed to gain entrance to York all might be lost. Then I think of the courage it took to walk between the Barbican walls and into the ancient city without their men, knowing that many of the citizens were against them. This was the only time Richard probably felt unease in York, almost like an unwelcome stranger in the city he would come to know so well.

Austin Friars

The Austin Friars in York were of the order of St Augustine. Originally from Tickhill, they were in York by July of 1272 and built their friary on the banks of the River Ouse in Lendal. Richard lodged here at the friary several times. While he was here, the friars offered him gifts of several gallons of wine, along with other things. The friary must have held pleasant memories for him, because in 1484 he appointed an Austin friar, William Bewick, as the 'surveyor of the King's works and buildings'.

All that remains of the Austin Friars in York is a bit of limestone wall by the River Ouse and a few remnants in the Yorkshire Museum (which also holds the Middleham Jewel). After the Dissolution, the house was surrendered to the king's men. At that time, the order held the prior, nine priests and four novices. Two chalices and seven spoons were sent to the king's jewel house and the golden age of the Austin Friars was over.

To see the remains of the Austin Friars masonry, you will need to go into the pub Lendal Cellars. The pub has a display on the lower level that shows the masonry and gives a bit of history about the priory.

York Guildhall

Located on the east bank of the River Ouse, the guildhall was a place Richard visited several times. Erected in the mid-fifteenth century, it was built by the joint effort of the mayor and commonality, along with the Guild of St Christopher. The hall was used for many purposes, including plays.

The original guildhall was largely destroyed by an air raid in the Second World War and was rebuilt as close to its original form as possible. Inside the medieval guildhall, ten octagonal pillars of oak resting on stone bases supported a timbered roof, decorated with grotesques and the royal arms of Henry V. At the west end of the hall, a dais was enclosed by a wooden screen. It was here at the guildhall that Richard watched the Creed play on 7 September 1483. While not much is known about the play itself, the account rolls of the Corpus Christi Guild state that the play was for the instruction and information on the Christian faith and was for the glory of God and the instruction of the people.

Richard and Anne joined the Corpus Christi Guild in 1477 and as members would have joined in the procession of the pageants of Corpus Christi. The religious festival of Corpus Christi was held on the Thursday after Trinity Sunday, and it was a day of plays and pageants performed by the trade guilds located in the city. Large scaffolds were placed on wheels and divided into two stages, with the upper stage being uncovered. This allowed for the movement from one station to the next. In 1399, twelve places had been fixed for the performances, but this restriction was removed in the fifteenth century.

On the morning of the Corpus Christi festival, the people who were joining in the procession met at the gates of the Priory of the

Holy Trinity in Micklegate. The clergy, including the Master of the Guild, were first, carrying the shrine. Following them were the Lord Mayor and aldermen in their ceremonial robes, accompanied by city officers bearing torches. Next came the members of the trade associations carrying their torches and banners. Along their route, which took them to the cathedral and the Hospital of St Leonard, houses were decorated with tapestries and flowers.

In his book *Corpus Christi Pageants in England*, Matthew Spencer included a detailed description of the shrine when it was sold in 1547:

> First, the said shrine is gilded, having six images gilded, with an image of the birth of our Lord, of mother of pearl, silver and gilt, and thirty-three small images enamelled standing about the same, and a tablet of gold; two gold rings, one with a sapphire, and the other with a pearl, and eight other little images, and a great tablet of gold having in it the image of our Lady, of mother of pearl …
> (translated into a modern version)

Visiting the Guildhall Today

The guildhall is no longer open to the public, except on special occasions. However, you can still look at the outside of the structure, which is located behind the Mansion House. While seeing the same Creed play as Richard would require a time machine, you can book an event and enjoy the ambience of the guildhall. York guildhall postcode: YO1 9QN.

York Minster

Few cathedrals are as evocative as the Cathedral and Metropolitan church of St Peter in York, which is York Minster's full name. The largest Gothic cathedral in England, it dominates the city of York. Not only a cathedral, as it contains a bishop's seat, it is also a minster, because it was founded by a missionary. The history of this place goes back to Roman times, and the ruins of a Roman basilica were found underneath the current minster. It is likely that Constantine was proclaimed emperor here in the basilica.

After the Romans left, the basilica fell to ruin. Centuries later, Edwin, a Saxon king of Northumberland, converted to Christianity and erected a wooden building for his baptism. Following his baptism, he ordered a stone building dedicated to St Peter to be erected. After the building was damaged by fire, it was rebuilt, but fell once again to a fire. The Norman church was built in the same spot and remained there until 1187 when it, too, was destroyed by a fire. Construction would take more than 200 years, but the building was finally completed in the Gothic style.

Richard and York Minster

Upon hearing of the death of his brother, Richard's first public act was to hasten to the minster. On this spot where people had worshipped for centuries, he proclaimed his loyalty to his new king, Edward V. Ever since Richard's brief reign, people have strenuously debated whether or not he had already decided to claim the throne even as he outwardly pledged his loyalty to his brother's son, the son Edward had entrusted to him above all others. Proponents of Richard claim that his loyalty to his brother had been tested time and again and had never wavered. Others point to the fact that Richard immediately sent the young king's maternal uncle to Pontefract to be executed. This conflict regarding Richard's character will likely never be resolved to all parties' satisfaction.

As king, Richard began plans to fund a chantry at York Minster. This chantry was to be served by 100 priests, who would say prayers for him and the members of his family. An ambitious plan, it never fully materialised as his death precluded its completion. Altars had been built by the time of Richard's death, but they were apparently torn down. The affinity Richard had for the north makes it possible that he intended the chantry to be his mausoleum.

When Richard and Anne made their triumphant entry into York after his coronation, they were escorted to the minster, where they were met at the west door by the dean and the clergy, dressed in red silken copes. After they had been sprinkled with holy water, the Lord's Prayer was said. Next, services were held, including a prayer of blessing for the king. Following the service, the procession continued to the Archbishop's Palace.

The minster would play an important role in completing one of Richard's chief aims – the investiture of his son, Edward of

Middleham, as Prince of Wales. Upon arriving in York, Richard sent to London for quality items for the ceremony. He required one doublet of purple satin lined with Holland cloth, one doublet of tawny satin, two short doublets of crimson cloth of gold, many other gowns of cloth of gold and satin, banners, coats of arms and golden armour, along with 13,000 livery badges with Richard's device of the white boar.

On 8 September 1483, the procession arrived at the minster to find the High Altar festooned with silver and gilt figures of the twelve apostles, as well as other relics the king had provided. It may have been at this time that Richard donated a crucifix, bejewelled with rubies and sapphires, to the minster. The king and queen wore their crowns, leading to whispers that a second coronation had been held. After Mass, performed by the Bishop of Durham, the party moved to the archbishop's palace, where Edward was knighted and then invested as Prince of Wales by the girding on of the sword. A garland wreath was placed upon his head, a gold ring was placed on his finger and a golden staff was handed to him. The king also knighted his illegitimate son, John; Clarence's son, Edward; and the Spanish ambassador. Afterwards, a large feast was held in the palace. It must have been an exciting day for Richard, a proud father watching his dynastic ambitions start to take root. Sadly, this would be one of the last times the family would be together, as Edward would die shortly afterwards.

Richard would have gazed upon a minster that, from the outside, largely appeared the same as today. The Great West Window had the same stonework, even though today's version is an exact replica. Some of the panels in the window had to be replaced, but many of the originals remain.

Visiting the Minster Today

It is best to approach the minster on foot instead of driving. This gives you a feel of how it would have appeared to Richard as he approached it.

Entrance to the minster is through the west side. Look at the Great West Doors as you stand in line to get in to the building. Once inside, turn back toward the doors and look up at the West Window. The tracery of the window had to be replaced in the 1980s, but exact replicas of the stonework were made. The window that you are looking at is largely the same as it was in Richard's time.

As you move into the south transept you are in the earliest part of today's building. The minster has been plagued by fire, and the one in 1984 damaged the building, destroying the roof. The entrance to the undercroft, treasury and crypt is here, but these rooms are best seen last.

The tomb of Archbishop Richard Scrope is in the Lady chapel. Richard would have recognised the tomb of the archbishop, who was executed by Henry IV. Another fire in 1829 damaged his tomb, but it was restored in 1972.

The East Window was made in the early part of the fifteenth century. It contains 117 panels that depict the days of creation, as well as other events in the Old and New Testaments. Historical and mythical figures dominate the bottom row.

The shrine of St William would have stood behind the high altar. After Archbishop William Fitzherbert was canonised in 1227, his shrine became a popular pilgrimage site. Unfortunately, the shrine was dismantled during the Dissolution. St William's story is narrated in the St William Window in the north choir aisle. Fragments of the shrine are in the Yorkshire Museum.

In the south choir aisle, look for a glass panel picturing St Cuthbert holding St Oswald's head. This glass would have decorated the minster during Richard's time as well. In the choir, Richard would have recognised the badges and shields of the nobility, which include those of Bohun, Percy, Clifford and Neville. In the choir clerestory are the fourteenth-century windows decorated with figures of saints and kings. The elaborate archbishop's throne, called a cathedra, is located in the choir.

The Five Sisters Window in the north transept was built in the mid-thirteenth century. The window appears darker than the others, and it is the oldest complete window in the building. There are many theories about the name of the window, but my favourite is that five nuns wove a tapestry for the church which was used as a pattern for the window.

The chapter house entrance is in the eastern corner of the north transept. This part of York Minster was in use by the thirteenth century, and it is here that Richard met with city leaders to tell them he was granting a relief of some of the taxes they owed the crown. Richard would have seen walls brightly coloured with paintings, but the room looks much like it did in his time. Medieval carvings abound in this part of the minster, and it is worth taking time to discover each one. The spacious room is breathtaking, with no central column to block the view. The original ceiling panels are on display in the undercroft.

During the Dissolution, the chantries that dominated the minster were destroyed and many of the treasures held within were seized by the Crown. The minster lost much of its medieval look with the destruction of its shrines, more than fifty chantries and several altars. The nave was left bare, which emphasised the wide expanse of space. The original medieval bosses on the ceiling were lost in the fire of 1840, but most of the key bosses were replaced with exact replicas.

After absorbing the atmosphere of the minster with its soaring ceilings, medieval stained glass, elaborate tombs and vast expanse of space, it is hard to transition to modern times. Ease the feeling by visiting the undercroft, crypt and treasury first. The exhibitions here are among the best. Spend some time in the gift shop and then retrace your steps to the exit.

After exiting the building, spend some time wandering around the outside. As the Great West Door is the ceremonial entrance to the minster, Richard would have used it upon his visits. On the north-east side of the cathedral is St William's College. Richard would have seen this timber-framed building, which was the lodging for the chantry priests. It is now York Minster's conference area, but sometimes a few of the medieval rooms are open to the public. North of the minster is the green expanse of Dean's Park, which was created when the buildings nearby were demolished. The area around the minster, known as the Liberty of St Peter, would have been walled and gated during the medieval era. The Liberty functioned as its own city, with its own laws and jail. One of the surviving gates of the Liberty of St Peter is at the west end of the park.

Within the gates stands the Treasurer's House, which is now open to the public via the National Trust. Further along is York Minster's Library and Archives. This building, the former chapel, is all that survives of the massive medieval archbishop's palace where Edward was invested as Prince of Wales. There is a plaque on the building commemorating his investiture. The only other remnant of the palace is arcading, perhaps once forming a cloister walk, which is now part of the Kohima memorial.

For opening times, call the minster on +44 (0) 1904 557200 or visit its website at www.yorkminster.org/visit-york-minster.html. York Minster postcode: YO1 7HH.

My Favourite Place in York Minster

The entire building is breath-taking, and I have been known to spend hours inside. My favourite part of the cathedral is the choir screen. I love to stand before the screen and imagine Richard doing the same. His view would have been much different, as the figures were brightly coloured during the medieval period. Even though the nearly life-size statues represent kings of England, they are obviously not drawn to life. Still, I enjoy picturing each king's history as I walk up and down looking at them.

Monk Bar

Monk Bar is not likely a place that Richard would have visited. It makes our list, however, because for years it housed the Richard III Museum and because it was in York during Richard's time there. Today it houses the Richard III Experience, which is owned by the York Archaeological Trust.

Monk Bar was one of York's fortified gateways. The top storey of the Bar was added during Richard's reign, making it taller than the other gateways. Francis Drake called Monk Bar 'a handsome port, with a good quantity of large grit stones in the foundation to denote it ancient, as well as the arms of old France, quartered with England, on the battlements without'.

The Richard III Experience is informative for those unfamiliar with the York family. It offers an overview of Richard's life, as well as key battles in the Wars of the Roses.

Visitors can buy a reduced ticket to see both the Richard III Experience and the Henry VII Experience. For more information on visiting the Richard III Experience, see the website at richardiiiexperience.com/visiting/.

Holy Trinity, Micklegate

The Priory of Holy Trinity, Micklegate, was a monastery that stood near Micklegate. The priory was of the Benedictine Order and played an important role in the city. For a time, the shrine used in the festival of Corpus Christi was housed in the priory. Those taking part in the festival met at the priory gate, where the first pageant took place. The procession would have departed from here, and would have passed along crowded streets on its way to the minster.

The priory's gates are long gone, as are all the monastic buildings, with the exception of the priory church. According to the church, it is the only monastic building to have survived as a place of worship in York.

Visiting the Church Today

The church is open to visitors. Admission is free, although donations are welcome. To find out more about visiting the church and to see a virtual tour of the monastic buildings, visit the church's website at www.holytrinityyork.org/visit.

Cawood Castle, North Yorkshire

Located on shores of the River Ouse, Cawood Castle was one of the residences of the archbishops of York. The castle was also popular with royals. Edward I's second wife, Margaret, had planned to go into her confinement at Cawood, but the baby came earlier than expected. Edward I stayed here during his wars with the Scots. Later, Edward II and his wife, Isabella, stayed here as well. Henry VIII brought his 'Rose without a Thorn', Catherine Howard, to the castle and stayed for two days.

By the fifteenth century the castle had become more of a palace. George Neville held a feast here to celebrate his enthronement as the Archbishop of York. Richard, as Duke of Gloucester, attended the celebration.

The feast was extravagant, most likely to showcase the wealth and power of the Neville family. Richard was seated in the chief chamber. He was the only male at the table and his aunt and sister were seated with him. Also sitting at the table were Isabel and

Anne Neville, the Earl of Warwick's daughters. This may have been because Richard knew the girls and enjoyed their company, or it might have been more strategic on Warwick's part, as he may have already been considering a marriage between the king's brothers and his daughters.

The hall had been richly decorated and the cloth of estate was hung on the wall. Cushions made of silk and of cloth of gold were placed on the bench and a fire blazed, making the rooms comfortable and cosy. Cooks had laboured over the food, which included 2,000 pigs, chickens and pigeons, 104 oxen, 1,000 sheep, 200 pheasants, 100 stags, 4,000 cold tarts, 104 peacocks and a host of other meats and pastries, with 100 tuns of wine and 300 tuns of ale. The meal also included subtleties and sugar sculptures, including one of a dolphin, one of St George, and one of a dragon.

Visiting the Castle Today
The castle was slated for 'slighting' by Parliament following the Civil War, so most of this historical treasure has been destroyed. All that remains is the gatehouse with a domestic wing. The buttery-white stone of the gatehouse sets it off from the rest of the building. The gatehouse is much like it was in medieval times. When it was renovated, the parapet had to be reconstructed and the pitched roof removed. A flat roof was put in place to restore the gatehouse to its original look.

Cawood Castle is in the hands of the National Trust. It is not open for tourists, but you may book lodging in the gatehouse. It is located near the town of Cawood, south of York. As you stand and view the structure, think of these lines written about it by William Wheater in his book *The History of the Parishes of Sherburn and Cawood*: 'Come, then, with me and gaze awhile on this decaying scene, You know what things are now, but think! Just think what they have been …' Cawood Castle postcode: YO8 3SG.

Abbey of Stratford Langthorne, Stratford

The Abbey of Stratford Langthorne was located a few miles from London. Founded in 1135 by William de Montfichet, the abbey was a daughter house of the Abbey of Savigny in Normandy. It has long been believed that the house was absorbed into the Cistercian order in 1147, but recent research by historian Constance Hoffman Berman brings that date into question.

Montfichet richly endowed the abbey with two mills, woods, and eleven acres of meadow. The abbey was dedicated to the Virgin Mary and all saints.

Henry II confirmed the grants by Montfichet in a charter, along with those of Gilbert de Montfichet and others. Henry III gave a generous grant of free warren to the abbot and convent of Stratford in their demesne lands in West Ham, Leyton, Chigwell, Woodford, Montnessing (Gynges Munteny), and several others. They were also given a licence to enclose and clear the field and till the grove of Corpech in the parish of Leyton, as well as one to make a park. They were granted a weekly market on Tuesday at their manor of Great Burghsted and a yearly fair there on the feast of St Mary Magdalene held in July.

The abbey became wealthy, with about 1,500 acres in Essex alone. They also held lands elsewhere, including houses in London and land in Kent. They had pastures for 800 sheep, as well as liberties in the forest at Windsor. The abbot was summoned to Parliament under both Edward I and Edward II, which gives an indication of how powerful the abbey was. During the barons' rebellion under Henry III, the papal legate, Ottobuono Fieshci, stayed at Stratford Langthorne with the king during negotiations with the barons.

Nothing remains today of this great abbey, but a portion of the gate remained in the 1700s. It was described as a gatehouse with a great hall, built of brick with a small stone arch to the side. The plan of the abbey apparently followed that of most medieval monasteries. The abbey would probably have had a square cloister, enclosed by buildings, with the church to one side and the refectory on the other. The chapter house would have been located to one side of the cloister. Most Cistercian churches were built in a cross shape with a central tower. Several accounts claim that the abbey was moated, which was unusual. It would have been a great house, with lodgings sufficient for kings.

Richard stayed at the abbey as he accompanied his sister, Margaret, and her retinue to Margate, where she was sailing from to marry Charles the Bold, Duke of Burgundy. Charles Derek Ross, in his biography of Edward IV, says that the group stayed at Stratford by Bow, and that both Kendall and Scofield got this detail incorrect. However, as early as 1795, it was noted that a careful examination of the charters show most references to an abbey at Stratford by Bow are in fact a confusion with the Abbey of Stratford Langthorne.

The importance of the abbey to Richard's family is evident from a grant of Edward IV in the patent rolls. Edward's grant states that St Mary Stratford Langthorne is 'of the foundation of the king's progenitors and of the king's patronage' and granted it two tuns of red wine yearly in the port of London, one at Martinmas and the other at Easter for the celebration of Mass. This later changed to money. In December of 1476, Edward granted the abbot and convent of Stratford Langthorne a market on Wednesdays in Bellerica (Billericay) and two fairs there, one on the feast of St Mary Magdalen and one on the Decollation of St John with all liberties, free customs and profits. Both fairs were for three days.

It would have been a festive time at the abbey when Margaret and Richard were there. She was about to marry a powerful duke and help fulfil her part of the dynastic obligations of the House of York. Everything we know about Margaret shows her to be a strong woman, highly aware of her duties as the sister of the king. While the time would also have been bittersweet, as Richard was cognisant this journey might be the last time he spent with his sister, he would have realised what this marriage symbolised for his family. The Duke of Burgundy had Lancastrian ties but was uniting with the House of York. It was a reminder to all of how far the Lancastrians had fallen.

Visiting the Abbey Site Today

The abbey's once great lands are hidden today under a morass of industrial development, factories and railways. When you visit come via the Abbey Road station. Once off the station, there is an area called Abbey Gardens where excavations yielded some of the abbey ruins. On this spot was the northern part of the gatehouse. If you look at the rail lines, you can see where the main abbey complex once stood.

Visiting the West Ham parish church of All Saints, which once belonged to the abbey, is the best way to see remnants of the abbey. All that remains of the abbey building is the abbey window in the Long Porch and a carved skull stone from the charnel house. Postcode: E15 3HU.

Margate, Kent

Located about sixteen miles north-east of Canterbury, Margate is situated on the coast and was within the liberties of the Cinque Ports. A stream flowing into the sea earned the town the early name of Meregate. Richard and George may have come ashore here on their return from exile. However, Richard was certainly here on one occasion as it was from this small fishing village that Margaret of York departed to Sluys (Sluis) for her wedding to Charles, Duke of Burgundy. This marriage was one of several reasons the Earl of Warwick felt alienated from the king. He believed that his negotiations with the French were made a mockery of by this alliance with Burgundy. He also believed that the queen's family, the Woodvilles, had promoted the match. This was true, but it seems they did so to obey Edward's wishes and not through subversive actions.

The marriage of Margaret and Charles was not only preferred by the king, but also by the merchants, who did not want the profitable trade with Burgundy to cease. Additionally, the people's antipathy for the French played a role in this choice.

Despite Warwick's growing bitter feelings, he was one of the party accompanying Margaret to Margate. After spending several days at the abbey at Stratford Langthorne, the party moved on, finally arriving at the coastal town. Here, Margaret would part from her family and travel on to Sluys, where she would become the Duchess of Burgundy. Richard, Margaret and the rest of the family probably spent a few quiet moments alone remembering their childhood together. Perhaps they talked about the future of their family, their ambitions and what Margaret could do to promote the Yorkist agenda with the duke. It is easy to imagine Margaret sailing away as Richard and the remainder of her retinue were left behind, standing by the docks watching her leave. The chalky-white cliffs of the area would have been the last thing to fade away as she headed toward her new home.

Visiting Margate Today

Margate is now a pleasant seaside resort in the district of Thanet. There is little to see of the medieval town, but it is worth a visit to get an idea of what Margaret faced as she was leaving for a new life with her husband. Take time to visit the Margate Harbour Arm to get a view of the town from the sea. Margate Harbour Arm postcode: CT9 1JD.

Bury St Edmunds, Suffolk

The abbey of St Edmunds in Bury owes much of its existence as the richest and largest Benedictine house in medieval England to the fact that St Edmund was buried here. After Anglo-Saxon king Edmund decided to resist paying the Danish invaders, he was killed fighting them. The Christian king was eventually buried at the abbey in a wooden church. After the abbey became part of the Benedictine order in 1020, the wooden church was torn down and an enormous church was built to house his body.

His shrine quickly became a place of pilgrimage, adding tremendously to the abbey's coffers. The monks carefully cultivated the status of the shrine by copiously recording any miracle attributed to the saint. One story about the shrine involved a thief who would kiss the plate where offerings were placed, taking the money into her mouth. One day, her mouth froze and the money fell out. After the woman remained stuck to the table all day, she lost her desire to steal. Several people claimed to have been healed from various ailments, including blindness, and the number of pilgrims visiting the shrine soared.

In the Domesday survey the town of St Edmunds Bury, as it became known, contained thirty priests, deacons and clerks, twenty-eight nuns and poor persons, seventy-five bakers, ale-brewers, tailors, washer-women, shoemakers, cooks, porters, stewards and other merchants, thirty-four knights and 342 houses. It was a prosperous community and was expanding quickly. At one point, the abbey had eighty monks, 111 servants and eleven chaplains. The monks would have been busy as the monastery was responsible for producing one of the early Bibles. The Bury Bible is part of the collection in the library of Corpus Christi College, Cambridge.

Royalty often visited the shrine of St Edmund. Edward the Confessor was known for walking the last mile barefoot as the pilgrims did in order to venerate the saint. Both Henry I and Henry II stayed here, as well as King John. Three parliaments were held in the town. One of these, the parliament in 1446, held a few years before Richard's birth, is one that he would have heard about. The parliament came about through the manoeuvring of Queen Margaret and Cardinal Beaufort. It was here that Humphrey, Duke of Gloucester, who had served as regent for the king, was arrested. The day after his arrest he was found dead in bed. Richard, Duke of York, would later think of this when he, too, was summoned to a great council in Coventry. Remembering the fate of the Duke of Gloucester, he refused to attend.

When Edward IV came to Bury St Edmunds with Richard, it is likely he would have garnered the same reception that Henry VI did. Accounts of Henry's reception say that the alderman, burgesses and attendants, dressed in scarlet robes, came out to meet the king. He was received at the monastery by all the clergy, with the Bishop of Norwich and the abbot dressed in their pontifical robes. After an offering at the shrine, the king went to the abbot's palace, which had been richly decorated for his visit. An illustration of the shrine of St Edmund shows Henry VI kneeling before an elaborate reliquary of gold, which rested on a Gothic stone pedestal. The circular walls behind the pedestal had painted angels watching over the shrine.

Richard and Edward would have entered through the abbey's great gate. The impressive gatehouse with its intricate stonework was meant to impress. As the heavy portcullis raised, Richard and Edward would have passed under the embattled gatehouse and into the great court.

Richard was pious, probably owing to his mother's influence, and visiting the shrine would have been a momentous occasion for him. Imagine his anticipation as the great bronze doors of the church swung wide open to admit Edward and Richard as they made their way to pray at the shrine. After kneeling at the shrine and making his offering, Richard would have lodged in the abbot's lavish palace.

Visiting the Abbey Today

The Great Gate of the abbey still survives. The three-storey gatehouse is resplendent and gives an indication of the former opulence of the abbey. Stand in front of it for a moment to drink in all the intricate carvings that Richard would have seen. The gatehouse is approximately fifty feet long and sixty-two feet high and is greatly ornamented. Near the top are two decorations containing two interlaced triangles. Once you are inside, look up to see where the large portcullis would have hung. Upon entering the abbey precincts, a visitor would have seen the great court with the abbot's palace, which occupied the eastern side. Behind the palace was the abbot's cloisters. It is easy to imagine Richard walking through the cloisters, even though the building no longer remains.

The limestone church had great octagonal towers. The church, built in the shape of a cross, was more than 500 feet long with a nave that was thirty-three feet wide. The shrine of St Edmund was located in the east end in a semi-circle chapel. Beneath the shrine was the vaulted Chapel of Saint Mary, supported by twenty-four marble pillars. A fountain murmured peacefully within the chapel.

John Leland wrote of the town and abbey:

> The sun hath not shone on a town more prettily situated on a gradual and easy descent, with a small river flowing on the eastern part; or a monastery more illustrious, whether we consider its wealth, its extent, or its incomparable magnificence: you might indeed say that the monastery itself is a town, so many gates there are, some of them of brass; so many towers; and a church, than which none can be more magnificent, and subservient to which are three others also splendidly adorned with admirable workmanship, and standing in one and the same church yard. The rivulet mentioned above, with an arched bridge thrown over it, glides through the bounds of the monastery.

Today visitors entering through the gate come into the abbey gardens. A glorious panorama of beautiful flowers and herbs grace the area. It is worth wandering through the gardens before heading to the rest of the abbey site. The layout of the abbey can be difficult to discern, but informative panels throughout the grounds may help you to recreate the great abbey in your mind. Some structures are still extant, such as the picturesque Abbot's Bridge.

The Norman tower was a gateway into the abbey church. It was built in the early twelfth century and is now the bell tower for the Church of St James. Standing about eighty-six feet high and thirty-six feet around, the walls of its four storeys are more than five feet thick. The top two storeys of the tower are flooded with the light from twelve windows, three on each side of the tower. The tower was restored in Victorian times.

St Mary's Church

To get to St Mary's church, turn left out of the abbey's Great Gate and walk along the pavement. Built in the twelfth century, there is nothing now evident of the Norman structure. The church underwent several renovations, with portions being finished in the Decorated style. In the fifteenth century additions were made, including the paving of the church and increasing the width and length of the nave and aisles.

The best part of the church is its gorgeous angel hammer-beam roof. Angels project from the sides of the roof as if preparing to fly to Heaven. One of the angels on the north side is St Edward the Confessor with his sceptre in his right hand. On the south side is St Paul with a sword in his right hand and a book in his left. Also in the south aisle, a bit of ornamental decoration near the ceiling contains a bear and staff, the badge of the Beauchamps, which was later used by Richard Neville. A boss of a hart, which Edward IV adopted as his device, is also in the church, as well as the royal arms of both Henry VI and Edward IV, along with a symbol of a boar.

After the Dissolution, Henry VIII had his sister Mary's remains removed from the abbey and brought here to the parish church. Her tomb is still within the church with a plaque commemorating her. In honour of Mary Tudor, Queen Victoria donated a stained-glass window to the church depicting Mary's life.

The church is open from Monday to Saturday for visitors, but it is wise to call +44 (0) 1284 754680 or check the website for unexpected closures at www.wearechurch.net/visitors/365-2/.

St Edmundsbury Cathedral

The church of St James was built in the eleventh century. It is unknown whether or not Richard visited the church, but he would have seen it on his visit. A new chancel was built at the beginning of the fifteenth century, and the church received a new nave at the start of the sixteenth century. In 1914, the church became a cathedral with the creation of the diocese of St Edmundsbury and Ipswich. Massive renovations were undertaken, one of which was a new Millennium Tower, completed in 2005.

The cathedral is open daily and is free of charge, although donations are requested. For more information, visit www.stedscathedral.co.uk/visiting/general-information or call +44 (0) 1284 748720.

Visiting Bury St Edmunds Today

Bury St Edmunds has several pay-and-display car parks within a ten-minute walk of the city centre. Trains run to Bury St Edmunds from London Kings Cross and from London Liverpool Street. For more information see www.nationalrail.co.uk/. Bury St Edmunds's postcode: IP33 3TT.

Our Lady of Walsingham, Norfolk

Pilgrimage was a popular way of demonstrating piety in the medieval period. There were many shrines throughout England and the continent for pilgrims to visit. Some were much more popular than others, such as the shrines of St Edmund at Bury, St Thomas of Canterbury and Our Lady of Walsingham. Pilgrims came to honour God, to receive indulgences and to obtain healing.

Nestled in the beautiful countryside of Norfolk, the shrine of Our Lady of Walsingham was reputed to be one of the richest shrines in England. Legend states that the shrine was founded in 1061 by Richeldis de Faverches, who claimed that as she was saying her prayers she was visited by a vision of the Virgin Mary. Soon after she received two more visions of Joseph, Mary and Jesus, and was instructed to build a replica of the home in which Mary had received the news from the angel Gabriel that she was to bear the Messiah. Geoffrey de Faverches, Richeldis's son, endowed the church with the intention that it be made a priory and gave the church land from his manor. The priory was established in the middle of the twelfth century.

Our Lady of Walsingham quickly became a place of pilgrimage, destined to be as popular, or even more popular, than that of the later shrine of St Thomas of Canterbury. Pilgrims came from as far away as the Continent, and the main road they are believed to have traversed went through Newmarket and Fakenham and is still called the Palmers' Way. Many notable foreign visitors arrived, including John, the Duke of Brittany; Guy, Count of St Pol; and Desiderius Erasmus, who left an account of his visit. The shrine was often visited by royalty, including Henry III and Edward I. Two of Henry VIII's wives visited Our Lady of Walsingham, and Katherine of Aragon left money to it in her will. Richard of York came here as a pilgrim upon his return from Ireland.

Evidence remains in wills that the shrine was popular – several bequests are left for pilgrims to travel to Walsingham on behalf of the dead. In 1498, William Mauleverer left the priory, 'a litell ring ... that king Richard gave me'.

The 'holy house' of the shrine was described in 1847 as having

a fine perpendicular east front, consisting of two stair-turrets covered with panelling of flint and stone, with rich niches ... and fine buttresses connected by the arch and gable over the east window; but the window itself is destroyed. In the gable is a small round window, with flowing tracery, set in the middle of a very thick wall.

There is some confusion as to whether the writer meant to describe the larger priory church instead of the shrine. The priory church consisted of a nave with two side aisles, a chapel, a choir, and a square middle tower. The 'holy house' was attached to the priory church on its north side, while the chapter house was connected with the abbey and the cloisters. The pointed arches of the cloisters rested on octagonal columns, and the large refectory was nearby. A large stone wall surrounded the abbey grounds.

After the Dissolution, the statue of the Virgin was burned, and the house dissolved. The vast treasures of this magnificent shrine went to further the coffers of Henry VIII and the priory fell to ruin.

If Erasmus can be believed, pilgrims approached the shrine by a narrow gate. Upon entering, they would be taken to the first relic, where after paying, they were able to kiss the finger bone of St Peter. They then were taken to the wells, where they could take the waters. After this, they were taken to see the statue of the Virgin, which was the main attraction for the pilgrims.

Richard, in the company of Edward IV, Elizabeth and several of the Woodvilles, visited the shrine in 1469. Normally the pilgrims' final stop on the way to Walsingham was the Chapel of St Catherine of Alexandria, built in the early fourteenth century. The pilgrims would confess their sins in the little chapel and then remove their shoes to walk the last mile to the shrine barefoot. After reaching the abbey, the pilgrims would have entered its precincts through the gatehouse and porter's lodge on the high street.

Upon entering the chapel of the Virgin, the first thing Richard would have noticed would have been the pervasive odour of incense. As the chapel was dimly lit by long, slender candles, he would have carefully made his way to the altar, where to the right stood the statue of Our Lady, surrounded by gold and the jewels of the shrine. Kneeling, he would have prayed for a time before presenting his offering, which an awaiting priest would have immediately taken up.

Making his way to the outer chapel, he would have prostrated himself at the altar and prayed. The canon in attendance, attired with a surplice over his cassock and a richly ornamented stole with a decorative trim around his neck, would have also prostrated himself on the ground in front of the altar and worshipped before offering the Virgin's milk for Richard to kiss. The milk of the Virgin was encased in crystal to protect it from contamination and was set in a crucifix. The peace of the moment would have been a break from the turmoil of the past few months – turmoil that Richard would not escape for long. It was from here that Edward, Richard and the king's retinue departed to head north to deal with the rebels.

Visiting Today

There are several places of interest in the area today. To recreate the medieval pilgrimage, the first stop should be the slipper chapel of St Catherine of Alexandria. Today, this is the Roman Catholic Shrine of Our Lady. One site of particular interest is the beautiful Annunciation Window by Alfred Fisher, which was placed in the chapel in 1997. After visiting the chapel, take some time to wander within the shop and grab a quick bite at the café. Whether or not you remove your shoes and walk the last mile to Walsingham is a personal decision.

The original shrine is gone, but there is a marker for it on the abbey grounds. However, the Anglican shrine contains a replica of the holy house. The shrine of Our Lady of Walsingham sits at the far end of the house. The room is ringed with candles whose flickering flames signify prayer requests left by today's pilgrims. Take a moment to examine the medieval well which is next to the holy house replica.

To visit the abbey ruins, head up the hill to the Shirehall museum. Very little is left today, but the arch of the East Window can still be seen, as well as the marker showing where the 'holy house' once stood. The stones that mark the location of the west tower are still extant, along with the crypt. The crypt contains several educational panels that detail the history of the area. After visiting the ruins, make your way down the high street to the gatehouse and porter's lodge to see the main entrance to the Augustinian abbey. This is the door where Richard and Edward would most likely have entered following their visit to the slipper chapel. For more information about visiting times and prices, see the website: www. walsinghamabbey.com/Home.html.

The Anglican shrine postcode is NR22 6BP and the Roman Catholic shrine postcode is NR22 6EG.

Norwich, Norfolk

The area of Norfolk was once the home of the Iceni people, who were driven out by the Romans. After the Romans left, the town they had created was abandoned and a new town erected a few miles away on the River Wensum. The Danes took the land from the Anglo-Saxons and ruled for half a century. The town changed hands between the Danes and Anglo-Saxons a few times before they began to live in harmony. This tranquillity was eventually destroyed by the Norman invasion.

The Normans moved the town, erecting a large stone wall around it. From its excellent vantage point, the new castle overlooked the town. Construction started on an immense cathedral in 1096. The town was prosperous, attracting weavers from the Low Countries. Today, Norwich still contains several of the medieval structures these prosperous merchants built.

In the fifteenth century the town retained its stone walls, but many towers and gates had been added throughout the years. There were twelve gates into the city. A large building with a pointed arch, Nedham, later called St Stephen's gate, was the main gate into the city. It had two towers which were round on the outside but square on the side facing the city. The building was embattled, and the western tower had a postern gate for foot traffic.

Richard would certainly have recognised Norwich's medieval guildhall. Construction on the impressive building began in 1407 and it took nearly fifty years to finish. With his mind occupied by the unrest in his brother's realm, he probably had no time for a visit.

Francis Blomefield's history of Norwich indicates that grand pageants were held on Edward's entrance into the city. As Richard had been with Edward for his entire trip, we can assume that he was with him during his sojourn in Norwich.

The Halls, Norwich

Unfortunately, there are no surviving records indicating where Richard and Edward lodged while in Norfolk. One likely possibility is that they lodged with the Blackfriars. A Dominican order, the Blackfriars came to Norwich in 1226. Eventually they moved to the location previously occupied by the Sack Friars, where they built the monastery. After a terrible fire in 1413, the building was rebuilt, largely through funding by the Erpingham family. The friary's church was finished in 1470. Today's St Andrew's hall used to be the nave of the church, while Blackfriars' hall was the friars' choir.

The crypt of the Halls and the adjacent St Thomas à Becket chapel date back to the early part of the fourteenth century. While Richard would probably have not visited this area of the friary, he would have been aware of the buildings here as they joined the cloisters.

It is tempting to imagine Richard walking through the cloisters, with tapers providing dim light, on his way to a service in the priory church, dedicated to St John the Baptist. As he entered, he would have seen a room with a gorgeous high-beamed ceiling supported by pillars of limestone. Large windows were spaced along the walls of the nave. Sounds from the friars' choir would have filled the room as Richard made his way in to worship. His time in Norwich was short, but he probably attended at least one Mass.

Visiting the Halls Today

The Halls as you see them today are significantly changed since Richard and Edward were in Norwich. An extensive renovation scheme in the sixteenth century saved the St Andrews and Blackfriars Halls from demolition, but most of the cloisters and many other outbuildings were destroyed.

It is possible that Richard visited the friary church while in Norwich. The inside of the church was repaved during the building works, but the building itself still stands. A plaque inside the Halls commemorates the visit of Edward and Richard, as well as a later visit from Elizabeth Woodville. For the armchair traveller, a virtual recreation of the medieval church may be found at www. norwichblackfriars.co.uk/animations/.

The Halls are open to the public when not being used for a private event. To avoid disappointment, call +44 (0) 1603 628477. For more information on visiting the Halls, see the website at www. standrewshall.co.uk/About-The-Halls.

Bishop's Palace

Another place that Richard and Edward might have lodged is the Bishop's Palace, which stood to the north side of the cathedral church. Bishop Salmon rebuilt a palace on a grand scale upon the site of the original palace. Richard and Edward would have come through Bishop Alnwick's gate, a large, imposing edifice with two arched entrances.

Coming into the cathedral precincts, they would have entered the Bishop's Palace through an elaborate, intricately detailed porch. Once inside the great hall they would have seen a room 110 feet long and more than fifty feet wide. As the bishop's guests they would have been treated to a feast in the great hall. Large tapers would have lit the room as Edward took the place of honour at the table with Richard seated nearby. After the meal, if Richard and Edward decided to observe Mass in the cathedral instead of the bishop's chapel, they would have walked through a vaulted stone passageway that connected the hall to the north transept of the cathedral.

Visiting the Palace Today
The great hall of the Bishop's Palace was demolished, with only the ruins of Bishop Salmon's porch remaining. Part of the palace remained and was restored throughout the years. Today it is in the hands of Norwich School. The only way to see Bishop Salmon's porch is by visiting the Bishop's Gardens, a four-acre site that is only open to the public occasionally, generally starting the first Sunday in May. For more information regarding open days, visit the website at www.dioceseofnorwich.org/about/bishops/norwich/gardens/. The north side of Bishop Alnwick's gate can be viewed from the road. It is located on St Martin-at-Palace-Plain.

I suggest that you visit Norwich with a car as so many other sites are within driving distance. If you do, take advantage of one of one of the city's park-and-ride services. For more information, see www. norfolk.gov.uk/Travel_and_transport/TravelNorfolk/Park_and_Ride/index.htm. Trains from London Liverpool Street take about two hours to arrive at Norwich rail station. For more information, see www.nationalrail.co.uk/. Travel by coach is possible, but I recommend train or car. For more information on coach service, see www.nationalexpress.com/home.aspx or uk.megabus.com/.

While in Norwich, I recommend that you also visit Norwich Cathedral, Norwich Castle and Dragon Hall. All of these date from the time of Richard and Edward's visit and provide an idea of what Richard would have seen during his short visit to the city.

Castle Rising, Norfolk

Made famous by its association with Isabella, the wife of Edward II, Castle Rising is located in Norfolk. The Domesday survey lists Rising as part of the manor of Snettisham. With forty-one households, it was a large area that had a value of £50 in 1066 and £85 in 1086. First granted to Archbishop Stigand, by 1086 it was in the hands of Odo of Bayeux. After Odo, the Albini family took control of the area.

When William de Albini married Henry I's widow, Adeliza of Louvain, he married into the higher echelons of the aristocracy. After his marriage, he began a massive building project at Rising. The castle eventually fell into royal hands, and in the fourteenth century became one of the homes of Isabella, wife of Edward II. After Roger Mortimer was executed and Edward III began ruling without her help, Isabella began to stay at her holdings. It was long thought that she was a prisoner for the rest of her life, but if so, she was an unusual one. She was allowed to move between her holdings and to receive visitors, such as the king, who visited her at Rising several times.

Richard arrived here in late June for such a short time that he probably did not have time to enjoy the deer park south of the castle. On his approach, Richard would have seen the curtain wall with three towers standing sentinel on the great earthworks surrounding the castle. Passing over the stone bridge, he would have entered the bailey through the gatehouse. Moving through the richly ornamented forebuilding, he would have climbed the palatial steps that led to the arched entrance to the great hall. Once inside, with a fire roaring on the slab in the middle of the draughty room, he and Edward would have spent time discussing their plans.

Richard probably lodged in either one of the buildings to the south of the keep, formerly Queen Isabella's apartments, or in an upper chamber of the keep. Given his situation, it is doubtful he noticed his lavish surroundings, as he would have had more pressing matters on his mind. Having left without realising he would have to deal with the rebels, Richard was short on funds. Here at Rising he dictated a letter to one of his followers:

Right trusty and well beloved, we greet you well. And forasmuch as the King's good grace has appointed me to attend upon his highness into the North parts of his land, which will be me great cost and charge, whereunto I am so suddenly called that I am not so well purveyed of money therefore as behoves me to be, and therefore pray you as my special trust is in you, to lend me a hundred pounds of money unto Easter next coming, at which time I promise ye shall be truly thereof content and paid again, as the bearer hereof shall inform you: to whom I pray you to give credence therein, and show me such friendliness in the same as I may do for you hereafter, wherein ye shall find me ready. Written at Rising the 24 day of June. R. GLOUCESTER

After he dictated the letter, Richard obviously thought of an addition he wanted to make, and taking the pen from his secretary, he added a postscript in his own hand:

Sir I Say, I pray you that ye fail me not at this time in my great need, as ye will that I show you my good lordship in that matter that ye labour to me for.

This letter is the earliest example we have of a letter from Richard. Richard and Edward left Rising a few days later and pushed on for Fotheringhay, their brief sojourn at Rising at an end.

Visiting Castle Rising Today

Even in a ruined state, Castle Rising is imposing. From the car park, the route around the enormous ringwork takes you to the ticket booth and gift shop. After browsing for a bit, walk towards the Norman gatehouse, which still has grooves where the portcullis hung. You can also see the remains of a staircase that led to the tower, which has long disappeared.

Upon entering the bailey, it becomes evident that the keep was built more to impress visitors than with defence in mind. Built of imported stone, elaborate arcading on the outside left little room for the normal defensive measures found in many castles. Before heading into the forebuilding, look up to see the ornamentation and the two carved arches. Stone columns were probably once attached to the arches, adding to the magnificence of this building. More arches can be seen along the side of the forebuilding.

The Forebuilding and Great Hall

Once inside the forebuilding, stand for a moment and look up the great staircase. Built wide, it is a grand entranceway. Visitors entering the stairway would have no doubt of the great wealth of the owner. Look for the ornately carved capitals that adorn the columns along the sides of the stairs, as well as the archways across the staircase. At the top of the stairs is a lobby where guests would wait before entering the great hall for an audience with the lord. Look above the fireplace to see the remnants of the elaborate Romanesque entrance into the hall. This was blocked in at some point and a fireplace was added.

The great hall is a ruin, but parts of it grant a picture of what it would have looked like in its original glory. A recess in the south wall of the hall is believed to be the place where the lord would have sat. Luxurious tapestries would have adorned the walls and the lack of a fireplace tells us that the fire would have been kept on a slab in the centre of the room. You can still see the spaces where the supportive floor joists would have been placed. When there is no one else nearby, it becomes easier to use your imagination to step back in time and imagine Richard and Edward bent over a table near the fire, engrossed in their plans for dealing with the rebels, with their wine resting in front of them.

The Lord's Chamber

The slightly smaller room next to the Great Hall was the privy chamber. This is where Edward would have slept. Most likely, Richard would have had entrance to this room as well, as the king's loyal brother. After finishing the meal in the Great Hall, they probably retired to this room to discuss business, before Edward went to sleep and Richard made his way back to his own lodgings. This room would also have been decorated with beautiful tapestries and covered by carpets. For necessity's sake, Edward's chamber would have had a garderobe.

Chapel

Beside the private chamber is the chapel. Originally reached from the Great Hall, the chapel was one of the most important rooms in a castle. The architecture here is Norman. The room would most likely have contained crosses, chalices, pyxes, containers for holy water, and candlesticks – all common in castle chapels. The attending clergy would have had beautiful vestments. Richard and Edward may have worshipped in this room, with its walls adorned with wall hangings and paintings of biblical scenes in bright colours. An altar cloth and hangings would have adorned the altar. Everything the lord and his guests needed to worship could be found here.

Kitchen

The kitchen is a room that Richard probably thought little about. Used to his meals being brought to him, he would not have visited this kitchen, with its circular hearth and vents to let out the smoke. These features, along with the floor drain for cleaning the floor, are still visible. The meals for the castle's occupants would have been cooked here or reheated after being prepared in a separate building outside of the keep.

Upper Floor

The upper floor of the three-storey building contained two chambers. One is believed to have been a priest's chamber, as it lay directly above the chapel. The other chamber is directly above the entrance vestibule. Richard might have stayed here during his visit to the castle, as it would have been closer to Edward's private chamber. Look for the fragments of medieval tile here in the floor. Perhaps Richard's feet trod on these very tiles. It is fun to think about. Assuming this was Richard's chamber, it is important to keep in mind that the fire grate was not here in the fifteenth century, as it was added later.

Basement

It is unlikely that Richard would have made his way to the basement during his short stay at Rising. Most likely these rooms were used for storage. One of the rooms contained the castle's well, which would have made life easier for those in the kitchen.

Outer Buildings

In a castle of this size, it is a foregone conclusion that wooden buildings would have existed in the inner bailey to provide accommodations for guests and their servants. Walking around to the south of the keep, you can still see stone footings that were part of the rooms built when Queen Isabella came to the castle. Remains of a chapel, kitchen and lodgings are here. A survey from 1543 says that there was also a stable and other houses. Continue walking around the keep until you see the ruined Norman church, built around 1100. Richard would have worshipped in the inside chapel, but he would have seen this church on his visit.

My Favourite Place

At Castle Rising, two places vie for my favourite. First, I love the grand staircase. Standing at the bottom, I imagine the number of men and women from history that have ascended this very staircase. The fanciful part of me imagines that if time could thin for just a moment, I might be able to catch a glimpse of one of them – perhaps even Richard as he strides up the stairway behind Edward.

My other favourite place in the castle is the interior chapel. Despite its current state, I can rest on one of the stone benches, close my eyes and almost hear the prayers. Something remains here, perhaps an elusive sense of earlier grandeur. Others wander through, audio guides pressed to their ears before heading back out, often glancing back curiously at me, as if wondering why I am still there. Despite the curiosity, I stay and absorb the sacred ambience of the room. Castle Rising postcode: PE31 6AH.

Croyland (Crowland) Abbey, Lincolnshire

Founded in the early eighth century, Croyland, known today as Crowland, was established in memory of St Guthlac. At the time of its foundation, the abbey was said to have been surrounded by four rivers: Shepishee on the east, the Nene on the west, Southee on the south and Asendyk, on the north. In H. T. Riley's translation of *Ingulf's Chronicle of the Abbey of Croyland*, the chronicler claims the following poem was written when Ethelbald gave the abbey its charter. He does not, however, list the poet's name, lending one to wonder whether he wrote it himself:

> This abbey, Christ, I, Ethelbald, the king
> Of Anglia, by God's grace, have for Thee built.
> The isle of Croyland, of the king's demesne,
> That same, Oh Jesus! do I grant to Thee —
> The whole, great God, with its encircling streams
> On every side, I do to Thee present.
> Three hundred pounds the building to promote
> This year, I hereby pledge myself to give —
> And, in the following ten, one hundred pounds ...

The name Croyland means crude and muddy land, such as marshland. The name fit well, as the land would not support a foundation of stone. The abbey's chronicler says the king ordered huge piles of trees driven into the ground, and solid earth to be brought from nine miles away to be thrown into the marsh. The monastery was built upon this foundation. Not long afterward, it was destroyed by the Danes. Rebuilt, it was destroyed again by fire in the eleventh century.

This time, the monastery was rebuilt in the shape of a square with the church taking up the north side of the area. The brewhouse, bakery and granary shared the west side. Visitor apartments made up the south side. A hall for the monks was on the east, and was connected to the cloisters and the chapter house. The abbot's hall, refectory and another dormitory were also attached to the church.

However, in the twelfth century, the monastery was again largely destroyed by fire and rebuilt, this time in the Gothic style. After these three fires, the abbey prospered. The shrine of St Guthlac brought many noble visitors who made significant endowments. Also, the monastery had helped the king with gifts from its treasury and was subsequently held in high esteem. The marshes were drained and supplied the abbey with food. Given its natural protection in the fens, the Benedictine monastery was also protected from the ravages of wars.

Despite this protection, during the Wars of the Roses the monks became alarmed. The chronicler describes this:

Amidst the confusion of the civil war, Henry 6th came hither, to pay his devotions to St Guthlac, and staid three days and three nights; and, upon the defeat and death of the Duke of York the same year the northern men rose and committed the most dreadful ravages. The inhabitants of Croyland were so alarmed, that they brought their effects to the Abbey; the convent concealed all their valuables, and performed continual processions round the tomb of St Guthlac. They likewise fortified themselves in the best manner they were able; stopping the mouths of their water courses with stakes and breaking up their causeways, etc.

In 1467, the Quarto History claimed that there were showers of blood and armies of both foot and horse fighting in the air, conducted by St George with his red cross. It was at this time that Edward IV came north with 400 horses and men to deal with the rebels, spending a night at Croyland. Richard was with him and would have lodged here as well, most likely in the abbot's hall, which is no longer visible.

In 1818, the ruins were described in detail by Josiah Taylor. The north aisle, which is still used today as the parish church, was at that time newly painted. The ceiling was vaulted and plain, with several richly designed bosses including those of a head, a rose and a tree. The balustrade and pulpit were fashioned out of Norway oak, while the rood screen, once vivid with paintings, was now ancient.

Outside in the ruins, two huge buttresses stood with small pillars at the top. On these pillars, elaborately carved animals once stood. On each side of the middle aisle of the ruined nave there were nine pointed arches with fluted columns.

In the eighteenth century, the west front of the church was described as hugely ornamented, with many statues placed in niches and under richly embellished canopies. The statue of St Peter with his keys was placed over the window, with St Paul and his sword at his left hand. Both saints had figures placed beside them, one sitting, with a book and a knife, and one standing, holding a lance. Placed to the right were two more large statues, one holding a cross and one holding loaves. Under this was a king with a broken sword and a globe. A gowned figure holding a cross and a book stood next to him. Under these stood two more statues – one of a headless figure and one of a knight. At the bottom stood a young bishop in his pontifical robes and beside him was a figure in a mantle.

To the south side of the window were other statues, including a shaven figure holding a whip in his right hand and a blessing in his left, with a prostrate demon at his feet. This figure represents St Guthlac and would have been one of the most important statues in the monastery. Other statues stood gathered around him and under him. At the bottom, on a pedestal, was a statue of Adam and Eve, and another of an ornately carved angel, unfortunately headless, stood nearby.

In the arch above the door, the story of St Guthlac was told in a quatrefoil of sculptures. In the first leaf was a boat bringing three people to the island. In the centre was a demon, believed to represent the temptations that St Guthlac overcame. To the right were two figures, one sitting and one standing, believed to have represented the consecration of the saint by a bishop. In the left leaf, the saint was dying and an angel was descending to collect him. In the highest leaf, he was carried by angels to Heaven.

All the figures were said to have been elaborately painted in the bright colours of the time, but by 1818, these colours had faded. The stonework of the front was of a rough brown stone called Bernack rag, but the columns on each side of the door were Purbeck marble. From this description it is easy to picture the grandeur of the abbey in its heyday.

The north aisle of the abbey escaped widespread destruction following the Dissolution because it had been used as a parish church. The Lady chapel of the church, the fonts and the bosses are all medieval. The tower was built for Abbot Litlyngton in the fifteenth century. Richard would have seen the tower and the beautiful west front of the abbey while he was there. Perhaps he went inside the north aisle of the abbey, passing the twelfth-century font as he travelled up the aisle. He would have recognised the fifteenth-century font as well.

Visiting the Abbey Today

Once again, as with many abbeys following the Dissolution, the abbey here is mainly in ruins. Fortunately, the north aisle survived, since it served as the parish church that is today named church of the

Blessed Virgin Mary, Saint Bartholomew and Saint Guthlac. It is still possible to visit it and attend a service there. While the ancient name for the abbey is Croyland, today the area is known as Crowland. Be sure to check out the church bells, as it was here that legend says that the first bells were hung in Britain. Church literature says that the rope to ring the bells is the longest in England, at ninety feet. The tenor bell was cast in 1430, which means Richard would have heard the very bell you hear today.

After visiting the church, walk around to the west front to see the statues described in 1818. A great many of them still survive. The abbot's hall, where Richard and Edward IV stayed on their visit to Croyland Abbey, is believed to have been on the south-west corner of the front of the church. Take some time to walk around the grounds and marvel at how this area has changed since it was mainly marshland. A sign behind the church shows the length of the choir. At ninety feet, it would have extended further than the wall of the church graveyard today. The abbey would have been impressive, and today you can still see the abbey ruins rising up over the fens from quite a distance. The church offers an online tour of the grounds at its website, www.crowlandabbey.org.uk/360-tour/.

Near the centre of town stands Trinity Bridge. This triangular bridge used to cross both the River Welland and the River Nene. Today, it stands near the centre of town as a bridge that goes nowhere. As it was built in the fourteenth century, Richard and Edward likely would have crossed the bridge on their way to the abbey. The statue of Christ on the bridge once graced the gable of the nave's west front. Crowland postcode: PE6 0EN.

Sudeley Castle, Gloucestershire

Sheltered in the tranquillity of the rolling Cotswold Hills, Sudeley Castle exudes a peace that belies the busy place this once was. On this spot walked several kings and queens, their paths in time weaving Sudeley forever into the tapestry of England's history.

Medieval Sudeley
In 1442, Ralph Boteler, having been advanced to the dignity of

Baron Sudeley by Henry VI, began building Sudeley using money earned from his time in the Hundred Years War. Built in the shape of two courtyards surrounded by a moat, the castle was lavish. Constructed with golden-coloured oolitic Cotswold limestone, its windows were glazed with beryl. This was a castle built to impress more than to intimidate.

A staunch Lancastrian, Boteler had been constable of Kenilworth when Eleanor Cobham was taken there as a prisoner after a charge of witchcraft. He also took part in the arrest of Duke Humphrey of Gloucester, and he quickly rose to great heights in the Lancastrian government, eventually becoming Treasurer of England. He managed to hold on to his property for several years after Edward IV came to the throne, despite his Lancastrian sympathies. Eventually, Edward came into possession of the castle and granted it to Richard in 1469.

Richard held the estate for nine years before he transferred it to Edward in exchange for Richmond Castle. Afterwards, Sudeley remained in royal hands, falling back to Richard once he became king. The private apartments that Richard built were opulent, with soaring gothic windows to allow the rooms to be flooded with light. Richard seemed to have enjoyed large windows, as he placed them in several of his holdings. As these windows were built into an outer wall, it is evident that the rooms were built for comfort and not for fortification.

Standing and looking up at the ruins with the delicate tracery above the windows, picturing Richard is effortless. Rich tapestries or intricate wall paintings would have graced the plastered walls, and a roaring fire would have provided warmth as Richard worked tirelessly on state business. Perhaps he took some time away from work to peer out the windows on to the gardens below. As the picture fades and the vines winding through the ruins once more come into view, you will see the evidence of a bricked-in arch, probably dating from later renovations of the building.

Today, one of the castle's formal gardens, the Queens' Garden, is built on the Tudor parterre, which was probably built near or on the old castle gardens. Elaborately laid out, the riot of colour is a pleasing assault on the senses.

The acts of one person tied to the history of Sudeley would

have further implications for Richard. Eleanor Talbot Butler was the widow of Ralph Boteler's son, Thomas. The daughter of John Talbot, the Earl of Shrewsbury, Eleanor allegedly became mistress of Edward IV after her husband's death. The supposed precontract of marriage between Edward IV and Eleanor became the basis of Richard's justification for assuming the throne.

While I was unable to find evidence of a visit by Richard as king, he did pay for several tonnes of wine at Sudeley while staying nearby at Kenilworth. As he was using Kenilworth as a base, it is within the realms of possibility that he visited Sudeley then. According to the castle records, he stayed here while on his way to Tewkesbury for the battle with the Lancastrians. Regardless, the castle is important in Richard's life due to its ties with Eleanor Butler and for this reason has been included.

Much of what we see of Sudeley today is Elizabethan, built by Baron Chandos during his tenure here. The castle as Richard would have seen it was built by Boteler. Sadly, most of what Boteler built is in ruins or has disappeared.

Visiting Sudeley

The historic atmosphere of Sudeley engrosses visitors as soon as they turn on to the long drive to the castle car park. The view is beautiful, with lush greenery abounding.

Begin at the Visitor and Plant Centre, where you can pick up tickets for the castle. Stroll along the path to the romantic ruins of the tithe barn, which was built under Boteler's residency and partially destroyed during the Civil War. A lush rose garden has been planted here, its fragrant scents wafting through the air. The carp pond, filled with koi carp, was built in the early twentieth century.

Under the terrace of the castle lies an exhibition about Winchcombe Abbey's stones that history lovers will not want to miss. Winchcombe Abbey was founded in 798 but became a Benedictine monastery in 985 and was one of the most powerful Benedictine monasteries in England. After the Dissolution, the king granted the abbey to Thomas Seymour, who used some of the stones in building work at Sudeley. In 1996, several of these stones were found. The elegance of these stones tell us how grand the abbey was in its heyday. Given the abbey's proximity to the castle, it is likely Richard's gaze would have fallen on some of these same stones during a visit.

After tearing yourself away from the stones' display, make your way up the steps to the entrance of the exhibitions. More rooms than ever have been recently opened to the visitor, and there are displays related to Richard. Following the exhibition of Richard's facial reconstruction at Sudeley, Lady Ashcombe was inspired to commission another replica based on the portraiture of Richard. After spending some time gazing at the artist's impression of Richard's face, take in the rest of the displays. Mainly Tudor era and beyond, the artefacts and exhibits are quite interesting.

After exiting the castle, visit St Mary's church. The church built by Boteler was ruined during the Civil War, but later restored. Richard would have known this chapel and likely would have spent time here while at Sudeley. The church is best known as the final resting place of Katherine Parr, and the former queen's tomb and exhibition regarding her deathbed are interesting.

The pheasantry, housing a number of rare birds, and the herb garden should not be missed as you leave the castle grounds. Make sure you pass through the Visitor and Plant Centre again to browse through its Sudeley-related items.

For more information on visiting the castle during its open months, visit its website, www.sudeleycastle.co.uk/visit-us/prices-opening-times/. On Tuesdays, Wednesdays and Thursdays at 2 p.m., the castle offers a tour of the gardens with a garden expert. The price is included in the cost of admission, but slots must be reserved as you enter as group size is limited. Sudeley also holds special events throughout the year. Check the website for more details. Sudeley Castle postcode: GL54 5JD.

Part III

Edward's Right Hand

Given the uneasy peace between Warwick and King Edward, it was inevitable that hostilities would once again break out. Warwick and Clarence had gone to Calais, and it was unclear what they were planning. It is unlikely that anyone expected the alliance that would come out of the trip. Warwick and his once great enemy, Margaret of Anjou, were collaborating together with the support of King Louis.

Warwick planned to invade England and rescue Henry VI from the Tower. In exchange, he proposed a marriage between his daughter Anne and Edward of Lancaster. After Anne and Edward's betrothal, Anne was to stay with her mother-in-law, Margaret, while Warwick secured King Henry. The marriage was likely not consummated as the proper dispensation had not arrived. Margaret of Anjou was intelligent, and she may have wanted to see how Warwick fared before committing her son irrevocably to Anne. At any rate, Warwick's invasion, backed with financial help from King Louis, brought many men to his side.

This alliance would ultimately cause Edward to flee from his country to the Low Countries. Richard, loyally committed to his brother, would assist Edward in any way he could to help him maintain control of his kingdom. At that moment, flight was the only option.

King's Lynn, Norfolk

Originally known as Lynn Bishop or Bishop's Lynn, by the fourteenth century the town was the third largest port in England. The city grew along the bank of the Great Ouse and became prosperous. Shipbuilding and trade were priorities for the city, and the Hanseatic League established trade with Lynn. At the time of Edward's flight, however, the Hanseatic League was at odds with England.

Edward, Hastings and Rivers fled to Bishop's Lynn (today King's Lynn), where they boarded boats to flee to the Low Countries. It has long been thought that Richard went with them, but recent scholarship does not support this view. Lynn's *Corporation's Hall Book II* states that Edward came with Anthony Woodville, Hastings and Lord Say, along with many other men. It does not mention Richard by name, which it certainly would if he had been there. Josephine Wilkinson, in her book *The Young Richard*, also believes that Richard arrived later in Holland. She credits a letter from Charles which granted Edward money but makes no mention of Richard.

Perhaps Richard came to Lynn at a later time to depart, because he was definitely in the Low Countries later that year. Some historians speculate that he was busy gathering men for Edward's cause. Wilkinson says that when Edward IV departed the Low Countries for England the chronicler Adrian de But noted that 'Edward sailed across, together with his younger brother, the Duke of Gloucester, who had come to him from England with many men ...'

Richard was ashore in the Low Countries by the end of 1470, because his arrival was noted by the chronicler Jan van Naaldwijk. He was also mentioned in the accounts of the city of Veere.

Richard probably departed for Holland from Lynn, as Edward had done. He may have had to stay in Lynn longer than Edward in order to find a ship to take him to the Low Countries.

Visiting King's Lynn Today
Since we do not know where Edward stayed, nor whether for certain this was the port Richard left from, there is not much Richard-related in the city. One of the city's markers does relate to the York family, however.

A marker on the quay notes that this was the spot from where Edward fled to the Low Countries. However, the date on the marker is incorrect. It gives the date as 1460, instead of the correct date of 1470. Despite this small mistake, King's Lynn has quite a bit to offer those interested in history. The city has several great walking trails throughout the town, as well as several buildings that would have been here at the same time as Edward, and possibly Richard. Take time to visit Lynn Minster, which was certainly here at the time. King's Lynn South Quay postcode: PE30 5DT.

The Isle of Walcheren, the Netherlands

The former island of Walcheren would be host to at least two events in Richard's life. Richard likely arrived on the island at Veere as he fled England after Warwick's invasion. Later, Edward and Richard were both in Vlissingen preparing for their return trip to England.

Veere

After Edward fled into exile, Richard did not stay behind in England long. The next mention we have of Richard states he was in Veere, in Zeeland. Veere was a powerful trading city as it was a well-known port. The city had ties with Scotland which had been cemented through the marriage of Mary Stewart with Wolfert VI of Borselen. Mary was the daughter of James I and Joan Beaufort, and through her, Wolfert claimed the title of Earl of Buchan. When Richard came ashore, he was received by Wolfert. According to historian Maaihe Lulofs, the Veere records note in the second week of November, 1470, 'Item paid by order of my Lord of Boucham the bailiff of Veere which he had loaned when my Lord of Gloucester travelled in Holland ...'

Veere is a picturesque town today with a bustling marketplace. No longer a major centre of commerce and trade, it focuses on tourism. The vendors in the marketplace dress in period costume, adding historical flair to the business of buying and selling. There is little left from Richard's time, although a street in Veere is still called Warwijcksestraat. According to Lulofs, the street received its name after a gate was built in fear that Warwick would invade.

Today tourists tread where merchants used to unload their goods. The sea is mainly for pleasure now; sailboats and pleasure ships ply the waters around the town. Veere postcode: 4351 AV.

Vlissingen (Flushing)

Located between the Scheldt (Schelde in Dutch) River and the North Sea, Vlissingen, known as Flushing to the English, quickly grew into a major port. A harbour was created and the town prospered. The English became interested in the port with its strategic location and trade between the Dutch and the English grew.

It was from Vlissingen that the exiles would embark on ships back to England to regain control of Edward's kingdom. After their winter in the Low Countries, Edward and his men were going home.

The earliest surviving building from the fifteenth century dates from around 1489, so it was built after Richard and Edward were here. It is the Prison Gate, Gevangenpoort, which was one of the two towers at the west entrance of Vlissingen. Postcode for Vlissingen: 4381 BV.

Visiting Veere and Vlissingen Today

Veere and Vlissingen (Flushing) are very close. The two cities could easily be visited in one day by a determined traveller, but really deserve a day each to absorb the atmosphere. Both are on the former Isle of Walcheren. Driving in Holland is a delight, with its large, signposted roads. Reaching the Isle of Walcheren from Bruges involves crossing a toll tunnel.

Once in Vlissingen, walk towards the beach. From here you can watch ocean-going vessels depart, seemingly within a few feet of the beach itself. The town's maritime museum is interesting, although you will find nothing about Richard and Edward here. My favourite activity in Vlissingen is walking the seafront.

Unfortunately, there is nothing in either city to visit specifically related to Richard. Being in Vlissingen and staring out to sea, however, you can imagine the mix of trepidation and excitement that Richard and Edward would have felt as they boarded ships headed back to England.

The best way to visit the former island is by car. Alternatively you can take a train to Vlissingen and then take a bus to Veere. At this time there is no train station in Veere.

The Hague, the Netherlands

Richard travelled from Veere to meet Edward, who was staying at the home of Lodewijk (Louis) Gruuthuse in The Hague. Louis was the governor of the counties of Holland and Zeeland. Edward stayed at his house until Christmas. Richard probably stayed here as well.

Accounts from the archives show that it is likely that Louis's home in The Hague was in the complex of the Binnenhof. Unfortunately, it is not possible to point out exactly where Edward and Richard lodged while in the complex. Their sister, Margaret, also stayed at the Binnenhof on a visit in 1475.

Louis and his wife, Margaretha van Borsele, must have been pleasant hosts, as Edward later rewarded Louis for his help by making him Earl of Winchester. While guests of Louis, Edward and Richard would have seen his collection of illuminated manuscripts.

The Binnenhof has been a centre of politics in The Hague for centuries. This would have been a busy area, even in the fifteenth century, and Richard and Edward would have enjoyed entertainments and culture while planning their strategy to retake the throne. They would have seen the Hall of Knights, and may have spent time near the artificial lake known as the Hofvijver that was north of the complex.

Visiting Today

The Binnenhof is still the centre of politics in the Netherlands. Today visitors can see parts of this beautiful building by taking a guided tour through the Hall of Knights and the Chambers of Parliament. The tour often fills up so reservations are advised. The tours are in Dutch, but there are audio guides provided in several other languages, including English. For more information, see english.prodemos.nl/English/Visitor-Centre/Guided-tours. Binnenhof postcode: 2511 AA.

Sandal Castle, West Yorkshire

Richard and Edward arrived back in England in March of 1471. After leaving Kingston-upon-Hull, where he and his men had been denied entry, he made straight for York. Despite initial qualms from leading citizens of the city, Edward and Richard, along with a few of their men, were allowed within the city walls. Leaving York, they made their way south to Sandal and on to face Warwick.

Situated in a strong, defensive position above the River Calder, Sandal Castle was once a fortress big enough for a king, or at least for one who had the aspiration of becoming king. Richard's father, the Duke of York, held the castle during the early part of the fifteenth century. Sandal dominated the surrounding Calder Valley. Located about two miles from Wakefield, the castle gets its name from the earth that surrounds it, as Sandal is thought to mean sandy dwelling place.

Believed to have been built by William de Warenne in the early twelfth century, Sandal Castle was originally a motte-and-bailey castle that was rebuilt in stone. The castle was fortified with a moat, which was dug to help build the mound for the castle. The mound was about fifty feet high, and would have towered over the rest of the valley.

By the thirteenth century, the castle boasted two mills, a large deer park, a grange, a small pool with fish for the castle occupants and a garden. Based on surveys, it is possible to determine the layout of the castle. Covering the entire mound, the castle had a courtyard and a circular stone keep with several turreted towers. A large embattled curtain wall enclosed the outer ward of the keep. The castle's domestic buildings lay to the east of the keep. A strong circular barbican tower with ashlar facing, surrounded by a ditch, was connected to the bailey by a drawbridge. From a drawing based on the surveys, it appears that the barbican tower was embattled. The steep entranceway up to the castle was apparently walled.

Writing in the late nineteenth century, J. W. Walker based his description on the surveys of the castle. The castle's great hall was about seventy-seven feet long. He gives a detailed description of the hall:

The entrance to it was by an external stone staircase of ten steps opening onto a platform or porch, supported on pillars, which gave access both to the hall and to the long gallery, which adjoined the hall at its southern end. The hall was lighted by round-headed windows opening into the court; from the north end of the hall, where the dais was erected, a door opened into the withdrawing room, across its south end ran a screen, and the fireplace was probably in the outer wall ...

When the ruins were excavated in the 1960s and 1970s, the workers found a gargoyle in the form of a wyvern, a mythical creature said to have a dragon's head, a reptilian body, wings and a forked tail. Excavators believed this to be a king's beast from Richard's building works.

Sandal and Richard

As a child, Richard may have visited Sandal as it was one of his father's many holdings. Not much is known about Richard's movements as a young child, but perhaps he spent some blissful times here with his entire family gathered around. Perhaps Richard's family was able to spend a joyful Christmas here, one of innocence and family togetherness, before his young world would be turned upside down by the ravages of war and death, as the famed 'wheel of fortune' made its fateful turn.

The first event at the castle that had an impact on Richard's life was the Battle of Wakefield. After being declared Henry VI's heir and gaining control of the king at Northampton, the Duke of York faced a threat from Queen Margaret. She had travelled to Scotland and was trying to assemble troops. At the same time, her forces in the North were getting larger as men from the area rallied to her cause after hearing that York had been made the king's heir. The chronicler at Croydon said that the 'queen's northern supporters found this decree of Parliament ... detestable'. York travelled north with Richard's brother Edmund and the Earl of Salisbury to meet this double threat.

On 21 December 1460, the group stopped at Sandal. The castle had not been ready for their arrival and seemed to lack enough food for their stay, probably depleted after Christmas festivities.

The Lancastrians tried a surprise attack on 30 December. While it is hard to know what happened with any certainty, one theory suggests that some of the duke's men were out foraging for food when the Lancastrians appeared. Instead of staying within the safety of the castle, the other men joined the fray. The Lancastrians apparently waited until the Yorkists were on level ground before attacking with their full forces.

Richard, Duke of York, was slain in the battle. Young Edmund of Rutland was said to have been struck down on nearby Wakefield Bridge after the battle by Lord Clifford, who later earned the sobriquet 'The Butcher' for his actions. Hall's chronicle has Edmund pleading silently to Clifford for his life. Clifford responded by saying, 'By God's blood, thy father slew mine, and so will I do thee and all thy kin,' before driving his dagger into Rutland's heart. He then turned to the priest standing there and coldly told him to take word to Edmund's mother and brother. Salisbury, who was captured, was executed the next day.

The news of this triple loss would reach Richard's surviving family soon after that of his father's death, prompting Cecily to send Richard and George to the relative safety of the Low Countries. Sandal would bring back these memories for Richard as he rode up to the castle with Edward. Once again, he was returning from exile, except this time as an adult and in the company of his older brother. Edward's flight to Holland and the subsequent reinstatement of Henry VI as king was a great motivator for the two brothers. They each knew what was at stake in this struggle.

As their tiny force rode up the hill towards the castle, the success of the House of York was probably uppermost in each of the brothers' minds. Despite the fact that all hope seemed lost, they would trudge on. Once again, a superior Lancastrian force was nearby at Pontefract, but this time there would be no battle at Wakefield – no inglorious defeat of the House of York. Soon, the group would leave the castle, pick up supporters and head on toward battle.

As king, Richard would revisit Sandal. The castle would be one of the meeting places of his Council of the North. Sandal, along with Sheriff Hutton, was called the King's Household in the North. Here, the council would meet to dispense justice and hear disputes.

During his brief reign, Richard ordered improvements to the castle, but his defeat at Bosworth would put an end to Sandal's glory days. The castle already showed signs of serious neglect by Elizabethan times, and during the Civil War, Sandal was besieged twice by Parliamentary forces, who later stripped it of its defences.

Visiting the Castle Today

Sandal Castle is located near Wakefield. The castle has a car park and a visitor's centre. Admission to the ruins is free. While very little remains of the castle today, visitors can wander the area. Allow your mind to fill in the details as you meander around the mound and towards the Calder River. The views from the mound of the surrounding area are incredible.

Walk down from the castle to see the monument of Richard, Duke of York. This monument supposedly marks the spot where Richard was slain. However, it takes the place of an earlier monument, not on the same spot, which was destroyed during the Civil War. If possible, take advantage of the 2 p.m. tours that are available Wednesdays through Sundays. It is advisable to call ahead, though, to avoid disappointment. The castle has a website: www.wakefield.gov.uk/residents/events-and-culture/castles/sandal-castle. Castle postcode: WF2 7DS.

Coventry, West Midlands

After leaving Sandal, Edward and Richard headed south, where they planned to meet the Earl of Warwick. Along the way they recruited more men to Edward's cause before reaching the embattled walls of Coventry.

Surrounded by gently rolling hills and dales, Coventry is situated in an area of natural beauty. The city has its roots in early times, before the Norman conquerors came. The Earl of Mercia and his countess, Godiva (of legendary fame), founded and richly endowed a Benedictine monastery here, which quickly became one of the wealthy establishments in England. It was so wealthy that William of Malmesbury claimed the walls of the church did not seem big enough to contain all the gold and silver it held.

Built on the slope of the hill, the priory buildings sat between the cathedral and the bank of the Sherbourne. These buildings included the chapter house, the undercroft, the cloisters and other buildings necessary for the priory to function.

The city began to build walls in the fourteenth century. Soon massive reddish-hued walls surrounded the city, complete with twelve opulent gates to allow travellers inside. Along the circumference of the wall were embattled towers offering further protection to the inhabitants of the city. According to Leland the towers were not just defensive but were fair, perhaps built to showcase the wealth of the city. Coventry, along with its opulent priory, would become the scene of some of the biggest events in the Wars of the Roses.

Coventry and the Wars of the Roses

After Henry VI regained his mental capabilities the court spent quite a bit of time in Coventry. As the region enjoyed strong Lancastrian support, Margaret of Anjou and those loyal to Henry probably felt safer in the area. Several councils met in Coventry over the next years, including one in June of 1456, which the Duke of York attended. Soon afterwards, William Waynflete took the place of Thomas Bourchier as Chancellor of England. It was evident that York and his allies were becoming increasingly marginalised, while Margaret of Anjou was playing a larger part in the government.

When Margaret and Henry arrived in Coventry in September 1456, the brightly dressed citizens met them with ceremony. Prominent citizens were placed in the streets to speak words of welcome to the king and queen. As she and Henry entered through the Bablake gate (Spon gate), they were met with pageants. When they reached the Smithford Street Conduit, they were treated to the pageant of the Four Cardinal Virtues. As they moved through town, they saw pageants of St John the Evangelist and St Edward the Confessor. At Cheaping the pageant of the Nine Conquerors was performed. The final pageant was performed on a stage where St Margaret appeared, slaying a ferocious dragon. When Queen Margaret left the city, the mayor rode before her with his mace in hand, while the sheriffs with their white rods rode before the mayor. Prior to this, the honour had been reserved for the king.

In June 1459, a council was called to meet in Coventry, but

Richard of York, Salisbury, Warwick, and several others close to York were not summoned. Sensing a legitimate threat, the men retreated to Ludlow to determine their next course of action. The ultimate outcome of this decision would be exile; after the confrontation with the king at Ludford Bridge the men fled to Ireland and Calais.

Meanwhile, a parliament had been called to meet in Coventry. Following on the heels of the rout at Ludford Bridge, the parliament was a punitive one, earning it the moniker Parliament of Devils. Parliament was opened in the chapter house of the priory by Waynflete. Securing the attainder of York and his allies was a top priority. Most of the men who were attainted had already fled, and Henry VI offered others clemency for submission. Cecily seems to have appeared before the king, who placed her, George, Richard and Margaret in the custody of her sister, the Duchess of Buckingham.

Coventry and the Earl of Warwick

Coventry was also the scene of a conflict between King Edward IV and the Earl of Warwick, both of whom had once been attainted here at the Parliament of Devils. After Edward had blocked a marriage between Isabel, Warwick's daughter, and George, Edward's brother, George and Warwick began conspiring to gain a dispensation from the Pope for the marriage. Warwick wrote to his followers in Coventry to announce the upcoming marriage, which took place on 11 July 1469. A manifesto was issued which set forth the complaints of the men, including complaints against Earl Rivers and other Woodvilles. The ensuing conflict resulted in the murder of Earl Rivers and his son John near Coventry. The *Coventry Leet Book* says this occurred on Gosforth Green.

Years later Coventry was to be the scene of another conflict, once again between the Earl of Warwick and Edward IV. Edward had fled to the Low Countries following the uprising led by Warwick and George. Once Edward returned, he gathered followers and headed towards the Earl of Warwick, who was in Coventry awaiting reinforcements, mainly from George. Edward boldly went to Coventry and offered the earl a choice between a pardon and a battle. Short on men, the earl chose neither, instead staying inside the relative safety of Coventry's walls.

Shortly afterwards, Edward IV, with Richard by his side, reconciled with Clarence outside Windsor. He then marched back to Coventry and offered the earl the same terms. Again the earl refused, and Edward marched on to London to see his wife and his family, now with a new addition – a son he'd never seen.

After the death of the Earl of Warwick, Edward IV removed the city's liberties as punishment, and Coventry was forced to buy them back. The city worked hard to regain Edward's trust. When his son, Edward, Prince of Wales, visited the city a few years later, they held huge pageants for him and gave him fine gifts. The mayor, garbed in green and blue finery, presented him with a gilded cup. Edward then watched the pageants in his honour, one of which included Richard II honouring Edward as the rightful heir to the kingdom.

Richard and Coventry

Richard visited Coventry on his progress northwards. Standing outside the Bablake gate with his large retinue, Richard would have seen a highly embellished gatehouse of reddish-hued stone with two embattled towers. Entering through the gate, he would have passed the collegiate church dedicated to St John and made his way along the paved streets of the city. Most royal visitors to Coventry stayed in the priory, so he likely made his way there.

The feast of the Assumption of the Blessed Virgin Mary was celebrated while Richard was in Coventry. He likely observed Mass in the priory's cathedral. At more than 400 feet long, the cathedral was huge. Perhaps Richard even visited the chapter house where so much of his family's history had occurred.

Richard came to the city on at least two other occasions. The first was on his way to putting down Buckingham's rebellion, so he did not linger long. In June 1485, Richard came to Coventry to experience the Corpus Christi pageants. Coventry's Corpus Christi pageants were famous in England. People came from all over to see the famous mystery plays.

On the morning of the Corpus Christi festival, even before the mystery plays occurred, there was a procession of the guilds. Behind the guilds were the priests of the Trinity Guild carrying the Host, with a canopy of rich material over it. After the procession, the pageants followed, setting out the scenes of the life of the Virgin, who wore an expensive crown. The pageants were performed on two-storey scaffolds. The lower storey was for the performers to change their costumes, while the upper level was for the pageant itself. They began at the priory gate before making their way to the mayor at Cross Cheaping.

The Smiths' elaborate pageant was the trial, condemnation and crucifixion of Christ. It required, among other items, a gilded cross with a rope to draw it up and a curtain to hang before it; a red standard; gowns and hoods for the tormentors and a painted red cloth with silk fringe. As this was just one of the several pageants that day, it is clear how impressive each pageant would have been. This would be the last time Richard would visit Coventry, as in August he would face Henry Tudor across a field of battle.

Visiting Coventry Today

Coventry has much to offer a visitor and a visit could take several days. However, it is possible to see all the sites related to Richard in one day. If you decide to do a day trip, a good option is to visit by train from London. For information about tickets, see www. nationalrail.co.uk/. Trains leave from Euston station and depending on which train you take, the journey can be made in one hour. Another option is to drive. Coventry has a good park-and-ride program. For more information on the park-and-ride scheme, see the webpage at www.networkwestmidlands.com/parkandride/indexparkandride.aspx. Postcode: CV3 6PT.

St Mary's Priory and Cathedral

St Mary's Priory and Cathedral did not survive the devastating effects of the Dissolution. Little remains of this huge edifice, including descriptions of it. Frustratingly we cannot know for sure what the cathedral church looked like. What we can be sure of is that it was opulent, with ornate decorations. Even though we can no longer visit the church, it is possible to visit the site of the building. Portions of the west front still exist in the priory garden, as well as remnants of the bases of columns. After wandering through the garden, be sure to see the excellent display at the priory visitor centre.

The visitor centre contains a plan of the priory, including the location of the cloisters and chapter house in relation to the other buildings. Fragments of medieval tiles, ornate bosses and figures from the cathedral, chapter house and other priory buildings are displayed, along with detailed descriptions of each piece. The chapter house contained a wall painting of the Apocalypse, which is described in one of the centre's displays. Tickets are available at the visitor centre for tours of the undercroft, which was discovered during excavation work. This is a must-see to get an idea of the former size of the priory.

For more information about visiting the visitor centre, check out its web page at www.prioryvisitorcentre.org/. Priory Visitor Centre postcode: CV1 5EX.

St Michael's Cathedral

After the destruction of the priory cathedral, the city was without a cathedral until the twentieth century. In 1918, the medieval parish church of St Michael was consecrated as a cathedral. While Richard would not have visited the church, he would have seen it on his visits. Shortly after its consecration, German bombs destroyed the gorgeous red sandstone church. A decision was made to leave the church in ruins as a memorial, with a new cathedral built nearby. The ruins are still lovely and are a moving reminder to the destruction of war. Remnants of the medieval church can still be seen among the ruins. The south porch, the oldest surviving part of the medieval structure, still stands facing St Mary's Hall.

As he travelled through the city, Richard would have seen the tall spire of the parish church. Although it has been restored today, the spire was completed by the time Richard visited Coventry. The tower began sinking even before it was finished, and a complete restoration had to be done in the nineteenth century.

For more information about opening times, see the cathedral website at www.coventrycathedral.org.uk/. This website has information about both the ruins and the new cathedral. The cathedral suggests that visitors arriving by car should park in the Pool Meadow car park. The car park's postcode is CV1 5EX. The cathedral's ruins are just a short walk from the Priory Visitor Centre.

St Mary's Hall

Another building Richard would have seen and may have even visited is the Guildhall. St Mary's Hall is an impressive building chock-full of history. Although built in the early part of the fourteenth century, additions were made to the building throughout the following years until it reached its present size in the fifteenth century. The hall often received royal visitors, including Henry VI and Henry VII.

One royal visitor to the hall came against her will. According to the Guildhall, records show that Mary, Queen of Scots, was held prisoner here for a time. For the Richard enthusiast, though, the best portion of the visit is the large tapestry in the great hall. Commissioned during the reign of Henry VII, the tapestry is the 'Glorification of the Virgin'. The king represented in the tapestry is thought to be Henry VI. According to the Guildhall's information panel, Richard and several of his family members are portrayed. It takes some time to find each figure represented, but a close look will uncover Richard as Duke of Gloucester, George, Isabel, and Anne Neville.

The roof of the hall has been largely restored after it was damaged by fire in the Second World War, but many of the medieval carvings survived and were incorporated into the restored roof. Some of the carved stone corbels in the hall may have come from the priory as signs of weathering have been detected.

In the old council chamber, be sure to look for the pieces of medieval stained glass that used to be in the hall's east window. This glass, which dates from the fifteenth century, would have been in the east window when Richard was in Coventry. Also look at the great chair in the room. This ornately carved chair dates from at least the fifteenth century and, according to the hall, may have been the bishop's chair in the priory. If so, Richard would have seen it in its original location. The treasury room is worth a visit, too. The intricate oak carvings on the wall were once in the priory's guesthouse. It is possible that Richard once gazed at this representation of God, along with the Virgin and child and several saints and evangelists.

Admission to the guildhall is free, although donations are welcome. For more information about opening times, visit the

website at www.stmarysguildhall.co.uk/info/4/visit or call +44 (0)
24 7683 3328. The hall is located on Bayley Lane, across from the
ruins of St Michael's Cathedral. St Mary's Hall postcode: CV1 5RN.

Barnet, London Borough of Barnet

After Edward tried unsuccessfully to engage the Earl of Warwick
at Coventry, he continued on towards London, where he and his
retinue were received in the City. After getting control of Henry
VI, Edward went to see his wife, who had sought sanctuary. Then
he and Elizabeth sojourned to Baynard's Castle to spend the night
with Cecily. Most likely, Richard also lodged at his mother's home,
where the group heard divine service that night. The following
morning was Good Friday, and Richard would certainly have been
a part of the group of 'great lords of his blood' advising the king.

Leaving on Saturday, Edward, Richard and Hastings led a 'great
armye' out of London. Taking Henry VI along as a hostage, the
army trudged the ten miles towards Barnet. Edward's scouts located
Warwick's scouts in Barnet, and chasing them out of town, came
upon the main body of Warwick's army. Warwick was located on
what is today Hadley Green. Edward marched onwards, passing
through the town of Barnet, where he would not allow any of his
men to stay. Instead they made camp extremely close to Warwick.
The chronicler in the *Historie of the Arrivall of Edward IV in
England* stated,

> And, for it was right derke, and he myght not well se where his
> enemyes were enbataylled afore hym, he lodged hym, and all his
> hoste, afore them, moche nere[r] then he had supposed, but he
> toke nat his ground so even in the front afore them as he wold
> have don yf he might bettar have sene them, butt somewhat
> a-syden-hande, where he disposed all his people, in good arraye,
> all that nyght; and so they kept them still, withowt any mannar
> langwage, or noyse, but as lytle as they well myght.

Despite what the chronicler thinks, it would be very hard to keep
such a large army still, with little or no noise, especially as the

Above left: 1. Richard III, King of England. A seventeenth-century copy of an original painting of Richard.

Above right: 2. Edward IV. From all accounts, Edward and Richard enjoyed a good relationship.

3. Anne Neville with her husband Richard III. Anne was the daughter of the Earl of Warwick.

Above left: 4. Fotheringhay Castle, Northamptonshire. The fragments of masonry are all that is left of the castle where Richard was born on 2 October 1452. Behind the masonry is the mound where the great castle keep once stood.

Above right: 5. Church of St Mary the Virgin and All Saints, Fotheringhay. In July 1476, the bodies of Richard's father, the Duke of York, and his brother Edmund, Earl of Rutland, were reburied in this church. His mother, Cecily Neville, was also buried here.

6. North Range, Ludlow Castle. This would have housed the great hall and chamber block of the castle during the tenure of the York family. The entrance to the hall was through the richly ornamented pointed arch.

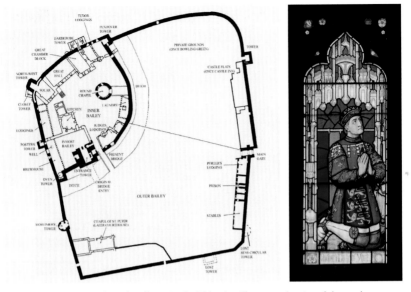

Above left: 7. Plan of Ludlow Castle. This plan illustrates the size of the castle.

Above right: 8. Richard's father, the Duke of York, represented in a stained-glass window at St Laurence's church, Ludlow.

9. Kasteel Duurstede, Wijk bij Duurstede. This large palace was once the home of Bishop David, illegitimate son of Duke Philip of Burgundy. Richard and George likely stayed here, at the castle outside of Utrecht, while they were in the Low Countries.

Top left: 10. Sluis Belfry, the Netherlands. Richard and George would have seen this fourteenth-century belfry while in Sluis (Sluys). Their time in the town was brief, as they were on their way to Bruges to meet Duke Philip. *Top right:* 11. Gruuthuse Museum, Bruges. This museum was once the home of Louis de Gruuthuse, who housed Edward and Richard while they were exiled from England. They visited here only briefly, spending most of their time at Gruuthuse's home in The Hague. *Bottom left:* 12. Bruges Belfry, Belgium. The tall belfry has dominated the Markt of Bruges for several centuries. The belfry as Richard would have seen it would not have had the octagonal tower that graces it today. *Bottom right:* 13. Église de Notre Dame, Calais, France. George, Duke of Clarence, and Isabel Neville were likely married in this church, once known as St Mary's.

14. Canterbury Cathedral, Kent. Richard visited the cathedral on several occasions, almost certainly lodging in the opulent Archbishop's Palace and visiting the shrine of St Thomas.

15. Greenwich, Kent. The Palace of Placentia would have stood on the spot where the Old Royal Naval College stands today. Most of Richard's visits would have been by boat along the Thames.

Above left: 16. Chichele's Tower, Lambeth Palace, London. The tower was begun by Archbishop Chichele in 1434. It was not as large in Richard's time, as the two top floors were added in the early part of the sixteenth century. A statue of St Thomas Becket once stood in the niche after the tower's completion in 1435. *Above right:* 17. Chapel entrance, Lambeth Palace, London. Chichele's Tower was built up against the entrance of the chapel, preserving its beautiful archway. Fragments of medieval tile can still be found inside the chapel. *Below:* 18. Middleham Castle, Wensleydale. Richard likely spent some of his childhood here in the palatial home of the Earl of Warwick. After Warwick's death, the castle passed into Richard's hands. His son, Edward of Middleham, was born, and probably died, here.

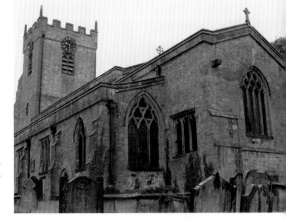

19. Church of St Mary and St Alkelda, Middleham. Richard intended to establish a collegiate church here, complete with a dean, six priests, four clerks and six choristers.

20. Pontefract Castle, West Yorkshire. The ruins of the King's and Queen's towers are on the hill, while the remains of the Norman chapel are in the foreground. Richard would have lodged in the elegant sandstone King's Tower, which is believed to have been connected to the Queen's Tower by the large great hall.

21. Walmgate Bar, York. This gateway into York was located on the principal road from Hull and was probably the entrance that Richard and Edward used upon their return from exile.

Left: 22. Micklegate Bar, York. York's main gatehouse, Micklegate Bar has stood for more than 800 years. Richard's father's head was placed on a spike here after his death. Today the bar is home to the Henry VII Experience.

Below left: 23. Holy Trinity Church, Micklegate, York. The parish church is all that is left of the Priory of the Holy Trinity in Micklegate. Richard would have visited the priory every time he participated in the Corpus Christi pageants as the procession started from here.

Below right: 24. York Minster, York. As the west front was the ceremonial entranceway to the minster, Richard would have entered through this great door on several occasions.

Above left: 25. Cawood Castle, North Yorkshire. Cawood Castle was one of the residences of the Archbishop of York.

Above right: 26. Relic from the Abbey of Stratford Langthorne, Stratford. Margaret of York's retinue stopped at the abbey on its way toward Margate.

27. Margate, Kent. It was from here that Richard's sister Margaret departed for her marriage to Charles, Duke of Burgundy.

Left: 28. Great Gate, Bury St Edmunds, Suffolk. Richard would have passed through this magnificent gatehouse on his way to the shrine of St Edmund.

Below left: 29. Norman Tower, Bury St Edmunds, Suffolk. Restored by the Victorians, the tower has stood here since the twelfth century.

Below right: 30. Entrance gate to Walsingham Abbey, Norfolk. Richard and Edward would have entered the abbey through this gateway on their visit in 1469.

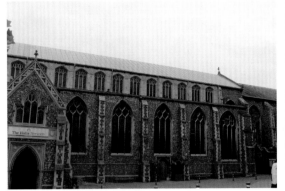

Above left: 31. The Halls, Norwich, Norfolk. A large Dominican priory once occupied this location in Norwich. Richard and Edward may have stayed here on their visit to Norwich.

Above right: 32. Blackfriars' Hall, Norwich. This building was the former Dominican friars' choir.

33. Alnwick Gateway, Norwich, Norfolk. This 1934 image shows Alnwick Gate, one of the entrances into the Bishop's Palace in Norwich.

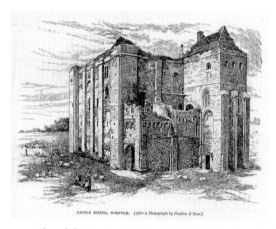

Above left: 34. Castle Rising, Norfolk. Richard's earliest known letter was written while at Castle Rising.

Above right: 35. Crowland (Croyland) Abbey, Lincolnshire. The west front of the abbey was richly ornamented. Some of the statues can still be seen today.

36. Sudeley Castle, Gloucestershire. This part of the castle is attributed to Richard.

37. King's Lynn, Norfolk. Edward IV departed from here on his way into exile. Richard likely left from here a few weeks later.

38. Veere, the Netherlands. Richard was here for a time while he and Edward made plans to regain England.

39. Vlissingen, the Netherlands. Richard and Edward IV departed from Vlissingen, known as Flushing to the English, on their way back to England to regain Edward's throne.

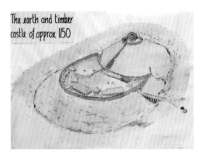

The earth and timber castle of approx. 1150

Top left: 40. Sandal Castle, West Yorkshire, in approximately 1150. This image gives an idea of the layout of the original timber construction. The stone castle largely followed this plan. *Top right:* 41. Sandal Castle. Richard, Duke of York, was killed near the castle by the Lancastrians. *Middle left:* 42. Spon Gate, Coventry, West Midlands. Spon Gate was one of Coventry's twelve gateways. *Middle right:* 43. St Mary's Priory in Coventry. Remains of the west front of the once opulent priory. *Bottom:* 44. Tapestry from St Mary's Guildhall, Coventry, depicting key figures in the Wars of the Roses. Richard, as Gloucester, is said to be the figure standing with his hand over his heart and looking back over his shoulder.

45. Church of St John the Baptist at Tredington, Gloucestershire. Tradition holds that Richard and Edward stayed in Tredington on the eve of the Battle of Tewkesbury.

46. Tewkesbury Abbey, Gloucestershire. Interior of the abbey.

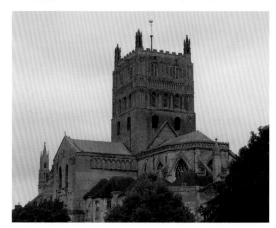

47. Tewkesbury Abbey. Lancastrian soldiers rushed to the abbey for sanctuary in the aftermath of the Battle of Tewkesbury.

48. Lower Lode Lane, Tewkesbury, Gloucestershire. Many Lancastrians drowned while trying to ford the river after the battle.

Above left: 49. Bloody Meadow, Tewkesbury. Lancastrian forces got bogged down here while fleeing for their lives and were cut down in large numbers.

Above right: 50. Barnard Castle, Durham. A view of the castle showing its large oriel window.

51. St Mary's church, Barnard Castle. Richard planned to make this church a collegiate foundation.

52. St Mary's church, Barnard Castle. A carving of Richard's emblem of a boar is shown here.

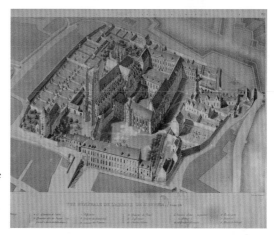

53. Abbey of St Bertin, St Omer, France. Richard would likely have stayed in the range of apartments abutting the nave while on his visit here with his sister Margaret.

Above left: 54. Westminster Hall, London. A nineteenth-century drawing of Westminster Hall, showing the hammer-beam roof constructed in the early part of the fifteenth century.

Above right: 55. Sheriff Hutton Castle, North Yorkshire. Richard imprisoned Anthony Woodville here before his execution.

56. Penrith Castle, Cumbria. Richard would have visited Penrith in his role as Sheriff of Cumberland.

57. Carlisle Castle, Cumbria. Richard was Governor of Carlisle Castle and one of its towers was named after him and bore his arms.

58. Carlisle Cathedral, Cumbria. Richard would have seen a much larger church when he visited Carlisle. Most of the monastic buildings were destroyed in the Civil War.

59. Berwick-upon-Tweed, Northumberland. This engraving shows the castle wall, which was built straight up the hill from the river to the castle.

Above left: 60. Eleanor Cross, Northampton, Northamptonshire. Tradition holds that this is the position from which the Archbishop of Canterbury watched the Battle of Northampton.

Above right: 61. St Albans Clock Tower, St Albans, Hertfordshire. The curfew bell in the tower dates from the fourteenth century.

62. Stony Stratford, Buckinghamshire. The site of the former Rose and Crown Inn where Edward V is believed to have stayed the night before Richard took him into his custody.

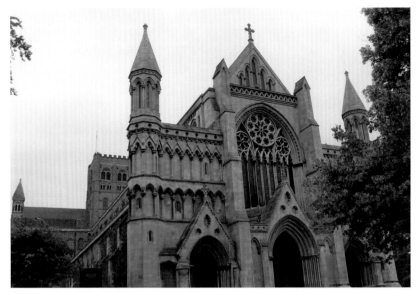

63. St Albans Cathedral, St Albans. Richard and Edward V likely lodged at the abbey here.

Above left: 64. St Albans Cathedral, interior. The medieval wall paintings were uncovered during renovations.

Above middle: 65. St Albans Cathedral. The Shrine of St Alban was a main pilgrimage site during the fifteenth century. Richard likely visited the shrine while in St Albans.

Above right: 66. St Albans Cathedral. Duke Humphrey of Gloucester's tomb rests next to the shrine. Richard may have considered the fate of Duke Humphrey as he made his decision about the throne.

67. St Albans Cathedral, Great Gate. This gateway was the principal entrance to the abbey precincts.

Above left: 68. Crosby Hall, London. Richard's home in London was located in Bishopsgate. *Above right:* 69. Baynard's Castle, London. An eighteenth-century depiction of Baynard's Castle. By tradition, Richard was offered the crown here at his mother's home. This interpretation shows how extensive the building was and how the castle would have appeared after Henry VIII enlarged it. Today nothing remains of this once great castle where so much history was made. *Below:* 70. Tower of London, London. The White Tower rises in the distance in this view across the Thames.

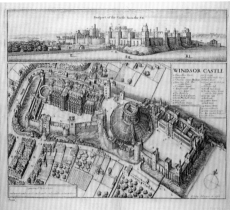

Above left: 71. Westminster Abbey, Westminster, London. Richard's coronation was held within the walls of the great abbey.

Above right: 72. Windsor Castle. A depiction of the castle by Wenceslaus Hollar in the seventeenth century. Richard would have recognised most of the castle as it stood in Hollar's time.

Above left: 73. Reading Abbey, Reading, Berkshire. Ruins are all that is left of the once palatial abbey where Elizabeth Woodville was presented as Edward's queen.

Above right: 74. Magdalen College, University of Oxford, Oxfordshire. Richard heard two disputations here in the hall while on his progress in July of 1483.

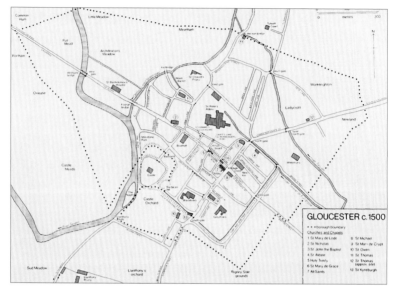

75. Gloucester, Gloucestershire. A map of Gloucester in 1500 which shows the location of the castle and abbey in relation to the gates. Richard would have entered Gloucester through the North Gate.

Above left: 76. The cloisters in Gloucester Cathedral, Gloucester. Richard would have walked from the abbot's lodge through the cloisters to get to the abbey church.

Above right: 77. Warwick Castle, Warwickshire. Richard stayed at the castle while on his first progress in 1483.

78. Nottingham Castle Gatehouse, Nottingham, Nottinghamshire. Richard would have passed through this gatehouse on his visits to the castle.

79. Nottingham Castle, middle bailey. The large, impressive royal apartments begun by Edward IV and finished by Richard III used to stand here.

80. Gainsborough Old Hall, Lincolnshire. Richard spent a night here while visiting Sir Thomas Burgh.

Top left: 81. Medieval Bishop's Palace, Lincoln, Lincolnshire. Richard would have stayed at the ecclesiastical palace on his visit to Lincoln in 1483 as the castle was serving as a gaol. *Top right:* 82. Exchequer Gate and Lincoln Cathedral, Lincoln. The fourteenth-century exchequer gate is in the foreground with the cathedral behind. The cathedral was begun soon after the Norman invasion and has undergone several renovations throughout the years. *Bottom left:* 83. King's House, Salisbury. Tradition has it that Richard stayed here on his visit to Salisbury. The vaulted stone porch is from the thirteenth-century building and would have been the principal entrance. *Bottom right:* 84. Salisbury Cathedral, Salisbury, Wiltshire. Richard visited Salisbury to put an end to Buckingham's rebellion and likely visited the cathedral while in the city.

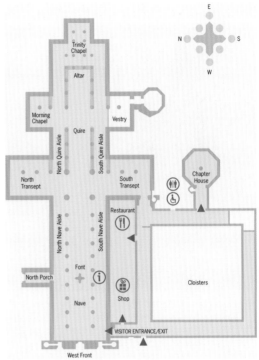

Above: 86. Effigy of Sir John Cheyne, Salisbury Cathedral. Cheyne fought against Richard in the Battle of Bosworth. *Right:* 85. Salisbury Cathedral plan. Richard may have visited the shrine of St Osmund, which was located in the Trinity Chapel. *Below:* 87. Entrance to Bishop's Palace, Exeter, Devon. This gateway was the principal entrance to the Bishop's Palace in Exeter when Richard visited to deal with the rebels.

Top left: 88. King's College Chapel, Cambridge, Cambridgeshire. Although Henry VI began building the college, a large amount of the work was completed during Richard's short reign. *Top right:* 89. Durham Cathedral, Durham. Richard and Anne often visited the cathedral and were admitted into the Fraternity of St Cuthbert. *Bottom:* 90. Scarborough, North Yorkshire. This view shows the castle perched on the hill above the town. The keep is on the left and Anne's apartments were nearby.

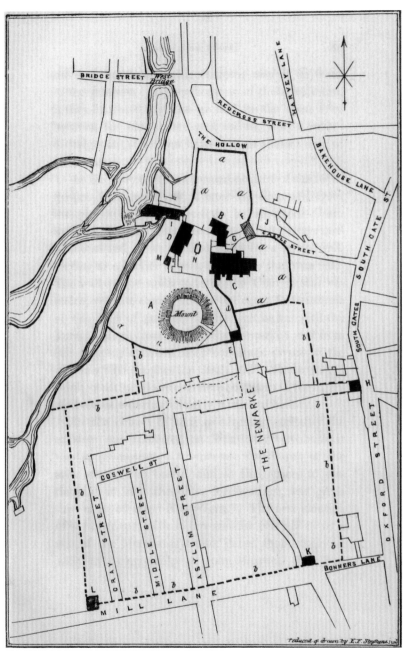

91. Leicester, Leicestershire. Plan of Leicester Castle and surrounding areas from 1859 showing the castle mound in relation to the Newarke.

92. Crypt of the Hospital of the Knights of St John of Jerusalem in Clerkenwell, London. The twelfth-century crypt is all that remains from Richard's time of the once extensive priory church of the Hospitallers of St John. Richard came to the priory to publicly denounce rumours that he planned to marry his niece, Elizabeth.

93. Leicester Newark Gateway, Leicester. Most likely the gateway that Richard's body would have passed through on its return to Leicester.

94. The church of the Annunciation of the Blessed Virgin Mary in the Newarke, Leicester. These arches are all that remain of the church and are located in the basement of the Hawthorn Building of the De Montfort University.

Above: 95. Richard III's reinterment at Leicester Cathedral, which took place on 26 March 2015. (Courtesy of Will Johnston, © Leicester Cathedral)

Right: 96. Richard's tomb, Leicester Cathedral. (Courtesy of Will Johnston, © Leicester Cathedral)

Loyaulte me lie

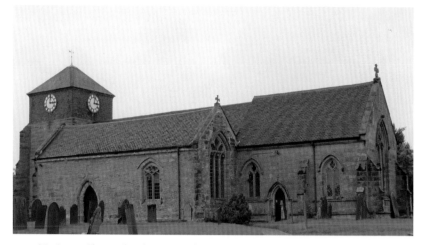

97. Sutton Cheney church, Leicestershire. Tradition holds that Richard may have taken Mass here before the Battle of Bosworth.

98. Bosworth, Leicestershire. This field is where the boar badge, Richard's emblem, was found. This image was taken from a vantage point not accessible to the general public.

horses would have made noise as well. Warwick definitely knew that Edward had arrived, although he may not have realised how close Edward's army was to his. The chronicler said that Warwick had more ordinance than Edward, and throughout the night constantly shot his guns, which 'thanked be God! It so fortuned that they alway ovarshote the Kyngs hoste, and hurtyd them nothinge, and the cawse was the Kyngs hoste lay muche nerrar them than they demyd.' The chronicler said that Edward did not allow his men to return fire, so that Warwick would not realise exactly where the army was located.

Edward divided his army into three main sections. While there is confusion about the location of Hastings and Richard during the battle, the most accepted account is provided here. Hastings held the left, Edward the centre, keeping wayward brother George close by, and Richard took the right. Richard's position was the hardest, as his division had to traverse rough terrain. In the darkness of the night, the armies did not line up directly opposite each other, leaving Warwick's right wing overlapping Edward's left wing. Also, Edward's right wing overlapped Warwick's left wing.

Primary accounts of the battles during this time usually differ in estimates, and the actual number of men at any battle is hard to pin down. Estimates of Warwick's men have been between 15,000 and 30,000, while Edward's are roughly estimated to be between 8,000 and 10,000. It is likely that the two groups were more evenly matched. The numbers of Warwick's men would probably coincide with what Alfred Burne proposed in *The Battlefields of England*. Burne suggested around 15,000 men for Warwick and 10,000 for Edward.

After a restless night, the battle commenced between 4 a.m. and 5 a.m. A mist had settled on the area, making it difficult to see. This would work to Edward's advantage in the end. As the battle began, Oxford seized on the fact that his men overlapped Hastings' and was able to outflank them and drive them back towards Barnet. Some of the king's men kept going until they reached London, where they shared the news that the king had lost. However, the mist kept the rest of Edward's men from seeing the flight of Hastings' group, so they were not discouraged.

The heavy fog worked in Edward's favour again as Oxford's men rode back into the fray. Oxford's banners resembled Edward's and in the confusion, Somerset's men fired on Oxford's men, thinking they were the enemy. Many of Oxford's men took up cries of 'Treason!' and fired back into Somerset's lines.

In the meantime, Richard was able to overcome the difficult terrain and push Warwick's army back. Then, his men turned around to help support the centre of the field. Edward pushed forward and his army overcame the centre of Warwick's army. Warwick turned to flee, but he was killed in his flight. The chroniclers disagree as to what befell the Marquis of Montagu. Warkworth's chronicle stated that Montagu was killed by one of Warwick's own men as he started to put on Edward's livery. However, the *Arrivall* said that he was slain in the battle. It is unlikely that, with the dense fog and the battle raging around him, one of Warwick's men was watching Montagu so closely that he was able to detect a change in livery.

In the aftermath of the battle, the Earl of Oxford escaped to Scotland. Exeter was terribly wounded and was left on the field for hours. Warkworth's chronicle said that he was eventually carried to a home where a doctor attended him, before he was taken into custody at the Tower. The bodies of Montagu and Warwick were placed in a cart and taken to London, where they were put on display in St Paul's for several days before being taken to the family vault in Bisham Abbey. Henry VI was taken back to the Tower of London.

The *Great Chronicle of London* says that Richard was the one routed by Oxford. As he was not experienced in battle, this is a possibility. Frustratingly, none of the other chronicles give the deployments. In the end, it does not change the outcome. Edward's army, of which Richard was an integral part, routed the Lancastrians and won the day.

Visiting Barnet Today

A good first place to start a tour of Barnet is the Barnet Museum in the town. It has restricted opening hours as it is entirely staffed by volunteers, but it is a good place to get an overview of the surrounding area.

Driving through Barnet is an experience! It is easy to miss some of the key sites associated with Richard III. At the junction of

Hadley Highstone and Kitts End Road is the Hadley monument to the battle. The sandstone obelisk is inscribed, 'Here was fought the famous battle between Edward the 4th and the Earl of Warwick April 14 Anno 1471 in which the Earl was defeated and slain.' The monument does not sit in its original location and does not mark the exact location of the fighting, but it is worth a visit as a tribute to those who fought in the battle.

Old Fold Golf Course is where much of the fighting is believed to have happened. It is possible to take a public footpath and walk along the area. It is hard to picture this peaceful golf course as the scene for such a bloody battle. Nearby, Hadley Green Road has an information panel that is worth visiting to get an idea of the Yorkists' lines.

Hadley Green Road postcode: EN5 5PP.

Tewkesbury, Gloucestershire

Richard and his men did not have long to rest after the victory at Barnet before Edward was raising fresh troops and pushing once again towards a Lancastrian army. Margaret of Anjou and her son, Prince Edward, along with the exiled lords, had landed. Upon hearing that Warwick was dead, Margaret was worried that their cause was over. Beaufort and Courtenay met with her and persuaded her that the cause was not lost and that men would rally around her. The group set out to raise troops among the men of Devon, Cornwall and other southern counties.

Edward set forth to meet Margaret's troops. Despite Lancastrian ruses, he was not deceived. Realising that Margaret's army would try to meet up with Jasper Tudor's men, he headed west. Trying desperately to trick Edward, the Lancastrians sent a group of scouts to Sodbury, hoping Edward would think the entire army was headed that way. It worked. Edward camped the night near Sodbury Hill, unsure of whether or not Margaret's army was nearby.

Once he realised where Margaret was headed, he sent a messenger to Gloucester telling it to bar the gates to the Lancastrians. Frustrated by this, the Lancastrians had to make for the next crossing at Tewkesbury. After their strenuous march, they were exhausted as they took up their position. The king reached the area later that day. Both armies camped that night about three miles from each other.

The next morning, the army of the king, separated again into three divisions, marched towards the Lancastrians. Richard held the front, Edward, with brother George nearby, held the centre, and Hastings guarded the rear. On reaching the Lancastrians, who had the benefit of slightly higher ground, the king's guns roared. Richard's archers let loose their arrows, and the battle began. For some reason, the Lancastrian division under Somerset left its defensive ground and made its way towards the king's army, where hand-to-hand combat broke out. Whether this was a strategic move to try and overtake Edward or whether he was incited to impulsivity is unclear. The outcome of his move, though, is quite clear. Overcome, Somerset's men moved back up the hill where they were attacked by others in the king's army. Somerset's men broke ranks and fled, many of them being cut down as they tried to escape.

Seizing the advantage, Edward turned on the Lancastrian centre, led by Prince Edward. These men began to flee as well. The York army surged forward, slicing down the fleeing men. Some of the escaping men drowned in the river, weighed down by their armour. What happened to Prince Edward is unknown. Later chroniclers, influenced by the passage of time and a new dynasty, have the York brothers falling upon him and murdering him. He could easily have died in the heat of battle, as this was his first military campaign. Either way, the heir to the Lancastrian throne was dead.

Many of the men escaped into the sanctuary of Tewkesbury Abbey. An old tradition, sanctuary, had protected Elizabeth and his heir when Edward was in exile. If this thought crossed his mind as he demanded the men inside be handed over to him, he did not show it. The abbot, fearful of repercussions, handed the men over. A quick trial was held in the toll house, with Richard and the Duke of Norfolk serving as judges. As expected, the men were found guilty. A scaffold was hastily erected and the men were swiftly executed. Margaret and Anne, her daughter-in-law and Richard's future wife, escaped with their ladies but were later captured. It seemed the Lancastrians were finished. At long last, Edward IV was secure upon his throne.

Visiting Tewkesbury Today

I recommend that you drive to the area so that you have a car to visit nearby sites of interest. There are many places to stay in Tewkesbury, and as it is so near the M5, there are also hotels nearby. The first place to visit is the tourist information centre, located at 100 Church Street. The centre has a battlefield walking tour leaflet that explains sites along the battlefield.

While obviously not a location that Richard would have visited, the heritage centre here has a well-developed exhibition on the battle. A replica of how the battle might have looked helps visitors get an idea of the scope of the battle in relation to the surrounding countryside. Details of each of the main participants in the battle are also supplied. It also has exhibitions on the history of Tewkesbury in general. Visiting the museum before you go to any of the sites helps you visualise where you are in relation to the other points of interest.

The layout of the town has not changed tremendously from medieval days. Surrounded by water, there were no town walls, as the rivers would have offered protection. The Severn, Avon, Carron and Swilgate are all near Tewkesbury. This confluence of waters would have made this area easy to flood, and it still floods today. Our first stop is slightly outside of Tewkesbury in the village of Tredington.

Tredington

Tredington is about two miles south of Tewkesbury and, in the fifteenth century, its church served as a chapel of ease for Tewkesbury. Tradition has it that Edward and his army stayed here the night before the battle. There is not much to back up the claim, other than the village's proximity to Tewkesbury and its location on a main road. The main primary source for the battle is the *Historie of the Arrivall of Edward IV in England,* which says that he 'lodgyd hym selfe, and all his hooste, within three myle of them'. The manor house that Edward lodged in is gone, but the church nearby is still standing.

The church of St John the Baptist at Tredington is primarily the same as it was at the time of the battle. There have obviously been renovations, but the main layout has remained the same. The church was built of ashlar stone and has a timber-framed tower, which was rebuilt in 1883. In the south porch is an elaborate arch above the doorway, embellished with alternating coloured stone in a zigzag pattern with the pillars continuing the pattern.

The layout inside the church is similar to how it would have appeared during the Wars of the Roses. The armorial bearings in the west end of the church symbolise families connected with the church, including the de Clares and the Neville lords of Warwick.

It is possible that Edward and Richard observed Mass here before the battle at Tewkesbury. They would not have seen any pews in the nave, as these are all Elizabethan. Their minds were probably focused on securing God's blessing for the battle before them, and they would not have noticed any of the church's decorative features.

Visiting the Church Today

The church is open during daylight hours. Make sure to pick up one of the informative church guides as you enter. St John the Baptist postcode: GL20 7AB.

Bloody Meadow

The bloody meadow is traditionally held to be the area where the Lancastrians were slaughtered as they attempted to flee en masse. The meadow is shaped in such a way that it would have been impossible for the Lancastrians to escape on either side, forcing them to press onwards, where they were bogged down in the soft soil. Defeated, exhausted and desperate to escape, they were easily caught by the triumphant Yorkists, who cut them down in numbers so high that the field earned the sobriquet 'Bloody Meadow'. The meadow is marked by a panel.

Lower Lode Lane

Some of the escaping Lancastrians made for the ford of the river at Lower Lode Lane. At least one author, Steven Goodchild, believes that Queen Margaret also fled this way toward Malvern. There is insufficient evidence to know exactly where Margaret was captured, but some believe she made it to Malvern Priory.

Lower Lode Lane is off Gloucester Road and is not far from the abbey. Follow the road until it ends. This was one of the crossing points for the river. Today you can take a boat across to eat at the pub.

Tewkesbury Abbey

The abbey can be seen from some areas of the battle site and a fanciful mind can picture it as a beacon of hope to the men running for their lives after the battle's end. Today, the abbey offers a picturesque view to its many visitors.

A religious building has occupied the site since the Saxon times, when a monastery was built here in the eighth century. In the eleventh century, Robert Fitzhamon founded the abbey. When he died, he was first buried in the chapter house, but was later reinterred in a tomb in the church. The building was consecrated in the twelfth century, and over the years passed through some illustrious families. Robert, Earl of Gloucester, Henry I's natural son and Matilda's half-brother, held the land and helped finish the abbey. It came down to King John, through his first wife. When he divorced her, he granted her family lands back to her. As she died with no issue, her sister inherited, and the lands fell to the de Clare family. Later, it would pass through the Despensers to the Beauchamps, before coming to Warwick and then, after his death, to George, Duke of Clarence.

A fire destroyed the monastic buildings in 1178, but did little damage to the church itself. Under Hugh le Despenser, the church underwent elaborate changes. Seven large windows, made of glass from Chartres, were installed and the choir was remodelled. Pointed arches were added to the columns. Many of the Despenser family are buried in the church. An elaborate canopied tomb contains the remains of Hugh le Despenser and his wife.

After the battle and executions of the Lancastrians, many of them were buried here in the church. Prince Edward is buried in the choir, while several of the lords are buried in the north transept. After his execution, George, Duke of Clarence, was buried here, along with his wife, Isabel, behind the high altar.

During the Dissolution, the monastery was forced to close. However, the people of Tewkesbury saved the abbey by petitioning to use it as a parish church. They were able to amass the large sum of money the king demanded within two years.

Visiting Tewkesbury Abbey:

I suggest you set aside more time than you think you will need when you visit the abbey. At first, much of your time will be spent simply absorbing the atmosphere of this place. Although I have been in many abbeys and cathedrals, I still consider Tewkesbury to be one of my favourites. The architecture is extraordinary. Vaulted ceilings, Norman columns, large capitals and ornate tracery abound. A sense of the historical relevance of the place seems trapped within the building.

Much of the stained glass you see, while beautiful, is not medieval. For the medieval stained glass, visit the choir. The gorgeous windows are of the late Decorated style. After admiring the exquisite glass, take a moment to look up. The soaring choir vault is painted and gilded; the bright colours set off the vaulting brilliantly. In later years, the choir was decorated with the Yorkist badge of the sun in splendour. Ironically, the burial place of Edward, the Lancastrian heir, lies directly below the badge. Before leaving the choir, examine the misericords. These resting areas in the choir stalls are often decorated with images, and Tewkesbury has some interesting ones.

Visit the chantry chapels and walk around the church before you leave. There is so much beauty and history contained here. The tombs are elaborate, and you will recognise many of the names. Make sure to spend time in the north transept, as the area is where many of the Lancastrian dead were buried. George and Isabel are in a vault behind the high altar. While near the high altar, look at the altar stone, which is made of Purbeck marble, and is said to be of thirteenth-century origin.

The church is a good place to have a meal or tea. The refectory has a wide assortment of cakes and home-cooked food. Spend some time relaxing here before heading out to the battlefield, or spend time recovering from your battlefield walk before heading onward to other sites of interest.

Obelisk

Before you leave Tewkesbury, it is worth taking the time to see the obelisk commemorating the Battle of Tewkesbury as well as other important events. To get there, turn right out of the abbey car park and walk across the bridge to the recreation area. At the top of the field you will see the obelisk. Each side of the obelisk has an informational plaque.

From here, the views of the abbey are incredible. It is apparent how immense the buildings once were, even with the outbuildings destroyed.

Part IV

Lord of the North

After the Battle of Tewkesbury, Edward made a jubilant entry into London with his brothers by his side. It would have been a sight to behold, the three York brothers riding together – the tall king, flanked on either side by his brothers, re-entering the capital of his kingdom. People lined the streets, cheering for the king and the men riding with him. Richard had proven his loyalty to his brother in battle, and now it was time to receive his reward.

In the years after Edward reclaimed his kingdom, Richard began to receive more grants of land and more responsibilities. He was appointed Great Chamberlain of England and Chief Steward of the Duchy of Lancaster in the North Parts and in the Palatine of Lancashire. He resumed the office of Warden of the West Marches, and he was given a grant in tail of Warwick's estates in the North, as well as many of the estates of John de Vere. He was consolidating power in the North and was quickly becoming a force in the area.

Not only did Richard begin to establish power in the North through grants from his brother, he was also looking toward marriage with a suitable heiress. To the horror and dismay of Clarence, Richard's eye fell on Anne Neville. The daughter of Warwick, Anne was entitled to a share in the estates that Clarence had been jealously guarding as his own. The thought that his brother would be able to share in this inheritance filled Clarence with rage. He quickly appealed to Edward, and a meeting was called at Sheen. Clarence told Richard that he could have Anne, but not her inheritance. Despite what Clarence felt, the marriage went through and the estates were partitioned. Richard and Anne had applied for a dispensation, but apparently married before it arrived. After the wedding, which may have taken place at Westminster, Richard and Anne headed back north to start their new lives.

Barnard Castle, Durham

Teesdale is a picturesque area of rolling hills and undulating streams that have graced this land for centuries. Richard would have travelled this terrain often, going to and from Barnard Castle. It is easy to see why this castle seems to have been one of his favourites. Not only does it sit high above the River Tees, commanding a beautiful view of the countryside, but it is both highly defensive and situated in a strategic location.

This area was granted to Guy de Baliol by William Rufus. However, the Baliol claim to the land was hotly contested by the bishopric of Durham. The bishops claimed that the land had originally belonged to them before the Earl of Northumberland wrested it away. When the earl was defeated by the king, the area reverted to the Crown. The bishops held that the land should have come back to them, but the family continued to claim the land.

History of the Castle

Guy built a timber castle upon a naturally fortified cliff above the River Tees. His nephew, Bernard, began building the stone fortifications seen today. He also founded the town and gave it its first charter. His son, another Bernard, finished the work on the castle. The town became known by the castle's name.

John de Baliol is probably the best known of the family. His marriage to Devorguilla of Galloway brought him titles and land. Legend has it that after John's death, his widow kept his heart in a casket with her at all times until her death. A stone effigy of her at Sweetheart Abbey depicts her holding his heart.

John de Baliol II inherited his father's titles. Edward I appointed him as the new King of Scotland, with the belief that he would be directly under the control of England. Edward miscalculated the loyalty of de Baliol, because once he became King of Scotland he renounced English authority. The ensuing war resulted in Baliol's imprisonment in the Tower of London; his lands were forfeited to Edward.

The Bishop of Durham saw his chance and claimed the land back for the Church. He held on to the land for a few years, but ultimately the king asserted his rights. He granted the land to Guy de Beauchamp, Earl of Warwick. Eventually, the land came to Richard Neville, Earl of Warwick through his marriage to Anne Beauchamp. Their daughter, Anne Neville, married Richard, Duke of Gloucester, and the lordship passed to him.

Originally, the castle had a large stone curtain wall surrounding it. Inside, it was divided into four areas called wards. The town ward housed the Dovecot Tower, where the pigeons nested. A source of food, eggs and fertiliser, pigeons were important to castle life. To the east of the ward is the Brackenbury Tower. An old story says that the tower was named after the constable of the tower, Robert Brackenbury. The North Gatehouse is to the north of the Dovecot Tower. The town ward was separated from the middle ward by a gatehouse and a drawbridge over a moat. Left of the bridge, look for the garderobe chutes at the base of the remains of the tower. These chutes would have emptied directly into the moat.

Richard and Barnard Castle

Richard would have spent most of his time at the castle within the inner ward. Today, it is hard to picture the once opulent setting. However, if you pause, you can still picture the Great Hall, with its beautiful tapestries covering the walls. Windows, most likely glazed and often shuttered, would have allowed light to flow into the room. Richard would have sat at the upper end of the hall, perhaps in front of a heraldic tapestry, boasting his ties to the king. Surrounded by his household, who would be seated at the tables slightly below the dais, Richard would have held lavish meals. According to the castle's guidebook, excavations of the castle revealed that one of these types of feasts had blocked the kitchen drains.

In his great chamber at the upper end of the hall, Richard would have taken light meals or played games. Likely he also met with important visitors in the room. Perhaps he and Brackenbury spoke together in this room, forging a friendship that would later lead to Brackenbury receiving great honours from Richard after he became king. Richard probably enjoyed the view from the oriel window that overlooked the river below. An emblem of a boar is carved above the window, lending weight to the theory that Richard was the one who added the window during the fifteenth century.

The ashlar Round Tower, thirty feet in diameter, was four storeys. The tower's vault was described as plain, without ribs or a pillar. Here is where Richard would have slept. Easily reachable from Richard's great chamber, this area would have been strictly for rest. A great bed with curtains would have sat in the room, offering privacy for its occupant. Anne's accommodations were likely on the second floor of the tower, as a survey in 1592 called this area the lady's chamber. Anne, too, would have had a great bed, curtained for her privacy, as some of her attendants would have slept in the room as well.

The outer ward, which is now on private property, contained the chapel and demesne land. Like most castles, Barnard had its own chapel for worship. This chapel, described by Leland as a 'faire chapel', was St Margaret's Chapel. Unfortunately, the area is now farmland and is not open to visitors. It is possible to view where the chapel once stood from the castle but nothing substantial remains.

The castle was already falling into disrepair by the time of the 1592 survey. This situation worsened under the ownership of the Vane family, who had the lead removed from the roof, allowing the castle to fall to ruin. The artist William Bewick, describing his Aunt Sarah bemoaning the fate of the castle, quoted her as saying, 'Oh! Misery! Can one thousand pounds worth of lead, iron, wood, and stone be more worth than a Castle which might receive a king and his whole train?' Most people standing here looking at the ruins of this once great fortress would wholeheartedly agree with Aunt Sarah.

Visiting Barnard Castle Today

The town of Barnard Castle is a delight to visit, although not necessarily to drive in. There is ample parking, however, and much to see and do. The castle is located behind the Methodist church.

For more information on opening times, visit the castle website at www.english-heritage.org.uk/daysout/properties/barnard-castle/.

After your visit, turn left out of the entrance and head down the path to the river. For stunning views of the castle, cross the bridge and turn right. Walk until you see a break in the trees or a path to the river. The views of the castle from across the river are not to be missed. From this angle it is apparent that the castle was built to be imposing, as it rises high over the surrounding land. Barnard Castle postcode: DL12 8PR.

St Mary's Church, Barnard Castle

As he had with the church of St Mary and St Alkelda at Middleham, Richard sought to turn St Mary's church at Barnard Castle into a collegiate church. In 1478, The *Calendar of the Patent Rolls* includes this licence:

> Licence for the king's brother Richard, duke of Gloucester, or his heirs or executors to found a college at Barnard Castell within the castle there of a dean and twelve chaplains, ten clerks and six choristers and one clerk to celebrate divine service and offices in the chapel within the castle for the good estate of the king and his consort Elizabeth, queen of England, and the said duke and Anne his wife and his heirs, and for their souls after death, and the souls of the king's father Richard, late duke of York, and the king's brothers and sisters, to be called the college of the said duke at Barnard Castell, and for the said dean and chaplains to acquire in mort main lands, rents, services and other possessions and advowsons of churches to the value of 400 marks yearly.

It is clear that Richard intended the collegiate church at Barnard Castle to be bigger than the one he wanted to establish at Middleham. While we do not know much about his plans for the collegiate church, as it was not completed, it seems reasonable to conclude that he would have wanted the church to follow the same guidelines as those established at Middleham. The dean and the chaplains would live there.

Richard undertook quite a bit of work at the church. He had the roof raised and windows placed in the clerestory. As Richard often put in windows, it appears that he appreciated lighted spaces. He also put in the chancel arch and added a north porch and a vestry to the church.

Visiting the Church Today

The church as you see it today has drastically changed from Richard's time period. Although roughly the same size, much of today's church is Victorian or later. However, there is still much to see related to Richard. Where the accessible toilet entrance is today was the north porch that Richard ordered built. The vestry was replaced by a Victorian vestry, but you can still see the heads that were carved on either side of the chancel arch. The head on the left wearing a crown is Edward IV, while the one on the right wearing a ducal coronet is Richard, as Duke of Gloucester. The carving of Richard is quite detailed, much more so than the one of Edward IV. With binoculars, it is even possible to make out wavy hair and a strong chin, much like the paintings of Richard.

On the back of the church near one of the windows is a carving of Richard's emblem, a boar. It is hard to see, but it is next to the window in the upper left-hand corner. St Mary's postcode: DL12 8NQ.

Abbey of St Bertin, St Omer, France

During the summer of 1475, large numbers of English troops began landing in Calais. An alliance between Edward IV and his brother-in-law, the Duke of Burgundy, had led Edward to bring troops to France in order to invade. On 4 July 1475 Edward landed at Calais with an army that Commines called 'most numerous, the best disciplined, the best mounted ... that ever any king of England invaded France withal'. In Calais, they were met by their sister Margaret. Charles had been delayed. After several days, Cora Scofield says that Margaret went on to St Omer accompanied by Richard and George. Edward and the troops would await Charles and reunite with them later in the month.

While we have no contemporary records as to where Margaret and her brothers stayed, it is most likely that they stayed either in the princess quarters or other appropriate lodgings within the Gothic abbey of St Bertin. Located on the banks of the Aa River, the abbey was one of the most important monasteries in Europe. The last Merovingian king, Childeric III, was deposed, tonsured and confined in the abbey, where he died in the eighth century. The abbey later joined the Benedictine order and prospered.

The princess quarters, which abutted the abbey's church, were built by Abbot Guillaume Fillastre. During the last time that Richard, George and Margaret would have together, they probably heard Mass at the high altar of the impressive abbey church. Pausing in front of the altar, they would have noticed the seven-foot-long altarpiece, exquisitely painted, gilded and covered with precious gems, which had been commissioned by Fillastre.

Today the church is only ruins, but thanks to antiquarians and models of the abbey grounds, it is possible to work out some of its former layout. Richard, accompanied by his siblings, would have seen a grand church with two courtyards. A large expanse of gardens surrounded the abbey, along with outbuildings such as the bakery and brewhouse. A pyramid fountain lay close to the cloisters.

The church itself was more than 360 feet in length, with a nave of more than 135 feet. The choir, transept, nave and tower were all completed at different times. The tower was finished by Fillastre, who was also responsible for the princess quarter of the monastic buildings. Several chapels dominated the building of the church. The chapel of St Denis was ornamented with gilded sculptures and its ceiling was painted with blue flowers.

The quarters that Richard would have stayed in as the guest of his sister would have been splendid. Built for the Duke of Burgundy, whose court was known for its courtly manners and sophistication, the chambers would have been constructed with both splendour and comfort in mind. After Edward's arrival, the blissful family reunion would come to an end, and the brothers would depart towards Fauquembergues, and from there would move on to Picquigny.

Visiting St Omer Today

I recommend that you visit the tourist office as soon as you arrive in St Omer and get a town map. Public parking is across the street from the cinema and close to the tourist office. All of the sites in St Omer are within a mile of each other, and buses are available. Check with the tourist office for the latest routes and numbers.

The ruins are all that is left of the abbey today. However, you can still visit the area where the abbey once stood. After it was closed, the abbey buildings were used as a quarry for other buildings and soon little was standing. Further damage was done during the Second World War.

Mosaic tiles and artefacts from the abbey can be found in the nearby Musée Sandelin. The museum is well worth a visit as it contains a rich variety of paintings and other exhibits, including weapons, from the medieval era and beyond. For more information about current opening times, see www.musenor.com/en/Les-Musees/Saint-Omer-Musee-de-l-Hotel-Sandelin. St Omer postcode: 62500.

Other Locations in France

Other locations in France were not included as a section as no extant sites directly related to Richard remained. I did want to acknowledge them, in case you might want to include them in your visit. Fauquembergues is nearby, and Picquigny, where the treaty was signed, is approximately a two-hour drive from St Omer. Amiens, with its magnificent cathedral, is near Picquigny.

Palace of Westminster and Environs, London

Richard would have been familiar with this palace, situated on the banks of the Thames. A royal palace has graced this area since Edward the Confessor's time. Under the Normans, the palace was enlarged and the Great Hall was added. Many of England's medieval rulers stayed at the palace, given its close proximity to London.

The old palace had the River Thames as its eastern boundary, Bridge Street as its northern, St Margaret's church precinct as its western, and Great College Street as its southern boundary.

Richard visited the palace many times, but he certainly was here in 1478 when his nephew, Richard of York, married the heiress Anne Mowbray. He would also have been with Edward on his triumphant re-entry to London after his exile. The palace likely held happy memories for him.

Other memories might have flooded his mind as he came into Westminster Hall to accept the throne, supplanting his nephew as King of England. It was here at the palace that he had once sworn fealty to Edward as the Prince of Wales. Even if his conscience was clear, believing his nephew to be illegitimate and unfit to rule, he may have felt a bit unsettled as he sat upon the King's Bench that day.

Richard's most memorable experience at the palace was probably after he was offered the crown of England. On being presented at Baynard's Castle with a petition requesting he assume the throne, Richard agreed. Afterwards he rode to Westminster Hall and took his seat upon the marble chair of the King's Bench.

As king, Richard erected a stone gateway by the north-western end of the palace. The gatehouse, called the High Tower, was across from the Abbey Sanctuary gate. The gatehouse was of great height, with spacious rooms in it. Unfortunately, it remained unfinished after Richard's death.

Visiting Westminster Today

Westminster Hall is the oldest surviving part of the Palace of Westminster. Built in the last decade of the eleventh century, the history of England permeates its walls. Standing in the centre of the cavernous room, a fanciful person can almost feel the history sliding past. Kings, queens, nobles and commoners have passed through this hall, both on momentous occasions and on everyday business.

As you enter the hall, pause for a minute. You may feel rushed to head into the Houses of Parliament, but stop and look around. The current hammer-beam roof above you was put in place in the early part of the fifteenth century. This is the same roof that would have sheltered Richard as he feasted following his coronation.

The statues of the kings that line the south wall are from the fourteenth century. Imagine them as they would have appeared to Richard, colourfully painted and gilded. On the south side of the hall was where the court of the King's Bench met. It was here that Richard came to accept the throne.

The only way to see Westminster Hall is to visit the Houses of

Parliament. At the time of writing, visitors enter into the Houses of Parliament through the hall. To get to the Houses of Parliament, take the tube to Westminster station.

For information on ordering tickets for a tour, see the website at www.parliament.uk/visiting/visiting-and-tours/. Postcode: SW1A 0AA.

St Stephen's Chapel

Tradition holds that the royal chapel known as St Stephen's Chapel was originally built by King Stephen. Later the chapel would be rebuilt and refounded by Edward I, with work continuing on the chapel until the reign of Edward III. Connected to the Palace of Westminster, the chapel was elaborately decorated. Richard's royal ancestors had worshipped on this spot for centuries.

Nothing remains today of this highly ornamented chapel, but thanks to the works of Edward Brayley and John Britton writing in the nineteenth century, and to the work of J. M. Hastings in the twentieth century, we know quite a bit about how the interior of the chapel appeared.

The chapel was divided into an upper and lower chapel. The lower was named St Mary in the Vaults. The upper chapel was for the king and the royal family, while the lower chapel was for the household and the courtiers. A two-storey passageway connected the Painted Chamber of the palace with the king's pew in the upper chapel. The doorway to his pew had the arms of England and France above it. Since St Stephen's was a collegiate chapel, stalls were necessary for the dean and chapter. These were placed in the upper chapel as well.

The exterior of the chapel was entirely covered with tracery. On each side of the area above the great east window was an arcade with richly carved statues.

Entering the upper vestibule, Richard would have seen elaborate arcading. As he made his way into the chapel he would have been in a room about ninety feet long, thirty feet wide and almost sixty-five feet high. Large piers divided the chapel into five bays. Each wall of each bay was ornately arcaded with columns of Purbeck marble. The area above each arch was heavily crested, with battlements above. The mouldings in the bay had painted heraldic arches, and the spandrels of the arches were painted with stars of gold on a blue background.

A plethora of colours would have assaulted his senses as Richard stood in the doorway of the vestibule. Paintings of angels and motifs of lions, fleurs de lis, and other gilded ornaments adorned the walls. Painted lifesize statues stood on pedestals. The mouldings of the chapel were light blue, but the bases, caps, canopies and bosses were gilded.

The stained glass of some windows told the biblical stories of Adam and Eve, Noah, Abraham, Joseph and the Israelites. Other windows had angels or knights. The heraldry of the nobility occupied several windows. There were many windows with delicate tracery within the chapel.

Beautiful paintings hung on the walls. The Ascension of Christ, as well as the stories of Jonah, Job, Daniel and other biblical figures were central to the chapel. According to Hastings, the clerestory of the chapel resembled a glazed triforium.

At the east end of the chapel, above the altar, was a splendid painting of Edward III being presented to the court of Heaven by St George. Behind the bowing king were his kneeling sons. The queen knelt behind them, with her daughters kneeling behind her. Highly conscious of the fact that his right to rule came through his descent from this imposing king, Richard probably felt immense pride when observing the painting.

The ceiling of the chapel was vaulted and made of wood. It likely resembled the lantern tower of Ely Cathedral. The ceiling beams were ornamented with large, gilded bosses.

The lower chapel was also richly decorated. The vaulting was elaborate, with small columns making way for elaborate arches. Courtiers looking up would have seen large bosses on the ceiling of this chapel as well. Ornaments of foliage, dragons and angels adorned the lower chapel, and arched doorways marked its entrances and exits. There is no reason to believe that the lower chapel was not as elaborate as the upper. As the courtiers would have worshipped here, it is highly probable that this area was just as sumptuously decorated as the upper chapel.

Before he was king, Richard would already know the chapel well. As a young man and a member of the royal family, he likely worshipped here whenever visiting his brother at the Palace of Westminster. As uncle to Richard, Duke of York, Richard attended the elaborate wedding of his nephew to the heiress, Anne Mowbray, held in St Stephens in 1478. That day the chapel was elaborately festooned with tapestries and azure carpets as the newly married couple heard Mass at the altar.

Edward IV's body lay here in the chapel for several days following his untimely death. His heir, Edward V, was at Ludlow with his maternal uncle, and Richard was far away at his castle of Middleham. Edward's death would have far-reaching consequences for the mourners gathered there, many of whom may have been worried about having a young boy as a king.

Once Richard was crowned king, he would have taken his place in the king's pew. He did not have to enter the chapel to reach the pew, as it was easily accessible through the Painted Chamber. Here he and Anne would have observed Mass during his days in Westminster.

Visiting the Chapel Today

Today, there is little left of the once ostentatious St Stephen's Chapel. For years it was used for the House of Commons and underwent much renovation to suit the members' purposes. Additionally, the area was rebuilt following a fire. The crypt below the chapel, St Mary Undercroft, is still in existence but is not open to the public. St Stephen's Hall and the porch are built where the chapel once stood. The entrance to the hall is through the public entrance to the Houses of Parliament.

The Houses of Parliament stand directly across from Westminster Abbey. Driving in London is not advised, due to both the congestion charge and the difficulty in finding parking. The city is easy to travel in with public transportation.

The best tube stop for St Stephen's is Westminster station, although Westminster is not far from any tube stop in the general vicinity. You can easily walk there from Trafalgar Square, experiencing the bustle that is London. On the way you will pass 10 Downing Street as well as the Queen's Horse Guards. Alternatively, you could take a boat from the Tower of London to Westminster Pier. St Stephen's postcode: SW1A 0AA.

The Painted Chamber

After Richard, the Duke of York, married the young Anne Mowbray, a feast was held to celebrate the marriage. One of the likely places for the feast was the Painted Chamber. The chamber was highly ornamented and would have made an elegant background for a marriage feast. Richard, as the king's uncle, escorted the newly married Anne to the feast.

The Painted Chamber was large, at eighty feet long, twenty feet wide and fifty feet high. It was covered in glorious paintings, hence its name. As Richard entered the room he would have noticed the elegantly painted tracery and wainscoting that garnished the ceiling. On a sunny day, the sun would cast a rosy glow through the four windows in the chamber, illuminating the decorative paintings that graced its interior. Even the arches over the windows were covered with paintings, mostly heraldic images. It is easy to imagine Richard pausing from his duties as king and admiring these magnificent works of art with their deep hues of vermillion, ochre, and verdigris. Depictions of biblical scenes filled the room; most were portrayals of war.

In the east end of the chamber the king's great bed once stood. Above the bed was a large painting of the coronation of Edward the Confessor. He would keep watch over the king as he slept through the night. By the time Richard became king, the king had a more private chamber for sleeping. Most of the time, the Painted Chamber was used for state business, with Parliament meeting here at times during the fourteenth century.

Visiting the Chamber Today

Unfortunately, the Painted Chamber has totally been lost to history. A fire devastated this area of the palace and the chamber was lost. Nothing remains on site of this beautiful chamber with its intricate paintings and wainscoting. However, fragments of the Painted Chamber were found and are on display at the British Museum. The fragments displayed are those of a winged seraph and a prophet. According to the museum, they had been removed from the building prior to the fire by Adam Lee, who was the 'Labourer in Trust' for the palace at the time he removed them. The panels can be viewed in person or at the museum's website:

www.britishmuseum.org/explore/highlights/highlight_objects/
pe_mla/p/panel_paintings_from_palace.aspx

Jewel Tower

Built in the fourteenth century to house King Edward III's treasures,
the Jewel Tower is one of the few remaining sections of the medieval
Palace of Westminster. The tower was known as the king's privy
wardrobe. It was adjacent to the king's privy garden, so Richard
would have seen its exterior any time he walked within his garden.

The king's collection of jewels, gold and silver were kept at the
tower. A moat, remains of which can still be seen today, protected
the treasures from thieves. The tower still contains a fourteenth-
century vault, as well as lovely vaulted ceilings with intricate bosses.

Visiting the Tower Today

Richard would never have entered the tower, but it is still worth a
visit to get a sense of the medieval palace. The tower is open to the
public. At the time of writing, the tower has an exhibit about the
history of the building, as well as a model of the medieval palace.

If you are leaving the House of Commons, cross the street and
then turn left on Abingdon Street. The Jewel Tower is a short walk
and will be on your right. For more information about opening
times and admission prices, see the Jewel Tower's website at www.
english-heritage.org.uk/daysout/properties/jewel-tower/.   Postcode:
SW1P 3JX.

Sheriff Hutton Castle, North Yorkshire

In 1382, John Neville was granted a licence to crenellate by Richard
II. The stone castle he built at Sheriff Hutton is believed to have
replaced the earlier castle built nearby during the reign of Stephen
by Bertram de Bulmer. Built on rising land at the edge of a ridge, the
stone castle would have commanded a view of the Forest of Galtres
and the Vale of York. About ten miles from York, the castle was in
a strategic location.

Since Sheriff Hutton was one of the Earl of Warwick's castles,
Richard probably visited as a young man. The castle is little more

than a ruin today, but in its time it was impressive. Leland described the castle, saying, 'I saw no house in the north so like a princely lodging.' As you visit the castle, imagine seeing it as it would have appeared through Richard's eyes. With a little bit of imagination, the ruins can come alive again.

On a clear day, the whitewashed quarry stone would have glistened in the sun as Richard rode up with the Nevilles. Arriving on the east side, the Nevilles' heraldic shields on the Warder's Tower probably caught his eye before he passed through the arch under the tower. Entering into the inner court, he might have stopped to look at the great towers all around, with apartments built up alongside the walls. He might have wondered why the south-east tower was the only one supported by a buttress.

The south-west tower was four storeys tall, with embattled cresting on the turrets. As Richard looked around, he would have noticed that the north-west tower was taller, at five storeys. The elaborate embattlements would have impressed a young man in training.

The castle was built in the form of a square, with a tower placed at each angle. There were three wards in the castle. Climbing the stairs into the great hall in the south-west tower, Richard might have paused to look around the inner ward. As the family had dinner in the great hall, Richard would have been able to see sunlight streaming in through the two arched windows, bringing to life the tapestries hung on the walls.

Exploring the area, he would have seen the double fosse in front of the south tower. Perhaps he was curious about why the moat, which doubled as a fish pond, did not extend around the entire castle. As a park was nearby, he would have been able to hunt whenever time allowed.

He would most certainly have observed services at the castle chapel of Holy Trinity and Our Blessed Lady. When Warwick or his constable were in residence, the priests would sing Mass there.

Whether or not Richard came to Sheriff Hutton as a young man is not certain. It is known that he visited the castle rarely as an adult. After the defeat and death of the Earl of Warwick at Barnet, Edward IV granted the castle to Richard. Richard's marriage to Anne, the daughter of the Earl of Warwick, solidified his claim.

Richard used Sheriff Hutton as a prison in which to hold Anthony Woodville, the queen's brother and King Edward V's maternal uncle. Woodville had been with Edward at Ludlow when they learned that Edward IV had died. Making his way to London with the young king, Woodville met Richard at Stony Stratford. Richard had Woodville and others taken into custody, and he imprisoned Woodville at Sheriff Hutton before having him executed at Pontefract Castle.

In May of 1484, Richard visited Sheriff Hutton. Burdened with grief, he spent a night here on his way to York, soon after the death of his son Edward. For years people believed that a monument in the parish church was to commemorate Edward. Doubts have been cast on the monument and most historians no longer believe it was for the king's son. As Richard rode off towards York, he would not have known that this one-night visit would mark the last time he saw Sheriff Hutton Castle.

Sheriff Hutton was also used as a residence for Edward, Earl of Warwick. The son of George, Duke of Clarence, Edward had lost his claim to the crown due to the Bill of Attainder against his father. However, both Richard and Henry VII kept a close watch on Edward, in case someone used him to start an uprising. Henry eventually beheaded the earl, and with him, the male line of the House of York was ended.

Vergil says that Elizabeth of York was at the castle as well. After Bosworth, Henry VII sent to Sheriff Hutton for her. Proponents of Richard say he sent the royal children to Sheriff Hutton to protect them during the invasion. Others say he was holding Edward and Elizabeth as virtual prisoners at the castle.

During the Tudor time period, the castle was used as a residence for another royal son. The illegitimate son of Henry VIII, Henry Fitzroy, kept a household here. After the Tudors, the castle fell into decline, and despite other royal visits, was eventually plundered for stone. It was also used as a farm, with a barn being built inside the castle ruins. This seems rather an ignoble ending for such a proud building.

Visiting Sheriff Hutton Castle Today

The castle is located about ten miles north of York. If you have a vehicle, it is an easy drive. Alternatively, you can catch a bus in York to Sheriff Hutton.

The landscape around the castle has changed significantly since Richard was here. At that time the area was part of the Galtres Forest, and forest would have stretched as far as the eye could see. Today, there is not much woodland left. It is a peaceful area now, but during its heyday, it would have been a lively place, humming with energy as people bustled to and fro.

Unfortunately, due to safety issues you can no longer freely walk among the ruins of the castle, but instead have to view it from a distance or make a prior appointment to view it. Hopefully some conservation work will be done in the future, allowing for a more 'up close and personal' view of this once regal castle of the North. The nearby parish church is worth a visit, as Richard would have seen it on his visits to the castle.

Penrith Castle, Cumbria

The red sandstone castle of Penrith was built by Ralph Neville. Neville, jointly with his wife, Joan, had been granted the lordship of Penrith in 1396. Possibly due to his advantageous marriage to Joan Beaufort, Neville's power in the North grew steadily and as the Warden in the West March, it was his job to make sure Penrith was secure.

One way to ensure Penrith's security was to build a fortification. Neville built the castle in a square formation with a projecting north tower. Built mainly of square blocks of red sandstone, the castle must have been a beautiful sight with the sandstone glowing in the sun. After the death of Richard Neville at Barnet, Richard was granted the castle by his brother. As Sheriff of Cumberland, he would have visited here several times to help maintain order and keep the county safe from Scottish invasion.

As he often did in his newly acquired buildings, Richard set about making improvements to the castle. English Heritage credits him with adding large windows, probably for his own apartments, as well as a new gatehouse and a tower. Antiquarian John Hassell credited Richard with even more when he said, 'Nothing worthy of remark occurs in history respecting this place, until it was inhabited by Richard III, who, when Duke of Gloucester, that he might more conveniently oppose the Scots, and keep the country in awe, resided here for some time ...'

Visiting Penrith Castle Today

Penrith is a ruin, as are many of the sites associated with Richard. Despite the centuries of neglect, enough of the castle is left to picture it in its glory days. Situated on a hill, the area would have had commanding views in its day. Today there are so many buildings built up around it that it is hard to see the view.

Only traces remain of the gatehouse and tower that Richard built, but you can see how large the windows would have been. The light would have illuminated the spacious private apartments. The floor the apartments were on has long since decayed, but you can stand on the floor beneath to get an idea of the scope of the rooms.

Under the Tudors, the castle fell into ruin, and by the sixteenth century, surveys show that it was partially in ruins. The great hall was decayed of both stone and lead for twenty-six yards long and nine yards wide, while the great chamber was decayed of both stone and lead for ten yards long and nine yards wide. The chapel with the chamber underneath was also ruined. After the Civil War, the castle deteriorated even more.

As you walk amid the ruins, try to picture Richard here administering justice. He probably would have sat on the dais of the great hall listening to those who had issues. Alternatively, he would have planned strategies to keep the area safe from the Scots.

Getting to the castle is easy. At the time of writing, there is free public parking near the town centre, and it is a short walk to the castle. On the way you will pass a pub that claims it was once the home of Richard III. The pub, named the Gloucester Arms, sits on the site of the fifteenth-century hall house, Dockray Hall. It is possible that Richard did stay at Dockray Hall while renovations were occurring at Penrith, but no direct evidence exists to prove this theory. Whatever your thoughts on this, it is still an interesting place to have refreshments while visiting the castle.

The castle is managed today by English Heritage and admittance is free during daylight hours. For updated information, check out Penrith Castle's website at www.english-heritage.org.uk/daysout/properties/penrith-castle/prices-and-opening-times. Penrith postcode: CA11 7JQ.

Carlisle, Cumbria

Carlisle was established on an immense vale with rich, fertile meadows surrounded by rolling hills and flowing rivers. Even with its natural fortifications, the town originally had a wall encompassing it, with three entrances on each on the north, south and west walls. Like many towns in the region, Carlisle saw its roots in Roman times, but lay in ruins after the Romans pulled out. It was later rebuilt but again destroyed by the Danes in 900. Sitting so close to the border of the two warring countries of Scotland and England, through the centuries the city has been bandied about like a ball between two feuding children.

Under William Rufus, the town was rebuilt and fortified with a castle and a formidable defensive wall. Henry I endowed an Augustinian priory here in 1101 and continued the work on the castle and wall that his brother had started. King David of Scotland took the city in 1135, and he may have been responsible for the completion of the fortifications. He visited the castle often and would later die here. Henry II was knighted here by David as they united in trying to remove Stephen from the throne. Despite a pledge to David from Henry II that he would allow the Scots to keep Carlisle, he demanded it back from David's heir, Malcolm. Malcolm reluctantly relinquished Carlisle to the English and once again Carlisle was an English town. For the next two centuries, the town would be subject to attack, often suffering burning and plundering as a result.

During Edward IV's reign, Margaret of Anjou and the Duke of Exeter burned the city gates and surrounding area. The city once again experienced the ravages of war, but this time between the two warring houses of England. Richard was Governor of Carlisle and Sheriff of Cumberland. Despite the fact that he had permanent deputies to oversee these duties, he visited the castle and undertook improvements to the buildings. One of the towers at the castle was named after him and bore his arms.

Carlisle Castle

More than 900 years old, Carlisle Castle still looks the part of a fortress. Given how often Carlisle was attacked, it is only to be expected that the castle would be heavily fortified. Royalty, high-ranking officials and prisoners all made this grey and red sandstone edifice their residence at different times in history. Richard's appointment as governor here would have been a great responsibility.

Even though William Rufus started the present structure, the buildings are believed to have been built on an earlier fortification, as Roman coins were found when Queen Mary's tower was demolished. The present castle was divided into an outer and inner ward by a rampart wall. In the inner ward stood the massive stone keep. The outer ward's entrance was to the south. Visitors would cross over the moat by way of a drawbridge, then enter through the de Ireby Tower, an embattled tower with a double gateway, defended with machicolations, strong gates and a portcullis. The walls surrounding the outer ward were almost ten feet thick and eighteen feet tall, with crenellations.

From the outer ward, visitors would make their way to the inner ward through another double gateway, the Captain's Tower, with a portcullis, complete with murder holes, where inhabitants could drop rocks down on invaders' heads. In the inner ward stood the chapel, the keep, the great hall and other outbuildings. Queen Mary's Tower was at the south-east part of the castle. It was ornate and most likely served as the residence for royal visitors or other important guests. Richard probably stayed here when he visited the castle, as his deputy would have been occupying the governor's apartments in the keep.

An elaborately decorated turret completed the tower. According to nineteenth-century accounts, the tower contained a small chapel with a groined roof, an apartment with oak roof beams supported by pendants, and the queen's bed chamber, which was a spacious, well-lit room, entered through a pointed arch. Without these nineteenth-century descriptions, the tower may have been lost to history, as it was taken down in the early part of that century for safety reasons. Some of the ornamental stonework was taken to the cathedral.

Queen Mary's tower is said to have been the lodgings of Mary, Queen of Scots, when she was kept as prisoner here during the reign of Elizabeth I. As she was allowed considerable freedom, Mary probably spent some of her most pleasant days as a prisoner here.

The square, stone keep contained the governor's apartments. Almost seventy feet tall from ground to top of the parapets, the structure was solid with thick walls. The entrance, guarded by another portcullis, opened up to a circular staircase, which led to each floor of the structure. A large fireplace filled Richard's apartment in the keep, but despite a warm and glowing fire, the apartment was dark and gloomy with only small windows for light. The keep was connected with King Richard's tower nearby via a subterranean passageway. This tower is believed to have been named for Richard III because he either built it or reinforced it. At one time, his arms were emblazoned on the tower.

Visiting Carlisle Castle Today

The castle is under the care of English Heritage. Entrance to the castle is through the de Ireby Tower, where you can see the remains of a Roman altar. The half-moon battery and military buildings in the outer ward are after the time period we are interested in, but still worth a look. Heading towards the inner ward, stop to visit the Captain's Tower, which has recently been reopened for visitors. This tower was built in the twelfth century, and is a well-preserved gatehouse. Once inside the inner ward, explore the keep and ramparts. An informative exhibition about the history of the castle and its inhabitants is included in the ticket price. While it is not medieval, the Cumbria Military Museum is also included in the ticket price. More information about pricing and opening times can be found at the castle website, www.english-heritage. org.uk/daysout/properties/carlisle-castle/directions. Carlisle Castle's postcode: CA3 8UR.

Carlisle Cathedral

The cathedral church is said to have been built on the site of a

Saxon church and was begun under the reign of William Rufus. Henry I endowed the church and established a bishop's see here, making the church a cathedral. Augustinian monks were placed in the monastery adjoining the cathedral.

The choir was rebuilt over a period of several years after a disastrous fire destroyed the earlier section. The triforium and clerestory were added and the tracery and moulding were put in place for the magnificent east window. A panelled ceiling was added to the roof bearing the arms of the families that had given money for the rebuilding, including the Nevilles, the Percys and the Lacys.

The church as Richard would have seen it had a short tower, topped with a small spire and covered with lead. Considerably larger than it is today, the nave of the church was built of grey stone with Norman arches and pillars, with both ornate and plain capitals. Entering the red sandstone interior of the choir, Richard would have seen eight arches, placed on pillars with grotesque capitals representing the seasons. The base of the clerestory was ornamented with quatrefoils, but it would have been the highly decorated east window that would have caught his attention. More than fifty feet high, the window dominates the choir, with its exquisite tracery and stained glass at the top depicting the Last Judgement of Christ. The choir held forty-six stalls, which were built atop red sandstone. Each stall, assigned to a canon, had a misericord, finely gilded with a trace of gold.

Carlisle was one of the churches that benefited from Richard's largesse during his brief reign. The *Calendar of the Patent Rolls* records the following grant to the church:

Grant to Thomas, the prior, and the canons of the cathedral church of St. Mary, Carlisle, a great part of the possessions of which have been destroyed by the Scots, of two tuns of red wine of Gascony yearly in the port of Kyngeston on Hull for use in their church, that they may pray for the good estate of the king and his consort Anne, queen of England, and for their souls after death and the souls of the king's progenitors. Grant to them from 1 April last of the tithes of the king's mills of Carlisle and other titheable things of the king within the city or elsewhere

within the places tithing to their church. And confirmation to
them of all their possessions and liberties.

Visiting Carlisle Cathedral Today

While Richard would recognise the church today, he would be
shocked at the difference in size. Most of the monastic buildings
were destroyed during the Civil War or afterwards. The west front
of the church was completely removed, as was more than ninety feet
of the nave. The buttresses that were added to support the south
wall were not there in his time. The spire of the tower was also
removed due to wear.

The inside of the church holds some differences as well. The
choir stalls were unpainted before 1485, and much of the medieval
stained glass in the east window is gone. The ceiling of the choir
has been repainted with a different scene. The Regimental Chapel
would not have been here in the fifteenth century, nor would the
Salkheld Screen.

Using this guidebook, take some time to search out the cathedral
that Richard would have known. Many of the stonework and
arches remain the same as they did in his day. Take some time in the
choir to look at the misericords. Each one is different.

The cathedral is open daily, but it is always wise to phone ahead
in case of closures for events. It is about a half-mile walk from the
castle, and is located near the west wall of the city. See the cathedral's
website for up-to-date information regarding opening times, www.
carlislecathedral.org.uk/. Carlisle Cathedral postcode: CA3 8TZ.

Berwick-upon-Tweed, Northumberland

Like Carlisle, Berwick was a border town that changed hands
between the Scots and the English several times, suffering raids
and plunder as a consequence. People have occupied this area since
ancient times. The Danes were in the area by the ninth century and
held the land until the Scots took over. The Scots held the land
until William the Lion lost the town to the English. Throughout
the next years, the town would undergo violent raids by the two
countries.

A terrible atrocity is said to have occurred at Berwick. Isabel, wife of the Earl of Buchan, had crowned Robert Bruce at Scone. Legend has it that for this crime Edward I had her imprisoned in a cage and hung from the walls of Berwick Castle for several years. Whether the legend of Isabel's cage is true or not, she was imprisoned here for several years.

In April of 1861, the Lancastrians brokered an agreement with Scotland where the Scots would provide the exiled Lancastrians military support, and the Lancastrians would give Berwick to the Scots.

Berwick and Richard

Following a marriage treaty with Scotland in 1474, the relations between the two countries had become peaceful. For several years, each of them had kept the terms of the truce. But for some reason the Scots broke the treaty and started raiding into England. A messenger was sent to Scotland to tell the king that he was in breach of the treaty and that if he did not pay reparations for the breach, Edward IV would make war on Scotland. Edward also demanded return of Berwick and that the Scottish heir be handed over as a guarantee that the marriage would go forward.

In preparation for war, Richard was appointed lieutenant-general with the power to recruit men to the king's cause. He spent much of that year preparing for war and leading a siege of Berwick. He also managed to lead a successful raid into south-west Scotland, setting fire to Dumfries and other towns. While Richard was busy with preparations, Edward sent agents to speak with James III's brother, the Duke of Albany, offering to help him take control of the throne. Albany, whom Richard's biographer Paul Murray Kendall called 'Clarence in a kilt', jumped at the chance. In June of 1482, Richard, Edward and the Duke of Albany met at Fotheringhay to set out terms of an agreement. In exchange for Edward's formal recognition of Albany as the lawful king of Scotland, Albany agreed to cede Berwick to the English and pay homage to Edward, among other stipulations.

Richard returned north, gathering together a large army. Berwick, realising the futility of holding out against such an immense army, opened the town gates to the English. The men in the castle, however, remained steadfast and would not relinquish their fortress. Richard left a small contingent at Berwick and headed north with the main body of the army. Scotland was in no position to stop him. Some of the nobles had taken the king and imprisoned him in Edinburgh castle. Richard's men easily captured Edinburgh, and to his credit, he kept the men from plundering the town. As he made preparations to attack the main Scottish force, word came that the nobles wanted to end the war. They offered to renew the truce between the countries. However, Edward and Albany had agreed that Cecily would be Albany's bride, so Richard had to tread carefully. He negotiated the terms to include the repayment of Cecily's dower.

Faced with rebellious nobles, Albany decided that he no longer wanted to claim the throne of Scotland. He made an agreement with the nobles that he would renounce his claim to the throne if he was promised full pardon, with all his titles and lands restored. Albany's defection put Richard in a delicate position. The objective had been to place Albany on the throne. Now Richard was faced with either occupying Edinburgh at high cost or retreating with the promise that the Scots would keep the peace and repay Cecily's dower. He chose the latter, and received a promise from Albany that he would abide by his agreement with Edward.

One of the war's aims was achieved, however. Berwick Castle finally fell to the English, as the town had already done. The Croyland chronicler said that the king was grieved by the loss of so much money 'although the recapture of Berwick alleviated his grief for a time'.

Visiting Berwick Today

Very little is left of Berwick Castle from the fifteenth century. Even the walls that once surrounded the town were torn down and new ones, covering a much smaller area, were put in place during the Tudor reign. Some of the Elizabethan walls trace the medieval wall, but not all of them are in the original location. Few signs of the original wall remain, but you can walk the Elizabethan ramparts to get a view of the town and surrounding countryside.

The castle is also a ruin with very little left to help you picture it the way it was in the fifteenth century. It is highly worthwhile to walk the river path to the castle though. In addition to its natural beauty, the path allows you to see the wall that was built straight up the hill. The placard at the bottom calls these the 'Breakneck Stairs' and after one view, it is easy to see why. Follow the path back towards town to the stairs leading up to the train station. Edward I's great hall is said to have been where the train station is now, but the build up of the area makes it hard to get a good idea of the scope of the castle.

Getting to Berwick by car is easy and parking is nearby. Another option is to take the train from Edinburgh or London Kings Cross station. For more information, visit www.nationalrail.co.uk/. Berwick-upon-Tweed postcode: TD15 1BN.

Battle of Northampton

Part V

The King's Uncle

Richard learned of his brother's death while he was in the North. Whether or not he decided in that moment to take the throne or whether his decision was gradual is still hotly debated. Ultimately, he did make the decision to take control of the king before he reached London. His time as 'the king's uncle' would be short.

Northampton, Northamptonshire

Northampton has been an important city in England since the time of the early Britons. As many towns did, Northampton fell under the control of the Danes. During the eleventh century, the Danes burnt the town and killed many of the inhabitants. Simon de Senlis was granted the land by William the Conqueror and it is believed he fortified the town with walls when he built the castle. Strategically located, Northampton was an important town in medieval England as it commanded one of the main roads north of London.

The walls that surrounded Northampton were apparently large enough for six people to walk comfortably side by side. Under Edward I the walls were embattled and steps were put in to allow people access to the walls. Northampton's walls had four gates: north gate, south gate, east gate and west gate. Over the arched gates of the south, north and west gates were chambers. The east gate was taller than the others, and it was ornamented with coats of arms and elaborate stonework. The south gate would have been the entrance from London, and it was strongly fortified.

The castle stood outside the west gate. It sat on high ground surrounded by a deep trench on the sides not adjacent to the river. Overlooking the town and river, the keep towered over the area. The castle's lands included a meadow and an orchard. By the fifteenth century, it served as the area's gaol.

Battle of Northampton

When Richard was still a small child, a battle was fought at Northampton that allowed his father to return to England. The Duke of York had escaped to Ireland following the debacle at Ludlow, where the Yorkists had to flee to exile before the king's troops. Richard's brother Edward and the Nevilles had fled to Calais.

In June 1460, Edward and the Nevilles returned to England and, after a brief stop in London, headed out to meet the king. The king moved from Coventry to Northampton, where he camped on the outskirts of the town. The two armies met on 10 July, and after negotiations between the two parties failed, the battle began, largely on the lands of Delapré Abbey.

The battle was short, ending within thirty minutes because one of the Lancastrians, Sir Ralph Grey, had been secretly collaborating with the Yorkists. He ordered his men to put their weapons down, allowing the Yorkists easy access to the camp. Although losses were minimal that day, several Lancastrian lords lost their lives trying to protect the king. Among these men were Humphrey, Duke of Buckingham, and the Lords Egremont and Beaumont.

The Yorkists treated the king with respect, but he was, for all purposes, a prisoner. This victory allowed the Duke of York to return and in October he was named the king's heir, removing Prince Edward from the succession. Margaret of Anjou would not countenance her son being disinherited and before the year was out, the Duke of York would fall at the Battle of Wakefield, changing Richard's life forever.

The King's Uncle at Northampton

Within days of learning of his brother's death, Richard was on the move towards Northampton. Perhaps fearing a Woodville plot, Richard had decided to take his nephew into his custody. This move was understandable if Richard did fear the Woodvilles. The young king had grown up surrounded by his maternal relations, while he had met Richard only a few times. His loyalties would be easily influenced by his mother and maternal uncles. Richard appears to have been determined not to let this happen. Some confusion surrounds the events at Northampton, as some accounts have the king's half-brother, Richard Grey, at Northampton with Rivers, but others place him at Stony Stratford with the king.

On 29 April, Richard and Buckingham met Anthony Woodville, Earl Rivers, at Northampton. Some chroniclers say the meeting was prearranged, while Croyland says that Rivers was sent there by the king to meet the dukes.

The men had a comfortable dinner at Richard's table, where they had pleasant conversation. The next morning the men headed toward Stony Stratford, where the king was housed. A few miles from the village, Richard and Buckingham seized Rivers. After entering the village, Richard went to the king's quarters and arrested Grey and Thomas Vaughn, who was the king's chamberlain. He ordered these men sent north under guard. He then made his obeisance to the king, telling him that the men had threatened Richard's safety. Whether or not Edward V believed Richard, he was in no position to argue.

The King and Northampton

During Richard's second year as king, he issued a letter patent to the city. Northampton had apparently become impoverished, with many parts in a ruinous state and with many citizens in poverty. Describing in the letter patent how he had learned of the desolation of the town, he had decided to remit fifty marks of the farm to the town.

Visiting Northampton Today

The great fire of 1675 in Northampton destroyed many of the medieval buildings in the town and Charles II ordered the walls and the town's gates to be destroyed. Not much is left of the city Richard would have known.

Due to destruction of many records by the fire, it is hard to determine where Richard stayed on his trip to Northampton in 1483. Perhaps he stayed in an inn or in a private citizen's home, but it is just as likely that he lodged at one of the friaries in the town. Northampton had friaries from all the Mendicant orders. Humphrey Stafford, the Duke of Buckingham's father, was buried in the Franciscan church. Given his ties to this friary, perhaps Buckingham suggested they stay with the Grey Friars. It is doubtful that they would have stayed at the castle as it was already showing signs of ruin.

Unfortunately, both the friary and the castle are totally demolished. Nothing remains of the castle except for a few crumbling bits of masonry and a plaque that has become so weathered it can't be read. You can still walk to the top of the mound and look around, but the trees surrounding the mound compromise the view.

Northampton has a museum within the city centre. It's worth a visit to see the medieval section. There is little on the Wars of the Roses, but it provides information on the town during the fifteenth century.

Another place worth a visit is the battlefield. Unfortunately for history enthusiasts, much of the battlefield has been lost to a golf course. If you drive along the A508 from town, you can still see the Queen Eleanor Cross, south-west of the battlefield, from where the Archbishop of Canterbury watched the battle. With the trees in the way it is impossible to see the view the archbishop would have had of the battle lines. From the cross, take the footpath and walk through the woods. You are walking near where the Yorkist lines are believed to have been.

Delapré Park is accessible to the public and there is a footpath to the battlefield site.

While little is left of the Northampton Richard would have known, the historical significance of the town is undeniable. That alone makes it worth a visit. Delapré Park postcode: NN4 8AW.

Stony Stratford, Buckinghamshire

Close to Northampton lies Stony Stratford, a town that maintains a medieval feel. A small market town located near the River Ouse, Stony Stratford was on a main coaching road. It played host to royalty several times throughout its history. Edward IV stayed in Stony Stratford while he was wooing Elizabeth Woodville.

On the night of 29 April 1483, the young Edward V lodged here with his half-brother, Richard Grey. In the morning, Edward and his retinue prepared to leave to find larger accommodations in order to house all the men in both his party and his Uncle Richard's party. He had no idea that Richard had already arrested Anthony Woodville.

Woodville had spent the night before enjoying a meal and conversation with Richard and Buckingham. The next morning, he was arrested before he could make his way back to Stony Stratford. After his arrest, Richard and Buckingham headed to the inn where the king was staying and arrested Richard Grey and Thomas Vaughn.

Next, Richard and Buckingham made their way straight to young Edward. Treating him with all the courtesies due a king, Richard explained how Woodville and Grey had conspired to keep him out of the government and told the king that he had arrested the men for protection. Despite the king's assertions that the men were honourable, Grey and the others were sent north. With no other choice, the young king acquiesced to his uncle's authority.

Much has been said about what was in Richard's mind at the moment he decided on such a drastic move. Richard's supporters say he was left with little choice. The Woodville faction would have closed ranks around the king and shielded him from other voices. Richard would have been shut out of the government and may have been in danger. Richard's detractors say that he had already made the decision to usurp his nephew's crown, and this was just his first strike in his battle plan. Whatever your view, it is clear that Stony Stratford played host to this crucial moment in Richard's life.

Visiting Stony Stratford Today

The main reason to visit Stony Stratford today is to see the town where the young king spent the night and was subsequently taken into Richard's custody. Stony Stratford is very proud of its historical connections and makes it easy for visitors to locate items of historical significance through its informative website. The town's website includes information on free places to park, as well as downloadable leaflets on various walks throughout the town. I recommend that you visit the website at www.stonystratford.gov. uk/Visit_The_Area/Visitor_essentials to get valuable information.

Upon your arrival in Stony Stratford, you will want to head for the Market Square. Turn left in front of the library and then turn right on to Church Street. From here, it is a short walk to the high street, where you turn right again. After passing New Street on your left and The George on your right, you will see a red building on the left. This is the former Rose and Crown Inn, where it is believed that Edward V lodged while in Stony Stratford. A small plaque on the building tells the story.

Although it does not have many places to visit associated with Richard, Stony Stratford is still worth a visit. It was the site of a pivotal moment in Richard's life – when he had to decide whether to trust the Woodvilles or to seize the young king for himself. There is quite a bit to see here, and it makes for a relaxing afternoon. There are river walks, as well as several shops and restaurants in the area. Stony Stratford postcode: MK11 1AH.

As a side trip, you might want to take a trip to Grafton Regis. Formerly known as Grafton Woodville, the village was renamed by Henry VIII to Grafton Regis. As Elizabeth Woodville was born here, it has an important Wars of the Roses association. Nothing remains of the manor home of the Woodvilles today, but the parish church is still there. The church's tower was added by John Woodville, the great-grandfather of Elizabeth Woodville. To arrange a visit, it is necessary to contact the church.

St Albans, Hertfordshire

As Richard and Edward V drew near to St Albans on their journey towards London, Richard's mind had to be filled with memories of how often this town had played a role in his family's drama. It was here that the opening battle in the Wars of the Roses occurred; it was here his mother suffered the attainder of her husband after Ludlow; and it was here the Yorkists suffered a defeat at the hands of the Lancastrians. Now he rode in with his young nephew, who was the new king. How would his family's newfound dynasty handle the problems associated with a child king?

St Albans has been a settlement since the ancient Britons lived here. Occupied by the Romans, it was one of the larger Roman settlements in England. Known as Verulamium, it was an important centre of government, commerce and trade for the area.

During Boudicca's revolt, the town was virtually destroyed and its inhabitants slaughtered. Afterwards, it was rebuilt and expanded. A large fosse was built around much, if not all, the town to help protect it from further uprisings. The fosse was no protection against the next attacker – fire – which destroyed large portions of the town. The town prospered under the Romans and even for a time after the Romans left. At some point between the Romans and the Normans, many people settled the area around the abbey, leaving what had been *Verulamium*. The new town stood on a hill about 100 feet above the plain surrounding it, with the River Ver flowing nearby.

Despite the change in power structure from Saxon to Norman, Saint Albans continued to thrive. Royalty often passed through the town. Empress Matilda (Maud) stayed here on her way to be crowned in London. Eleanor, wife of Edward I, came to visit here during his reign. Her funeral procession would also come through St Albans on its way to London. The first battle in the Wars of the Roses would also take place here.

The First Battle of St Albans

In 1455, King Henry VI recovered from his illness and released the Duke of Somerset from the Tower. He then dismissed York as the Captain of Calais and gave the post to Somerset instead. Already reeling from losing his status as Protector, York retreated to Sandal Castle. Summoned to appear before a council in Leicester, York feared that Somerset and his allies were trying to force him into an oath of submission or worse. Gathering his friends and allies together, he marched towards the king and his lords. The two armies met at St Albans with the king's forces inside the town and York's men in Key Field nearby.

Letters were sent from York to the king declaring his loyalty and affirming that he had only gathered his forces for his protection against his enemies. Apparently his letters were intercepted before they reached the king. Negotiations began, and York requested that the king deliver the men that York accused of being his enemies. The king refused, and one chronicler says he replied:

> ... I shall knowe what traytor dar be so bold to reyse apepull in myn owne lond, where thorugh I am in grete desese and hevynesse. And by the feyth that I owe to Seynt Edward and to the Corone of Inglond, I shal destrye them every moder sone, and they be hanged, and drawen, and quartered, that may be taken afterward, of them to have ensample to alle such traytours to be war to make ony such rysyng of peple withinne my londe and so traytorly to abdyde her Kyng ...

With this proclamation, York knew hope was lost and the battle began in earnest. The king's forces had barred the main roads and many of them were in the area near St Peter's church. Despite several attempts, the forces could not be overcome. The Earl of Warwick led his men up through the gardens along Holywell Street. One chronicler says that they broke down through the houses and entered St Peter's Street, blowing trumpets and shouting 'A Warwick! A Warwick!'

After the fighting was over, many of the Lancastrian leaders were dead, including the Duke of Somerset and Lord Clifford. The king was taken to the cathedral and treated with all respect, but was now under the control of the Duke of York. Many of the fallen were interred in St Peter's church, but most of the nobles were interred at St Albans in the chapel of the Virgin.

After the first battle of St Albans, York was able to revive his position as Protector briefly. When he tried to fix the royal finances through an act of resumption, he was removed as Protector in early 1456. A few years of an uneasy peace followed before the renewal of hostilities. When a council was summoned to meet at Coventry in June 1459, York and his supporters were not invited.

Afraid they would face indictments from the council, the men decided that force was necessary to receive time with the king. More battles ensued, eventually leading to the death of York at Sandal Castle. Following this, St Albans was once again enmeshed in the fray.

The Second Battle of St Albans

Warwick had captured Henry VI during the Battle of Northampton, and then he had returned to London. Learning that his father and York had been killed, he began steps to create a large Yorkist army. He released soldiers from jail and enlisted Burgundian gunners before heading towards St Albans to block roads that Queen Margaret could take to London.

Warwick stationed his men to block possible routes to London, and he also stationed some men on St Peter's Street to protect against a surprise attack. Other men were stationed nearby at Dunstable. Information about these positions was sent to Margaret from a traitor among Warwick's men. Margaret's army surrounded these men at Dunstable and they counted them to make sure that not one escaped to warn the Yorkists.

After a long, hard fight, the Lancastrians defeated Warwick's army. Several of his men had switched sides in the middle of battle. Warwick managed to escape and meet up with the Earl of March. Henry was found by a tree and rejoined his wife and son, spending the night at St Albans Abbey. One death that day would have a profound impact on British history. Sir John Grey, the husband of Elizabeth Woodville, was killed during the battle, after having been knighted just the day before. This would make Elizabeth a widow and free her to later marry Edward IV.

Although Richard would not have seen the fighting, these two battles played a significant role in his family's fortunes. Arriving in St Albans with Edward V, he may have thought about his family's history with the area. On this day, however, he would be ushering in a new era in his family's dynasty, and St Albans was simply one of his stops along the way to London.

St Peters Church

St Peters was originally built in the tenth century but apparently needed to be rebuilt by the end of the fifteenth century. The building is mainly Perpendicular in style with a clerestory on each side of the nave. The tower was a later addition and not extant in medieval times. In the north aisle a window contains the remains of fourteenth-century glass that has the arms of Edward III's son, Edmund. Richard was descended in the male line from Edmund, as well as in the female line from Edward III's third son, Lionel. It was through Lionel that Richard of York and Edward IV had based their claim to the crown.

The church was in the thick of the battle during the first engagement at St Albans and many of those who fell that day were buried in the graveyard of the church.

While Richard probably never stepped foot in this church, it is worth a visit due to its association with the Duke of York's struggle to be part of the government.

Clock Tower

The clock tower at St Albans was built in the early part of the fifteenth century and is the only surviving example of a medieval clock tower in England. According to the museum, it had a mechanical clock from its inception. The large square tower would signal curfews and alarms for the citizens with a curfew bell, which dates from the fourteenth century. During the first battle of St Albans, the tower rang the alarm. Richard would have seen the tower and heard the curfew bell on his visit to St Albans with the king.

St Albans Cathedral

When Richard visited St Albans, the cathedral was still an abbey, as the town did not receive its city charter until 1877. The abbey was named for a young soldier named Albanus (better known as Alban) who, during the time of Christian persecution under the Romans, gave shelter to a Christian named Amphibalus. After listening to Amphibalus teach about Christ, Albanus converted to Christianity. When the Romans came looking for Amphibalus, Albanus traded clothes with him and was taken in his place. He was later executed for professing his Christian faith.

A church grew up on the spot where Albanus had been martyred. First a basilica and then later a Benedictine monastery stood there.

The present church replaced the earlier Benedictine one and was begun in 1077 by the Normans. It was built fairly quickly as ready materials were available from the old Roman city. The abbey became powerful, and many early chroniclers, including Matthew Paris, were monks here.

Today, the monastic buildings of the church are gone. The lodgings where it is possible that Richard and Edward passed the night are no longer there. The chapter house, the cloisters, the abbot's lodge and other buildings that were part of the monastery were on the south side of the church.

After the Dissolution, much changed in the church. At one point, a street went through the church separating it from the Lady chapel, which was converted into a school.

The cathedral had to undergo major renovations in the nineteenth century and much of its appearance changed. As Richard and Edward V came into town, their first view of the abbey would have been the tower with its embattled parapet topped with a spire, resting on a stone base covered with decorative mouldings. The glint of the whitewashed church with its lead roofs sparkling in the sun would have been a cheerful sight. Perhaps the large Perpendicular window with medieval stained glass caught their eyes as they headed toward the monastic buildings.

Visiting today, you no longer see the western porches with their Norman arches and embellishments, as the renovations changed the entire look. On the south side, instead of the buttresses, Richard would have seen a cloister walk with exquisite arcading. The porch over the abbot's door was part of the reconstruction and would not have been here.

Although much of the interior appearance of the church has been altered since the fifteenth century, some of it would still look familiar to Richard. The tracery inside the Lady Chapel would be recognisable, as would the plain Norman and Early English piers. The rood screen behind the altar with its two fourteenth-century doors was here, but it has been renovated several times.

After flakes of plaster chipped off the wall, remnants of gorgeous medieval paintings were uncovered. A set of crucifixions are among the paintings that still remain. The transepts used to contain apsidal chapels, but these, along with the Norman gables of the transepts, were removed during the sixteenth century. At one point there were twenty-six altars in the nave.

The Shrine of St Albans was a drawing point to the church, and pilgrims came from far away to visit. They would enter the church, buy their beeswax candle, and make their way towards the shrine. On feast days, chamomile would be underfoot to elicit a clean scent in the air. The pilgrim could have observed the grandeur of the building, although he would not be able to visit every part of the church.

The shrine was found in more than 2,000 fragments and was reconstructed using paintings and drawings of other shrines. The Purbeck stone of the shrine is topped by a bright red canopy and still retains some of its monuments.

In the south aisle of the saint's chapel stands a monument that probably would have given Richard pause when he visited here with Edward. The monument to Humphrey, Duke of Gloucester, might have reminded Richard how dangerous and ineffective a young king could be.

Humphrey was the youngest son of Henry IV and was protector of England during the minority of Henry VI. This would have struck a chord with Richard, as he was being placed in a similar situation. Eventually, Humphrey was arrested at Bury St Edmunds, and following what appeared to have been a stroke, died.

Duke Humphrey's tomb is in the saint's chapel near the shrine. While his coffin is in an underground burial chamber, a visitor may still catch a glimpse of it through the grate on the floor. The chapel is open on the side of the shrine, but is separated from the south aisle by an iron grille. The traces of red and blue paint that remain make one think it was painted to match the nearby shrine, which also has these colours.

Humphrey's coat of arms can be seen on the chantry as well as one of his badges. On each side of the chantry's canopy are seventeen niches. The north side is empty of the statues, but the south side is filled with statues of kings. According to Jane Kelsall, author of *Humphrey Duke of Gloucester: 1391–1447*, although monuments usually contain an effigy, there is no record of any figure of Humphrey being made. It is possible one was made but destroyed during the Dissolution.

As the Lancastrian dead were buried in the Lady chapel, it is also worth a visit. Unfortunately, there are no memorials to the men who fell as these were destroyed years later.

Two other sites in the church are related to Richard's period. At the altar, ask a verger to remove the carpet that covers the floor brass commemorating Sir Antony Grey, the son of Edmund, Lord Grey of Ruthin, whose switching of sides led to a Yorkist victory at Northampton.

Great Gate

As you leave the church, be sure to look for the Great Gate. This structure is all that remains of the abbey's gates. Built in the fourteenth century, it was the principal entrance to the abbey, built to impress guests. Richard and Edward probably entered through this gate. Standing in front of the gate and looking up, the opulence of the abbey becomes evident. In its time the gate has served both as a gaol and a school.

Visiting St Albans Today

St Albans has much to offer history lovers. The cathedral is open daily, unless a special event has been planned. Before driving or travelling long distances, it is best to check ahead. The clock tower is located near the high street and is only open to visitors on Saturdays, Sundays and bank holidays. It is best to check the museum site at stalbansmuseums.org.uk/Your-Visit/Clock-Tower before visiting to confirm opening times. St Peter's church is open during daylight hours, but you should check before visiting to confirm.

As you walk through the town, be cognisant of the fact that some of the battle took place along the streets. The Lancastrians were based in the marketplace and along other streets, including Cock Lane. A plaque on Victoria Street marks the area as the site of the Castle Inn where traditionally Edmund Beaufort, Duke of Somerset, was slain. The citizenry must have been alarmed by the carnage within their town.

St Albans is a great day trip from London as it is only twenty minutes from the St Pancras International station by rail. You can check the timetables at the First Capital Connect website:

www.firstcapitalconnect.co.uk/plan-your-journey/timetables/
show-all/. By car, the city is a short stop from the M1 at junction 6,
from the A1(M) and the M25 at junctions 21A and 22. There are
plenty of car parks scattered throughout the city.

Upon arrival, I recommend heading straight to the tourist
information centre located in the town hall. It is open every day
except Sunday. Before heading off to see the sites, take some time to
learn more about the history of the town at the Museum of St Albans.
Other sites of interest nearby include the Verulamium Museum and
the Hypocaust and Roman mosaic. St Albans postcode: AL3 5DJ.

London

London has been occupied for thousands of years. The land that
forms the city has seen entire groups come and go. In the first
century, a group of Romans under the command of Caesar invaded
the area and forced the inhabitants to accept Roman rule. The
Romans built a great wall around the city and it prospered. The city
had a large basilica, public baths, and temples. A centre of commerce
and trade, London was filled with soldiers and merchants. London
appears in the records as a place of commerce and trade even after
the Roman withdrawal. After accepting Saxon rule, Londoners built
a cathedral church and a king's hall.

The Danes arrived in the ninth century. The *Anglo-Saxon
Chronicle* says at this time there was 'great slaughter in London'.
In 851, the chronicle records that 350 ships came to the mouth of
the Thames, landed and stormed Canterbury and London, putting
the king of the Mercians to flight. The Danes were beaten back
with 'the greatest slaughter of the heathen army that we ever heard
reported to this present day'. Eventually, the Danes prevailed, and
held the area until King Alfred was able to recover it.

Under Edward the Confessor and into the Norman Conquest,
London was seen as a central area with authority. A legal statute
confirmed that London was the head of the kingdom and of the
laws, making it a powerful place to be. With the Norman arrival, the
Tower of London, a massive edifice, would be erected, emphasising
the importance of this city on the Thames.

The London that Richard and Edward V arrived in was a lively place. The upper storeys of half-timbered houses leaned over the narrow streets, cutting out the light. Shops lined the streets, with the calls of 'hot pies' filling the air. Alleys led off in all directions. People filled the road as they ambled to their destinations. Church steeples soared above the cacophony of the city. Many areas were filled with courtyards and houses where the lords and their retinues stayed. Merchants crowded into areas with people of similar trades. Vessels of all types filled the river, from small boats to large barges, gilded and flying bright banners. Stone towers stood at both ends of the bridge that led into the city, often decorated with the heads of traitors.

The city was a prosperous one, according to Dominic Mancini:

> On the banks of the Thames are enormous warehouses for imported goods: also numerous cranes of remarkable size to unload merchandise from the ships. From the district on the east, adjacent to the Tower, three paved streets lead towards the wall on the west; there are the busiest ... and almost straight ... here are to be found all manner of minerals, wines, honey, pitch, wax, flax, ropes, thread, grain, fish ...

The number of merchants from other countries meant that several languages would be heard as one walked the streets, much like today.

London had opened its hearts and gates to Edward IV, proclaiming him king and supporting him in his fight against the House of Lancaster. Now, this great city opened its gates to welcome his son as their ruler. Richard had sent messengers from Northampton to explain his actions to the citizens and lords. After receiving word that Richard was in control of her son, Queen Elizabeth immediately sought sanctuary with her remaining royal son and daughters.

Leaving Northampton on 3 May, the party spent the night at St Albans. Early the next morning, the royal party left the town bound for London. Met by the mayor and aldermen of London, along with several of the leading citizens, the new king was greeted warmly by the Londoners. As he entered his city, Edward was cheered by the crowd. It was a great procession; the mayor and aldermen were dressed in scarlet, while the 500 citizens were in bright violet. This sharply contrasted with the black worn by Gloucester and his men. Four cartloads of weapons and armour rolled in with the procession. Richard pointed these out as proof that the Woodvilles had meant to kill him. Even as the crowd cheered the new king, tensions were high. Many of the citizens were concerned about what would happen. The queen was in sanctuary, the new king was installed at the Tower of London and the council was to meet to decide how to proceed.

The council formally appointed Gloucester as Protector. However, the council did not believe that Rivers and the others should be condemned as traitors since Richard had not been Protector when they were arrested. The new coronation date was set, and perhaps Richard was worried what would happen after the new king had his crown. Would the Protectorate be extended, or would the council take over? How long would he have before Edward V took over his reign in his own name? Would Richard be safe, having effectively removed the influence of the Woodvilles from the king? Or would the king's love for his maternal relatives triumph in the end? These thoughts must have raced through Richard's head in the time immediately following Northampton.

Crosby Hall (Crosby's Place)

After arriving in London, Richard went to his town house, Crosby Hall. The house was originally the home of Sir John Crosby, an alderman and grocer. Crosby leased the land from the Prioress Dame Alice Ashfield of the Priory of St Helen. This lease started on the nativity of St John the Baptist and ran for ninety-nine years. With his land secure, Crosby built a magnificent manor house at Bishopsgate Street.

Knighted by King Edward IV in 1471, Crosby's tomb shows his Yorkist ties. After he died in 1475, he was buried with his first wife in the church at St Helen, Bishopsgate. His tomb is badly damaged now, but earlier descriptions say that it was panelled with quatrefoils that were emblazoned with Crosby's arms. His effigy shows him wearing a collar with a Yorkist symbol of roses and suns alternating. The tomb was inscribed with:

Pray for the souls of John Crosby, soldier, alderman, and during a portion of his life Mayor of the Staple of the Town of Calais, and of Agnes, his wife, and of Thomas, Richard John, John, Margaret, and Johanna, children of the same John Crosby, soldier. He died 1475, and she 1476. To whose souls may God be merciful.

Some translations of the Latin separate Richard John into two people, but the original inscription did not.

In the fifteenth century, Bishopsgate Street was surrounded by open country, with only a few mansions. Lanterns hung on the street to light the way, but it was a quieter area than in the heart of the city.

The main entrance to Crosby Hall was through a gateway known as the Foregate. As Richard came in through the gateway, the main door of the great hall would have been in front of him, with the great parlour and state rooms on his left. On the right would have been the chapel and servants' quarters. The passageway then led under the minstrel's gallery and into the inner court, which held guest apartments.

The centrepiece of the home was the Great Hall. Not including the minstrel's gallery, the hall, built of stone, was fifty-four feet long, twenty-seven feet wide, and approximately forty feet high. Entrance into the hall was through a screened passageway from the lower end of the hall, under the minstrel's gallery. The hall had eight windows on the east, each having a four-centred arch. On the west, there were six windows that were approximately eleven feet high and five feet wide. The walls under the windows would have been covered with luxurious tapestries.

The oak ceiling had a flat painted arch, nine beams and was richly gilded and decorated with conical pendants. Sumptuously decorated brackets supported the arches. A lantern had been built in the ceiling for smoke from a central fire, but this appears to have been for decoration only as a large fireplace dominated one side of the hall. On the west side of the wall was a deeply recessed oriel window. The window had a richly groined roof and delicate tracery. The bosses on the window depicted flowers and foliage, but the large centre boss was emblazoned with Crosby's crest of a ram – argent, armed and hoofed. A smaller boss below displayed Crosby's shield.

No evidence has been found of a dais, but likely one existed, as the windows were set higher up to allow the cloth of arras to hang behind the lord's table. This dais would have been placed between the fireplace and the oriel window.

The ceiling of the hall stopped near the minstrel's gallery, which was above the screen. Too small to have been a chamber, this room was most likely used by the minstrels from which its name is derived.

Access to the church was through the garden on the north side. Adjacent to the garden was the two-storey council room. The bottom room was the anteroom, while the upper room served as a council chamber. For years, this room was mistakenly called the throne room because of the mistaken assumption that Richard III was offered the throne of England here.

The council room was also large. The ceiling of the room was divided into rows of square panels painted and decorated with corbels, spandrels and pendants. In this room, Richard met with the stream of men who wanted to present their cases to the Protector. He also met with his trusted advisers as he wrestled with decisions immediately after the death of Edward IV, and on his arrival into London with Edward V. Whether you see Richard as a scheming usurper or a man trying to do what he thought was right will determine how you view the events that transpired at Crosby Hall.

After Anne joined Richard in early June, meals were probably more elaborate and taken in state in the Great Hall. After dinner, the men would return to the council chamber to determine the Lord Protector's next course of action.

It is likely that during one of his meetings with his trusted friends, Richard and his advisers decided to execute Hastings. While at a council meeting at the Tower of London, Hastings was seized and executed without a trial. Whether Richard truly believed Hastings was guilty of conspiring against him or whether he just wanted him out of the way when he seized the throne is a matter of conjecture.

The decision to execute Anthony Woodville, Richard Grey, and Thomas Vaughn was also likely made at Crosby Hall. The three men were executed at Pontefract on 25 June 1483. Once Richard had executed these men, it was highly unlikely that Edward V would forgive him.

After Richard was made aware of a possible precontract between Edward IV and Eleanor Butler (other names have been mentioned as well) by Bishop Stillington, this would have become the main discussion in the room at Crosby Hall. If Edward V and Richard of York were illegitimate, and Clarence's son not eligible due to the attainder of his father, that left only Richard as the heir apparent.

Much has been theorised about this in other books. Did Richard really believe the boys were illegitimate? Did he just want the crown for himself? Did he strive to protect England from the problems associated with a young king? Was Richard scared of repercussions for the execution of Edward's maternal uncle and half-brother once Edward reached his majority? Whatever the answer is, it would most likely have been at Crosby Hall where Richard made his ultimate decision.

After Richard's death at Bosworth, the house passed through many hands, including, oddly enough, that of Thomas More, who would later write an incomplete biography of Richard III. Katherine of Aragon would also be a guest here after her arrival in England.

Visiting Crosby Hall Today

Crosby Hall is now a private home and is not open to the public. It also no longer stands in Bishopsgate. In the early part of the twentieth century, the Bank of India bought the land where Crosby Hall stood. After tremendous public outcry, the bank paid for the building to be taken down, each stone numbered, and then rebuilt in Chelsea on Cheyne Walk. A different type of stone was used to reface the building, so its appearance changed.

In 1988, the building was purchased as a private home and the hall was incorporated into the new home. The house is not open to the public. Postcode: SW3 5AZ.

If you would like to visit St Helen's Bishopsgate to see Sir John Crosby's tomb, the church is still open. Located near the building affectionately called the Gherkin, the church is accessible from several tube stops – Bank, Aldgate, and Liverpool. Alternatively, you can check bus routes and take a bus. Sir John's tomb is located south of the altar. For those readers interested in Shakespeare, the church was Shakespeare's parish church when he was in London. Postcode: EC3A 6AT.

Paul's Cross, London

Paul's Cross was an open-air pulpit in the north-east corner of the Old St Paul's Cathedral churchyard. Famous preachers would demonstrate their oratory skills here at the cross. The cross had also been a place of secular pronouncements throughout the centuries.

In the early part of the fifteenth century, the cross was rebuilt by Bishop Thomas Kempe. A hexagonal building made of timber covered with lead, the pulpit stood on a stone staircase and had a cross on top. Three to four people could fit inside, and a low stone wall was built around the outside. Londoners would crowd the area around the cross to hear the latest news, proclamations, and explanations of official policies.

On Sunday 22 June 1483, a crowd gathered around the cross to hear a sermon preached by Dr Ralph Shaa (Shaw), a student of divinity educated at Cambridge University. As a canon of St Paul's and as Mayor Edmund Shaa's brother, Dr Shaa would have been well known to those assembled. On this particular Sunday, Richard and several of his men also came to listen to the sermon.

Dr Shaa's voice rang above the noise of the crowd as he began his sermon based on the text of 'bastard slips shall not take deep root'. The crowd became quiet as Shaa began to explain how Richard was the only rightful heir to the Duke of York, and therefore, the crown of England. Sources differ as to what exactly was said. Polydore Vergil says that Shaa claimed that Edward was not the Duke of York's son, implicating Cecily as an adulteress, while other sources say that Shaa stated that Edward's sons were illegitimate.

One claim was that Edward had been precontracted before he married Elizabeth. This precontract made his marriage to the queen invalid, and tainted his children of that union as bastards. Whether it was this claim that Shaa put forth, or the one that Cecily was an adulteress or even both, we will likely never know. Richard's point had been made; he saw himself as the rightful inheritor of the crown, and now others might begin to do so as well. Two days later, Buckingham would stand in front of an assembly in the Guildhall to convince them to offer the crown to Richard. On 26 June, a delegation headed towards Baynard's Castle to do just that. On 27 June, in the castle's chapel, the king gave the great seal to John Russell as his Lord Chancellor.

Visiting Paul's Cross Today

Paul's Cross was torn down during the Reformation. Today, a new cross stands in St Paul's churchyard, but it does not resemble the original. I like to go stand in the churchyard and think of all the people, commoners and nobles, famous and unknowns, who have passed over the spot.

From here, it is an easy walk to Baynard's Castle. Walk down Peter's Hill as if you are going to Millennium Bridge. Turn right on Queen Victoria Street and then left on White Lion Hill. The large grey building is Baynard House. It stands on the former site of the castle. Castle Baynard Street is also close by, but is not meant for pedestrian traffic.

Baynard's Castle

Baynard's Castle has an unusual history, as it was the name of not one, but two castles in London. The earlier castle was built by one of William the Conqueror's men. The castle was forfeited and granted to Robert FitzWalter, the son of the Earl of Clare. Another Robert sided with the barons against King John and the castle was destroyed. After gaining King John's good graces, this Robert rebuilt the castle, most likely further along the bank. In the thirteenth century, another Robert FitzWalter gave the original land to the Blackfriars. After a fire burned the castle down, Humphrey, Duke of Gloucester, built a new one on the banks of the river. After Gloucester's death, the castle reverted to the crown. Henry VI gave it to Richard, Duke of York. It was here that York was placed under house arrest until he swore never to rebel against the king.

In 1460, Edward IV, then the Earl of March, and Warwick entered London. Warwick stirred a crowd gathered, asking them if they would accept Edward as their king. The pro-Yorkist crowd shouted 'Yea!' A selection of delegates came to Baynard's Castle where Edward was lodged to tell him. This event, coupled with Edward's subsequent military victories, made it safe for George and Richard to return home to England and enjoy their roles as the king's brothers. Their first stop in London would have been to spend time with their mother and Margaret, who were at the castle. Edward IV was not in London on the day of their arrival.

Years later, in 1483, as Richard was housed at Baynard's Castle, history repeated itself for another York brother. Buckingham presented the case to the people for Richard to be king. The next day, certain lords in the land decided that a petition should be drawn up proclaiming Richard to be the rightful heir to the throne. Buckingham and the delegates presented the petition to Richard at Baynard's Castle in the audience chamber. He agreed that on the next day he would accept the crown. How he must have celebrated that night at Baynard's Castle!

Very few descriptions remain of the castle in Richard's time, as the Tudors largely transformed the medieval castle into a palace. The castle was built on Roman fortifications and was large enough to be considered a sentinel on the banks of the Thames, much like the Tower of London. Made of either ashlar or sandstone, the castle was set in a sizable shape with four wings enclosing a square courtyard. From viewing several prints it becomes evident that more octagonal towers were positioned on each side of the building facing the river. In between the towers were windows that were placed in pairs with one above another. Towards the right tower stood a bridge with broad stairs leading down to the river. A garderobe, or privy, was in the south-east tower, with chutes allowing drainage from all three floors. A cobbled pathway led to the street-side entrance.

Arriving by boat, Richard would have walked up the wide staircase leading to the dock and then through large wooden doors into the castle. Once inside, he would have trod on brightly coloured Norman tiles decorated with birds facing back to back, as well as glossy, marbled tile. If Cecily was in residence, he probably would have greeted her in the Great Hall. Tapestries would have hung on most of the walls, both as decorative pieces as well as a practical way to insulate the room. The home would have included a chapel, along with several chambers for the family, with the upper storeys reached by a broad staircase.

Baynard's Castle under the Tudors
Henry VII enlarged Baynard's Castle, adding three new brick wings

towards the west and inserting a large octagonal tower in the centre. He had the side fronting the river refaced in stone and added gabled projections in between. The palace became a showcase for state purposes.

Some sources say that Arthur, Henry VII and Elizabeth of York stayed here the night before Arthur married Katherine of Aragon. Jane Grey was proclaimed queen at Baynard's Castle and a few days later the council departed from here to proclaim Mary Tudor queen. During the reign of Henry VIII, the castle became a place of great feasts and entertainment. Katherine of Aragon, Anne Boleyn and Anne of Cleves all resided here at some point while married to Henry. During Elizabeth's time, the castle belonged to the Earl of Pembroke, who treated Queen Elizabeth to a lavish display of fireworks from the castle.

Today, all that remains of this magnificent riverside castle is a plaque showing where it once stood. The Great Fire of 1666 destroyed most of the castle and the surrounding houses, although at least one of Baynard's towers remained standing for several more years. In Edward and Richard's time, the king's Great Wardrobe was located near Baynard's Castle.

Tower of London

For nearly a thousand years, the Tower of London has been a landmark in the city. From its position on the north bank of the Thames, it has been witness to some of the greatest events in British history. In more than 900 years of the Tower's history, the buildings that make it up have served as fortress, prison, menagerie, execution site, depository for the royal jewels, repository for records and armoury.

Richard would have been familiar with the layout of the Tower. Building of the structure started under William the Conqueror and was finished by 1100. Built to dominate the land surrounding it, the White Tower was immense. At ninety feet tall, it was far larger than any of the surrounding buildings. As he had with his other castle building projects, William had demonstrated Norman power and established his monarchy.

Throughout the years, other monarchs would add to the Tower. During Henry III's reign, two new waterfront towers were built to serve as lodgings for the royal family. In addition, Henry had a curtain wall built reinforced with nine towers and a moat. Edward I filled in the existing moat and added an additional curtain wall and a new moat. By the time Edward IV came to rule, the Tower consisted of a massive group of buildings and towers, whose general layout is much like what we see today. Unfortunately, some of the medieval buildings have been lost to time.

Richard and the Tower

Several momentous events in Richard's life happened here at the tower. Many chroniclers writing after the fact implicated him in murders and other dark deeds that occurred within the walls of the fortress. Many of the buildings of the Tower hold special significance for those interested in Richard.

St Thomas's Tower

This tower was built by Edward I to provide royal accommodation and to create another watergate for easy access to the Tower from the river. This entrance, now known as Traitor's Gate, later became the main entrance for prisoners accused of treason.

The first room in the tower is the King's Great Chamber. As this room is unrestored, it is harder to picture. Walk over to the small turret overlooking the river to see the remains of the garderobe. Likely the king's bed would have also been within these rooms. Entering into the next room you will see what was the king's private hall. By the time of Edward IV, this area was no longer used as royal apartments, but this room allows you to see how bright and colourful the later royal apartments would have appeared.

Wakefield Tower

Once you are inside the Wakefield Tower, look for a painted timber screen. Behind the screen is a beautiful tiny chapel. A stained-glass window floods light down on to the tiled floor where a memorial stone states, 'By tradition Henry VI died here'. While this is certainly possible, Wakefield Tower had not been used as royal lodgings for quite some time. In fact, St Thomas's Tower took its place, and then was in turn supplanted by Lanthorn Tower as the king's lodgings. Even though he was a prisoner, it is likely Henry VI would have been installed either in the Lanthorn Tower or St Thomas's Tower instead. Exit the Wakefield tower via a spiral staircase and walk out on to the south wall walk.

Before heading to the Lanthorn Tower, take some time to look out over the grassy area before you. If you look to the south-west corner of the White Tower you will see the remaining foundations of a gatehouse. This was the Coldharbour Gate. Visitors to the inmost ward of the castle would have entered through here. The area below you was the area where the Great Hall stood.

Lanthorn Tower

This present building is a reconstruction built in the nineteenth century. Built on the same site as its predecessor, this was the likely lodging place for Henry VI and probably the scene of his death.

Henry VI had lived in relative obscurity at the Tower since he had been captured several years earlier. Most likely, Edward IV had allowed him to live because his death would simply have allowed his son, Prince Edward, to claim the throne. After the defeat of the Lancastrians at Tewkesbury and the death of Prince Edward in its aftermath, this threat had been eliminated. The only threat standing in Edward's way now was Henry VI, so it is likely that he gave the order for Henry's murder.

Contemporary chronicler Philip de Comines lays the deed at Richard's feet, saying that Richard 'slew this poor king Henry with his own hand, or caused him to be carried into some private place, and stood by himself while he was killed'. The Croyland chronicler does not ascribe blame, but says, 'May God have mercy upon and give time for repentance to him, whoever it might be, who dared to lay sacrilegious hands on the Lord's Annointed!'

The *Great Chronicle of London* says that 'the Duke of Gloucester was not all guiltless', while Fabyan says that 'the most common fame went that he was stabbed with a dagger by the hands of the Duke of Gloucester'. It is doubtful that he died of 'melancholy' as the *Arrivall* claims. Evidence from an exhumation of Henry's grave in 1911 shows a fractured skull to be the cause of death. No matter who killed Henry, it is likely that the crime occurred on this spot.

A few days after his arrival in London, Edward V was moved to the king's lodging in the Tower. This was not unusual; monarchs typically stayed at the Tower before the coronation. The fact that his mother was in sanctuary at Westminster probably was foremost in his councillors' minds when they decided against lodging him in the Palace of Westminster.

When Richard and Anne came to the Tower on 4 July prior to their coronations, Richard would have lodged here in the Lanthorn Tower. Probably arriving by barge, the couple would have been feted with pageants along their way. After you descend the Queen Elizabeth's stairs, face the White Tower. Directly to your left is where the Great Hall once stood.

The Great Hall

One of the places in the Tower complex that has disappeared to history is the Great Hall. Constructed during the reign of Henry III, the hall would most likely have resembled others of that date. Windows, with glazed frames, were under arches set on slender columns. The room would have been whitewashed, with a wooden, high-beamed roof.

After the arrival of Richard and Anne to the Tower before their coronations, a large dinner would have been served. A group of men had been summoned to be created Knights of the Bath, just as Richard had upon his brother's coronation. According to Anne Sutton and P. W. Hammond in *The Coronation of Richard III: The Extant Documents*, these men would have served Richard at his table for the first course. Afterward they would have been led off for the preparations. Later, Richard would have ordered that Viscount Lovell bring the knights into the esquires' chamber in the hall to be advised regarding their duties as a Knight of the Bath. Next, the men would have gone to the chapel of St John to remain in prayer.

The next day, after Mass, Richard, sitting under the cloth of estate in the Great Hall, would have concluded the ceremony by creating each man a knight. Later, the newly created knights would have come into the hall for a meal. Anne and Richard would then have made their way to their chambers to finish getting ready for their procession to Westminster.

The White Tower

Halfway up the staircase that leads to the entrance of the White Tower is a break in the wall. In 1674, the bodies of two young boys were found buried under the remnants of the staircase that can be seen here. The bones were believed to have been those of the young princes, Edward and Richard. The younger prince, Richard, Duke of York, had been brought out of sanctuary to join his elder brother at the Tower.

At some point between then and Richard's coronation, the boys were moved from the king's lodgings to the White Tower. Tradition holds that the boys were kept in the Garden Tower, which became known as the Bloody Tower, but it is much more likely that they were placed in the White Tower. High-level prisoners had often been kept in the White Tower, including Charles, Duke of Orleans. If the boys were murdered, it would have happened in the White Tower.

Once you are inside the White Tower, enjoy the exhibitions on the ground floor before heading up to the first floor where the Chapel of St John the Evangelist is located. Stand out of the entranceway and take a few minutes to look at this room. Most visitors move quickly into the next room, so you might have a moment or so alone. Picture the room whitewashed, with typical bright colours painted on some areas. Imagine the room with light streaming in through the medieval stained glass that Henry III installed in the chapel's windows. Looking at the columns, you will see carvings along the capitals and bases.

Once Edward V was placed in the White Tower, he began going to confession daily, perhaps in this very room. Years later, the body of his sister, Elizabeth of York, would lie in state in this room following her death from childbirth.

Leaving the chapel, you will enter a larger room. According to Tower historians, this floor was the king's lodging before newer buildings replaced it as the royal accommodation. This larger room may have been used for public meetings, while the smaller room may have been a private chamber. This might be where the two princes were kept once they were moved to the White Tower.

Hastings and the Tower

In his book on Richard III, Paul Murray Kendall says that the council chamber was in an upper room of the White Tower. On Friday 13 June, two council meetings were called. One occurred at Westminster, while one convened at the Tower. At the Tower meeting were Hastings, Stanley, Morton, Buckingham and others. During this meeting, Hastings was accused of treason and, according to contemporary sources, dragged out to the green beside St Peter ad Vincula. Hurriedly shriven, Hastings was beheaded without a trial. The other men accused, including Stanley, were not beheaded and were eventually released. Some people assert that Richard had Hastings beheaded because he would have objected to Richard taking the throne, while others say Richard truly believed that Hastings was conspiring with the Woodvilles. The result was the same, whatever led to the action. The blood of Hastings was spilt on Tower Green.

From the White Tower, head to Tower Green. A sculpture of a glass pillow was erected on the site of the scaffold to commemorate the people beheaded here. The execution of Hastings was done so quickly that no scaffold was erected for him. The *Great Chronicle of London* says that his head was struck off on a squared piece of timber. Anne Boleyn's name on the memorial may be in error, as some historians believe that she was beheaded closer to the Waterloo Barracks.

Another name on the list of people executed here is Margaret Pole, Countess of Salisbury. Margaret was Richard's niece, the daughter of George, the Duke of Clarence. She was executed here in 1541 during the reign of Henry VIII. The details of her execution tell of a gruesome end. Evidently an inexperienced executioner was commissioned to carry out her sentence. His first blow apparently hit her shoulders and it took several further blows to remove her head from her body. A later story circulated that the poor woman ran around the block screaming, frantically trying to escape the executioner's blows.

More's Cell

Although he was not an adult during Richard III's reign, Thomas More is often quoted as a primary source of the time. His unfinished work on Richard paints the king with harsh strokes. Years after Richard's death, More was executed by Henry VIII. If you turn your back to the scaffold site and face the Queen's House, the door right at the corner leads to the cell in the Bell Tower where he was supposedly imprisoned.

At least one historian disagrees with the belief that this cell was the location for More's incarceration. Geoffrey Parnell, who was the official Tower historian, went on record in 2000 stating that there was no evidence More was kept in the lower portion of the Bell Tower. Having been inside this cell, I certainly hope he was not. Even today, it is a damp, dark place.

Bowyer Tower

One of the most interesting and controversial events in the Tower's history supposedly occurred in the Bowyer Tower. Following the death of Isabel Neville, George, Duke of Clarence, arrested one of her servants, Ankarette Twynho, and accused her of poisoning the duchess. Twynho was subsequently executed. George was also upset with Edward as he had not been allowed to marry Mary of Burgundy or Margaret of Scotland.

Clarence was arrested in June 1477 and put in the Tower. At this time, he was probably housed in comfortable lodgings in the White Tower. In January 1478, Parliament met to arraign the duke on charges of treason. Clarence was sentenced to death. Tradition has it that he was drowned in a butt of malmsey wine. While this cannot be substantiated and is most likely legend, it also cannot be ruled out.

Tradition also maintains that Clarence met his death in the Bowyer Tower. Clarence's daughter and son were both later imprisoned in the Tower and subsequently executed. Edward was executed by Henry VII; Margaret was executed by Henry VIII. On George's son's death, the legitimate male line of the Plantagenets became extinct.

To get to the Bowyer Tower from Tower Green, walk in front of the Waterloo Barracks and go up the stairs. The tower has large gargoyles on each one of its turrets. There is not much to see to evoke the time period, but it is worth the quick detour to see where Clarence may have died.

Visiting the Tower Today

Almost every tourist in London takes time to see this ancient site. Spending less than a full day at the Tower means you only scratch its surface, but most visitors only have a few hours to allocate for a tour. Knowing exactly what you want to see and planning your visit to get the most out of your time is key to enjoying your trip.

The best time to come to the Tower is as soon as it opens. I pre-purchase my ticket so that I can enter quickly. I usually find one of the tour-bus operators and buy a fast-track ticket from them. If you are interested in seeing the Crown Jewels, now is the time to go in order to beat the crowds. After seeing the Crown Jewels and visiting the sites associated with Richard, it is well worth taking a Yeoman Warder tour if you have time. Taking a Yeoman Warder tour is the only way to gain entrance into the chapel of St Peter ad Vincula unless you visit the Tower late in the afternoon. Even though the sites related to Richard are probably the ones you would want to visit first, there are so many other interesting areas of the Tower that are worthy of exploring. The prisoners' graffiti preserved in the Beauchamp Tower is fascinating.

A further event to consider participating in is the Ceremony of the Keys, a 700-year-old ceremony conducted at the Tower each night. Entering the Tower after dark, you will bear witness to the ceremony of the locking of the Tower gates. For more information on how to secure tickets, visit the website at www.hrp.org.uk/TowerOfLondon/WhatsOn/theceremonyofthekeys.

The Tower is in the care of Historic Royal Palaces. For more information about opening times and admission costs, or to purchase tickets online, visit the website at www.hrp.org.uk/TowerOfLondon/admissionsprices/toweroflondonadmission. The closest tube stop to the Tower is Tower Hill. Tower of London postcode: EC3N 4AB.

Part VI

King of the Realm

Once Richard decided to accept the citizens' petition and take the crown for himself, he set events in motion that ultimately led to the Battle of Bosworth. From his grand coronation to his death at Bosworth, Richard had a short reign, but he is one of England's best-known kings.

London: The Coronation

A grand and majestic exhibition, a coronation was an elaborate affair and had been for centuries. Richard has been maligned for his extravagance, but it is fair to state that he was only following in his predecessors' footsteps. The procession was one stage of the coronation. It allowed the citizens of London to see the king leaving from the Tower. At the head of the coronation train were lords and knights, then the alderman of the city, dressed in vivid scarlet. The newly created Knights of the Bath would follow, along with other members of the train. Directly in front of the king would be the 'king's sword', along with the Earl Marshal of England and the Lord Great Chamberlain.

According to Anne Sutton and P. W. Hammond in *The Coronation of Richard III: The Extant Documents*, the king wore blue cloth of gold with nets under his purple velvet gown, furred with ermine.

Four knights carried a silk brocade canopy of red and green above his head. Behind the king rode more lords and knights. The queen, her hair streaming down her back, wore a circlet of gold and pearls on her head and rested on cushions of cloth of gold. She was carried on her litter by two palfreys covered in white damask, with saddles also covered in cloth of gold. Anne, her jewels glistening in the sun, was clothed in damask cloth of gold furred with miniver and garnished with annulets of silver and gold, and was carried under a canopy similar to Richard's. Following behind the queen's henchmen and horse of estate came the noble ladies. The women were carried in four-wheeled carts, pulled by horses covered in crimson cloth of gold, crimson velvet and crimson damask, fringed with gold.

Houses along the way would have hung rich tapestries outside their windows. The citizens of London would have lined the procession route, standing on streets that had been cleaned and covered with gravel. The procession was slow as it stopped in Cheapside, at the Standard, the Eleanor Cross and the Little Conduit, along with other stops where stations were set up for speeches and performances in honour of the king and queen. The procession route would have followed those of previous coronations and would go through Cheapside, St Paul's, Ludgate Hill, Fleet Street and then the Strand, ending at Westminster Hall. Here, the king and queen would have been served 'of the voyde', which meant they partook of wine and spices beneath the cloths of estate in the Great Hall. Afterwards, the monarchs would have retired to chambers to change clothes and then take an evening meal.

In preparation for the joint coronation, a stage would have been set up between the choir and altar at Westminster Abbey. Steps would have led up to the stage on both the west and east sides. St Edward's Chair, with Scotland's Stone of Scone underneath, would have sat here for the king, and a richly decorated chair would have been set up on a lower part of the stage for the queen. At the presbytery another pair of chairs would have been set up for the royal couple upon their entry into the abbey.

Early on 6 July 1483, Richard would have arisen, bathed, and then been clothed by his Great Chamberlain, the Duke of Buckingham. Dressed in his white silk shirt, a coat of red sarcenet and silk breeches and stockings, covered by a red floor-length robe of silk and ermines, Richard must have appeared regal. He would have gone to the hall to be raised by nobles into the marble chair of the King's Bench. Anne would have joined him here. She was dressed in a robe of crimson velvet with a train, kept in place with silk and gold mantle laces, covering her crimson kirtle, which was laced down the front with silver and gilt. Together, they must have looked an imposing pair.

Based on compilations of several sources, it is easy to picture the scene. The floor of Westminster Hall shimmered in red cloth. Into the hall came the ecclesiastical procession with the regalia, which was handed over to the nobles for the procession to the abbey. Trumpets heralded the start of this. The abbot and the convent of Westminster were followed by the Chapel Royal, singing as they went. Following them were other abbots and bishops, with meters on their heads and crosses in hand.

The newly created Knights of the Bath trailed the bishops, with a parade of nobles following them. The Earl of Northumberland came bearing the first sword. Lord Stanley followed, bearing the mace. Next came the Earl of Kent and Lord Lovell, walking side by side. The Earl of Kent, on the right, bore the second sword, while Lord Lovell bore the third sword. The Mayor of London, Edmund Shaa, followed, carrying the crystal mace of the City of London. The Duke of Suffolk carried the sceptre, followed by his son, the Earl of Lincoln, who bore the 'crose with the ball' (the orb). The Earl of Surrey carried the sword of state in its ornamented scabbard. The king's crown was carried by the Duke of Norfolk.

Two bishops carrying the chalice and paten of St Edward preceded Richard into Westminster Abbey. The entire route from Westminster Hall to the west door of the abbey was covered in ray cloth. The bishops of Bath and Durham walked alongside the king. Richard, barefoot, walked under a canopy of red and green silk brocade interwoven with gold threads, carried by the barons of the Cinque Ports. His train was carried by the Great Chamberlain, the Duke of Buckingham. Once inside the church, Richard passed the throne set up on the south side of the stage, which was covered in a silken canopy.

The queen's procession, with the Earl of Huntington carrying the queen's sceptre, Viscount Lisle carrying her white rod ornamented with a dove, and the Earl of Wiltshire carrying her crown, followed in the path of the king's procession. Anne also walked under a canopy, with her train carried by Margaret Beaufort, the Countess of Richmond. She was followed by the duchesses of Suffolk and Norfolk, wearing their robes of estate, their hair crowned with coronets of gold. Twenty other ladies followed behind them. Finally knights and squires brought up the end of the procession. Once inside, the queen passed to the north side of the stage.

After the lengthy coronation service, Richard and Anne returned to the Palace of Westminster for a well-deserved rest, and since they had fasted all day, a chance to eat. While the monarchs were resting, tables and chairs for the evening meal were being set up in the hall. A lavish feast would conclude the coronation ceremonies for the day. The first course was served on dishes of gold and silver. Beef, mutton, roast, capons, custard, peacocks, and roe deer, along with many other dishes, made up the first course. Richard and Anne entered the hall dressed in fresh robes of crimson velvet embroidered with gold and made their way to the dais.

At the beginning of the second course, Robert Dymoke, as the King's Champion, came into the hall on a horse trapped in white and red silk. He came riding up before the king and made his obeisance. The herald asked the assembly, 'If there be any man who will say against King Richard III why he should not pretend and have the crown'. Everyone was silent, and then in one voice cried, 'King Richard!' The King's Champion threw down his gauntlet three times and then again made his obeisance to the king. After being offered wine, he turned the horse and rode out of the hall with the cup in his right hand as payment for his service. Afterwards, the heralds and four kings of arms came from their stage. The senior herald announced Richard as the King of England and France and Lord of Ireland. The ceremony ended so late that the third course could not be served. Hippocras and wafers were served to the king and queen, and they departed from the hall.

Christmas of 1484

Richard celebrated Christmas at the Palace of Westminster in 1484. Festivities abounded, as the Christmas season was not just celebrated on one day, but over several. Large feasts would be held, and afterwards mummers would put on plays. People would be singing and dancing, as well as playing games.

During the festival of Twelfth Day, Richard wore the crown at the royal banquet. Edward's daughters were allowed to be at court to enjoy the festivities. Rumours abounded that the king's niece, Elizabeth, was dressed like Anne. This led to further rumours that Richard was planning to marry Elizabeth after Anne died. The rumours became so widespread that Richard needed to appear before his council to denounce them. He also appeared before the leading citizens of London in the great hall of the hospital of the Knights of St John in Clerkenwell to deny the rumours.

Westminster Abbey, London

To reach Westminster Abbey from the Palace of Westminster, make your way carefully across the street through the morass of crossings. Westminster Abbey will be on your left.

The area that Westminster Abbey rests on was once called Thorney Island. As its name suggests, this marshy area was overgrown by thorns. In fact, the ancient manuscripts deem it 'in loco terribili'. It must not have been too terrible, as both a church and a medieval palace were built in the area.

One theory about the establishment of a church on this spot is that the king of the East Saxons, Sebert, erected a church here in honour of St Peter. This church was supposedly built early in the seventh century. While the earlier foundations cannot be conclusively proven, it is known that in the middle of the tenth century, St Dunstan established a group of monks here in the order of St Benedict.

During his reign, King Edward the Confessor established a larger church here next to the abbey. The church had a central tower and transepts, with a high nave vaulted with ribs resting on pillars and arches. The timber ceiling was covered with lead. King Edward would die in 1066, perhaps before he was able to see his church consecrated. He was buried before the high altar of the church, and soon miracles were being ascribed to him.

Henry III ordered the building of much of the church as we see it today. During his reign, the original eastern tower was taken down, rebuilt and connected to the western part. In 1269, the eastern part of the church seems to have been finished.

During the divine service, the choir, garbed in silk, sang Mass. Light from flickering wax tapers illuminated the chest carrying the body of Edward the Confessor, as it was removed to be placed in a new shrine. The ceremony was lavish, and the chest containing Edward's remains was carried by King Henry and his brother, with Henry's son, the future King Edward, and other nobles supporting it as it was conveyed to an elaborate shrine of gold, decorated with precious jewels, situated behind the high altar. The ceremony ended with a magnificent feast.

Henry III gave many gifts to the abbey during his reign. One was the standard of a dragon of red and gold, with eyes of sapphire and a tongue that appeared as if it were continuously moving. This standard was to be prominent in the church when the king was in attendance.

While you are in Westminster Abbey, look for the tombs of Sir Thomas Vaughan, Sir Humphrey Stanley and Sir Humphrey Bourchier. Bourchier's tomb is in St Edmund's chapel, while Stanley's brass is on the floor of the chapel of St Nicholas. Vaughan's canopied tomb is found in the chapel of St John the Baptist.

The coronation that took place for Richard and Anne had basically the same order of service as the one that prevails today. Most of the regalia would have been placed on the high altar, with the exception of the state crown, which would have been taken to the altar in the chapel of St Edward. The golden feretory of St Edward the Confessor is gone, but the base where it once rested is still behind the high altar.

Visiting Westminster Abbey Today

Westminster Abbey is one of the busiest tourist attractions in London. It takes careful planning to be able to see what you want without being surrounded by other tourists. Either be the first person in the line or go later in the day. Entrance today is through the Great North Door, located on the side closest to St Margaret's church. For more information about visiting hours and costs, see www.westminster-abbey.org/visit-us.

Walking Richard's Coronation Route

The City of London has kept much of its medieval street plan, although many of its buildings were destroyed by the Great Fire and other disasters, including the disaster of 'progress'. The streets Richard's procession would have taken would have been much narrower and darker than the streets along which you will be walking. With a bit of imagination, though, you can 'see' the buildings towering over the road, many almost touching. You can 'hear' the cacophony of sounds that the large procession and cheering citizens would have made.

Leaving from the Tower, walk up past the ticket booths to the road. Cross the road and turn left. Continue walking until you reach Mark Street. At the beginning of Mark Street the procession would have halted to change knights carrying the canopy. Along many of the stops, there were planned performances to honour the king and queen. Head up the street until you reach Fenchurch Street. Take a left here. Follow along Fenchurch until you reach Gracechurch. Take a right on to Gracechurch and continue on until you see Leadenhall Market on the right. In the fifteenth century, the market here sold mainly meat, cheese, grains and poultry. While the present building is Victorian, it kept to the original street pattern.

Continue on to the top of the street and then turn left onto Cornhill. At the corner of Cornhill and Gracechurch is St Peter Cornhill. This church has a legend that it is the oldest church site in London, said to have been founded by the first Christian king of the island, Lucius, in the second century. As doubtful as that legend may be, there has been a church here for many centuries. In the fifteenth century, the church had a stone building that housed a library. The present church is not the one that Richard would have seen as his procession stopped here to see another presentation by the citizens. The medieval church burned down in the Great Fire, and this edifice is of Wren's design.

Cornhill likely received its name due to the fact that it was the primary market in the city for corn. The street would have been lined with stalls from which the factors would sell their corn. The houses on the street were mainly occupied by drapers. In Richard's time a conduit ran through here, carrying water from the area surrounding

London. By the time of Richard's coronation procession, the cistern had been enlarged by Robert Drope in 1475 and castellated with stone and lead. Continue down Cornhill until you are able to turn right on Cheapside. Here, at the confluence of Cheapside and the former Poultry Street, stood the Great Conduit. During coronation processions, the conduits of Cheapside ran with wine.

Although we do not know exactly what pageant the citizens put on for Richard III and Anne here, we have records of other celebrations from which we can get an idea. When Margaret of Anjou passed by here during her marriage procession, a pageant representing five wise and five foolish virgins was enacted for her pleasure. For Anne of Bohemia, a castle of towers was erected, with young women blowing gold leaf down on the queen and her retinue. As Richard's niece, Elizabeth of York, rode by on her coronation route, children placed along the street and dressed like angels sang to her as she passed.

Cheapside, or West Cheap, was one of the most important streets in the City of London. Goldsmiths and mercers sold their luxury wares here. Historically the central focus of procession routes, it was one of the widest streets and was lined with buildings three and four storeys tall. As Richard and Anne progressed down the street, the buildings would have been draped in luxurious cloths of velvet and silk as their owners crammed into the windows to watch the procession pass by. Flags and banners would have flown, and the wealthy citizens would have worn bright and colourful clothing with their jewels shining brightly.

Richard's procession continued along Cheapside. The standard stood in the middle of the road near the church of St Mary-le-Bow. As Richard passed by, he might have remembered it as the place where Jack Cade, the Kentish rebel, was beheaded by Lord Say. As the procession neared Wood Street, an elegant cross could be seen. The Eleanor cross, named such as it was erected at the places where Eleanor of Castile's body lay on its way to be interred, was ornate and intricately carved, containing several statues, including one of the queen and the royal coat of arms. It was rebuilt in the middle fifteenth century and a water spout was added. At every coronation, it was newly gilded.

Elizabeth 'Jane' Shore, Edward IV's mistress, was born to a merchant who lived in Cheapside. She was supposedly beautiful, with blond hair and grey eyes. She was also said to be cheerful and fun-loving. Richard required her to do penance before the cross dressed only in her kirtle, before placing her in jail for conspiracy against the Protector's government. She would have known these streets very well. This route also carried the body of Henry VI on its way to St Paul's, after his death in the Tower. It is doubtful that Richard was thinking about either of his former enemies as he headed along his coronation route.

Continue on your way towards New Change Street. The little conduit in Cheapside stood facing Foster Lane and Old Change Street. Likely, another pageant was performed here for the king and queen before they turned towards St Paul's. At New Change Street, turn left and head towards St Paul's Cathedral. At the corner of New Change and St Paul's Churchyard, turn right and head along the street beside the church. This is not the same church that Richard would have known, as it was destroyed in the Great Fire and rebuilt, but this is the same area.

From here, Richard's procession would have headed on towards Ludgate, then along Fleet Street. In 1440, the Duchess of Gloucester, Eleanor Cobham, was forced to walk this street in penance for witchcraft she had supposedly performed against the king. The second wife of Humphrey of Gloucester, she would spend the rest of her life imprisoned in various castles for this charge of witchcraft. As you pass by the dragon statue on the Temple Bar monument, you are leaving the City of London, known as the Square Mile.

As you leave Fleet Street and come on to the Strand, Richard's procession nears its end. As you walk down the street, you will pass the Savoy. A magnificent palace by the same name once stood near here. Continue walking and soon you will see Somerset House on your left. In Richard's time, the Bishop of Chester's Inn stood on the east end of this site. The procession passed here and then on to Whitehall before reaching the Palace of Westminster.

Windsor Castle, Berkshire

Richard set out from London on his first progress. Stopping first at Greenwich, he came to Windsor before moving on to Reading

Abbey. Windsor Castle was founded by William the Conqueror as one of the fortifications surrounding London. The first building on the spot was a wooden structure. Its close proximity to London, combined with the nearby royal hunting forest, made it a favourite of the early kings, and it quickly became a royal residence. In the twelfth century, the castle was rebuilt in stone. Its plan has largely stayed the same throughout the years, although the interior has undergone substantial renovations, fundamentally altering its appearance.

Unlike many of the buildings associated with Richard, much of the castle is familiar enough that he would recognise it. Richard would be able to identify much of the external part of the building. The Round Tower was shorter in his day as it was heightened as part of the renovations. He would not have seen the range that contains today's Royal Library or the entrance gateway to the Lower Ward, as these were added by Henry VIII. If he were to walk around today's Lower Ward, he would also not remember the houses on the south side, which were added during the reign of Mary I. The current entrance on the south side between the York and Lancaster Towers was not added until 1824; prior to that, a gateway, complete with a portcullis, was reached via a bridge over the ditch.

Throughout its years, the castle has been the birthplace of kings, a royal prison and a place of refuge. Lancastrian Henry VI was born at Windsor. Kings of France and Scotland have been kept here as prisoner, albeit prisoners who received royal treatment.

The Yorks and Windsor

Edward IV lavished money on Windsor Castle as part of his refurbishment of several castles near London. He made elaborate improvements to the castle, which included hanging sumptuous cloths of arras on the wall. He seems to have visited Windsor often, preferring to be there for St George's Day whenever possible. The castle has several associations with both Edward and Richard's reigns.

After the Battle of Barnet, where Warwick was killed, Edward rode victoriously into London. However, he quickly learned that Margaret of Anjou and her son Edward had landed and were drawing considerable numbers to them. He dispatched runners to several counties telling men to meet him at Windsor. After celebrating St George's day at Windsor, Richard and Edward headed to meet Margaret's army.

Louis Gruuthuse, who had sheltered Richard and Edward during their exile in the Low Countries, came to visit Edward at Windsor. Cora Scofield reports that Gruuthuse's reception was pleasing:

> Lord Hastings and other noblemen took him at once to speak
> with the king and queen, and later they supped with him in the
> three chambers 'richly hanged with cloths of Arras and with beds
> of estate' which had been set aside for his use. In the evening the
> king accompanied his guest to the queen's chambers ...

Richard probably was not at this meeting between his brother and their Low Countries host, as his presence would have been recorded. The next day, Edward took Lord Gruuthuse to mass in the chapel. Later the men went hunting in Windsor Park. Edward took no shortcuts in impressing Louis.

The Order of the Garter

The Order of the Garter is the oldest chivalric order in England. Some confusion surrounds the dating of the order, but most agree that it was established by 1348. The Order consists of the sovereign and twenty-five knights, and its patron saint is St George. Legend says that the Order was founded after a lady (of various names) dropped her garter, which Edward picked up to give back to her. Seeing the looks of those around him, he said, 'Evil unto him who thinks evil of it.' From this he got the idea to form an Order using the garter as an emblem. It is more likely, however, that the Order stemmed from war with the French.

During Richard's time, a celebration was held every year for the Order. The celebrations would include the installation of the new knights and a service in St George's Chapel. Some notable members of the Order in Richard's day include George, Richard, Anthony Woodville and William Hastings. Charles, Duke of Burgundy, was also a Knight of the Order. During Richard's reign, the new Knights of the Order included Thomas Stanley, Thomas Howard, Edward

Brampton and Francis Lovell. Both Lovell and Howard were degraded, although Howard was later reinstated. When a knight is degraded, it means he is stripped of his honour.

St George's Chapel

One of only three Chapels Royal, St George's Chapel has played an important role in the spiritual life of those entering its doors for centuries. A church has stood here since at least the reign of Henry III, who established a church in the Lower Ward dedicated to Edward the Confessor. Today very little is left of that church, but it stood on the site of what now is the Albert Memorial Chapel. When Edward III established the Order of the Garter he also founded the College of St George. The chapel is the spiritual home of the Order.

Centuries later, Edward IV, noticing the state of decay the chapel was in, began an extensive renovation program. He almost completely rebuilt the chapel, although it would not be completed until the sixteenth century. He doubled the size of the college, as well as the number of priests and choristers which served the chapel. Exorbitant sums were spent on rich vestments and hangings, on elaborate statues, on intricate carvings and on the wall decorations.

When Edward left detailed instructions for his chantry in his will, he probably did not expect to have them implemented so soon. His funeral train left London for Windsor, where he was laid to rest in St George's Chapel. Later, Richard had Henry VI's body brought from Chertsey Abbey to be reinterred in St George's Chapel, ironically directly across from Edward's tomb.

Wars of the Roses in St George's Chapel

The splendour of St George's Chapel will take your breath away. There are several points of interest on our tour, but if you have time, do not limit your tour to just those. The sheer brilliance of the architecture alone deserves time to be absorbed.

Entrance to the chapel is through the south door. Moving through the south nave aisle, make your way to the nave. While construction of the nave started during Richard's lifetime, he would never have seen the splendid stone vaulting that spans it as it was not completed until the sixteenth century.

Move on to the north nave aisle, stopping at the Rutland

Chantry. Here, a memorial brass on the east wall of the chantry chapel honours Thomas St Leger and his wife, Anne, Duchess of Exeter. The magnificent tomb is that of their daughter, Anne, and her husband, George Manners. Thomas St Leger was Richard's brother-in-law as he had married Anne, Richard's sister. Anne was dead by 1476. Thomas St Leger took part in Buckingham's rebellion and was executed by Richard. When mtDNA testing was performed on the bones found in Leicester, the DNA it was compared with came from Anne's descendants.

In the north choir aisle you will see the Hastings Chantry on the right. William, Lord Hastings, had been a faithful servant and friend of Edward IV. After Edward's death, Hastings spoke out for Richard to be protector. For a time, Richard and Hastings seem to be working towards the same ends. However, on 13 June 1483, Richard had Hastings executed at the Tower for allegedly conspiring against him. Whether such a conspiracy existed or not has been debated by historians and will not be revisited here. However, the Hastings Chantry is stunning and contains four scenes from the life and death of St Stephen.

Leaving the chantry, make your way up the north choir aisle until you reach the tomb of Edward IV. Edward and Elizabeth's grave is marked with a stone slab that was placed on the grave below the elaborately decorated chantry chapel centuries after their deaths.

Retrace your steps back into the choir. Above the stalls in the choir hang the banners of the Knights of the Garter. Below each banner is a crest on top of a helm. Unlike the banners and other regalia, the stall plates on the back of each seat are not removed upon the death of the knight. Many of the plates from the earliest Knights of the Garter still remain. The Sovereign's stall is bigger than the other stalls and contains a misericord from the fifteenth century which commemorates the Treaty of Picquigny. A replica of the misericord is found in the south choir aisle. The oriel window that looks out into the choir was constructed in the Edward IV chantry on the orders of Henry VIII. He had it built so Katherine of Aragon could view services held here.

As you make your way down the south choir aisle, look for the tomb of Henry VI. A large marble slab marks the spot where the king was reinterred. Miracles were said to happen at his tomb, so an alms box was placed there to collect money from pilgrims. On the way out of the chapel, pause to see the Albert Memorial Chapel and the fragment of a medieval wall painting nearby.

Windsor Castle and St George's Chapel are prime tourist spots and are incredibly crowded in the summer. In addition, the castle is still one of the homes of the monarch, and at certain times, both St George's and some rooms of the castle may be closed. It is always best to check the website before visiting and arrive early. The website may be found at www.royalcollection.org.uk/visit/windsorcastle.

If you visit Windsor by car, you will need to park in one of the car parks in the town centre as the castle has no public car park. A list of the public car parks can be found online at www.windsor.gov.uk/visitor-info/parking. Windsor also operates a park-and-ride scheme. More information may be found at www.rbwm.gov.uk/web/tdbus_park_ride.htm.

It is easy to reach Windsor by train. From London Waterloo or London Paddington take the train to Windsor and Eton Central or Windsor and Eton Riverside. For more information see the National Rail website at www.nationalrail.co.uk/. Coach service to Windsor leaves from London Victoria. In addition, tour operators often offer day excursions from hotels.

Reading Abbey, Berkshire

After Richard had gained the crown, he set off, as England's kings had for centuries, on a royal progress. According to Richard's biographer, Charles Ross, Richard left from Windsor with a sizable train, which included five bishops, four earls, four barons and other nobles. His first stop was Reading. Richard likely housed in the abbey, as it was the traditional place for kings and queens to stay in when visiting Reading.

Henry I laid the foundation for the new monastery at Reading in 1121. Built on a ridge of a hill between the rivers Kennett and Thames, Reading Abbey commanded beautiful views of the surrounding countryside. The abbey was surrounded on three sides by a six-foot-thick wall, covered with freestone. The fourth side was protected by an offshoot of the Kennett. The abbey's precinct covered about thirty acres.

The abbey's church, built with Caen stone in cruciform shape, was immense. The nave was more than 200 feet long and forty feet wide, while the choir was almost 100 feet long. As the monks were of the Benedictine Order of Cluny, the church was probably highly decorated, with beautiful stained glass, elaborate wall paintings, and paved floors. The church had several relics, one of which was the hand of St James, which had been given to the church by Henry I. This highly prized relic was alluded to by the scallop shell, associated with St James, in the abbey's coat of arms. Reliquaries, decorated with precious jewels, would have housed the favourite relics of the monastery.

The Refectory

In September 1464, Edward IV met his council at Reading to discuss an upcoming conference at St Omer and the condition of the currency. This meeting may have occurred in the refectory as Henry VI's parliament had. It was here at Reading that Edward announced to his council that he had already been married for several months to a Lancastrian widow, Elizabeth Woodville. It is easy to imagine the scene. Edward, seated at the high table of the east end of the rectangular building, with his courtiers staring in shock, first at him, then at each other. A letter, written by John Wenlock, said that the king's announcement caused 'great displeasure to many great lords, and especially to the larger part of all his council'. The cavernous room with its ornamental arches probably could not contain the sounds of the council's displeasure.

However, as the marriage had already happened, the council had to make the best of it. On Michaelmas Day Elizabeth Woodville was escorted by the Duke of Clarence and the Earl of Warwick into the church at Reading Abbey. Amid the soaring columns, she was presented as Queen of England. A painting depicting this moment can be found in Reading Town Hall. There is no evidence that Richard was present at Elizabeth's presentation as queen, but given that so little survives of his movements as a young man, he may have been. Whatever his thoughts about his brother's wedding, he kept them to himself.

Royal Progress

When Richard arrived at Reading Abbey in 1483, he and his train would have entered through one of the abbey's four great gates, likely the Compter Gate. This gate, which faced the great west door of the church, is thought to have extended across the Forbury to St Laurence's church. Richard would have been received by the Abbot of Reading and housed in the abbot's lodge. As the abbot was a mitred abbot and peer of the realm, the lodge would have been luxurious. Even in times of financial difficulty, the abbot was said to have had forty servants.

One of Richard's orders of business was to make a grant to Hastings' widow, Katheryn Neville. In his grant, Richard promises to be a 'good and gracious soverain lord to the said Katheryn and to hir children and servauntes and to protect and defend the same Katheryn as our welbelovede Cousine and wydowe ...' He planned to do that by granting Katheryn the marriage and wardship of Hastings' heir, including the custody of Hastings' estates during the wardship, and by allowing her to keep other lucrative wardships.

Richard probably spent some time ensconced with his council while at Reading. A likely place for this business would have been the chapter house. Located east of the cloisters, the chapter house was a highly ornamented room which had eight rectangular columns projecting slightly from the wall. Each column had a carved capital and base. The vaulted room was about forty feet high. Richard and his council would have entered from the cloisters through the large door with enormous windows above it on each side. Once inside, they would have seen five huge windows at the opposite end of the room and walls decorated by frescoes and carvings. The room was often used for important business; parliaments had been held here, and it was the room where the abbot met with important guests.

Dissolution

Reading Abbey was closed following the Dissolution. Slowly,

the abbey buildings were mined for their stone. Once one of the richest abbeys in all of England, Reading fell into a state of terrible disrepair.

Visiting Reading Abbey Today

Unfortunately for medieval history enthusiasts, the ruins of Reading Abbey have become too dangerous for daily tours. The Friends of Reading Abbey are trying to get funding to help conserve what is left of this historical abbey.

In the past, the abbey ruins have been opened for abbreviated guided tours on certain occasions such as Water Fest. If you are visiting from a distance, it might be worth an email to find out if any such tours are planned. For more information, see Reading Museum's website at www.readingmuseum.org.uk/contact/.

The inner gateway is still in existence, having been heavily restored in the nineteenth century. It is doubtful Richard would recognise it as it is today.

Reading Museum, located in the town hall, is a good place to get further information on the abbey. Admission is free. Before entering the exhibitions, ask at the information desk to see the picture of Elizabeth. Be sure to ask specifically to see the painting by Ernest Board titled 'Marriage of King Edward IV and Elizabeth Woodville'. As we know that Edward and Elizabeth were already married before she was presented at Reading, the title is not quite accurate. However, the painting is well done, with vibrant colours. It is fun to stand in front of it and try to figure out which noble the artist meant to be Warwick. My guess is the one with the sour look on his face.

The museum houses some recovered stonework from the abbey, as well as a reconstruction of how the abbey might have looked. You can also feast your eyes on examples of medieval tile that would have graced the floors of the abbey.

Driving is difficult in Reading. The town operates a park-and-ride scheme that might be beneficial for a visit. For up-to-date information about visiting the museum, see its website at www. readingmuseum.org.uk/visiting/. Reading Museum postcode: RG1 1QH.

Oxford, Oxfordshire

From Reading, Richard headed to Oxford. Oxford is situated at the confluence of the Thames and the Cherwell rivers. The town was first mentioned in the *Anglo-Saxon Chronicle* as Oxnaforda, and it was already being visited by Anglo-Saxon royalty in the early part of the eleventh century. After the Norman Conquest, Robert d'Oilly was given the task of erecting a castle at Oxford for the king. He did so, building the large fortification on the western side of the town.

During the Anarchy, the war between Stephen and Matilda, the castle was witness to an extraordinary event. The empress was trapped in the castle, under siege by Stephen's forces. Realising she had to do something, Matilda outmanoeuvred Stephen by slipping out of the castle during a cold, snowy December night. Dressed all in white, she managed to escape through Stephen's lines and across the frozen river to safety.

The city's status as a university town got off to a turbulent start. After a tense incident involving the townspeople and students, residence halls were established for the students. The university quickly gained a reputation for academia in the medieval world, and students came from all over to study there.

Magdalen College

Magdalen (pronounced 'maudlin') College was founded as Magdalen Hall by William Waynflete in the mid-fifteenth century. Waynflete, the man who replaced Archbishop Bourchier as Chancellor of England, established parts of the college within the walls of St John's Hospital. The college was richly endowed with a large amount of John Fastolf's fortune, allowing it to expand quickly. Situated in the east of the city, the college backs up to a branch of the River Cherwell. A large deer park and grove make up part of the grounds.

The college was completely surrounded by an enormous wall, now called the Longwall. When Richard visited, mason William Orchard had recently finished the cloisters, hall, chapel and library.

Richard visited the college in July 1483 as part of his first royal progress. He came to Oxford from Reading and was received by the chancellor of the university, along with the regents and non-regents. With great pomp and ceremony, he was escorted by Waynflete, along with the President of Magdalen, Richard Mayhew, and students, into the college. After being greeted with kind speeches, Richard and many of his retinue spent the night at the college. It is likely that Richard dined with the president and Waynflete in the president's private dining area. Today, this room may be the location of the college's smoking room.

The following day was the feast day of St James the apostle, and Richard toured the college. He listened to two disputations on moral philosophy in the common hall, and afterwards rewarded the speakers with monetary gifts. On the following day, Richard toured the university prior to making his way to Woodstock. One anecdote states that the students crowned Richard with fragrant wreaths before he left. Richard clearly made quite the impression, since the chronicler of the college's register ended his account with 'May the king live forever!'

In October 1483, Richard stopped at Oxford on his way to deal with Buckingham's rebellion. An entry in the Magdalen College Chapel account book shows an offering made by the king on St Simon and St Jude's day.

Visiting Magdalen Today

The college welcomes visitors from 1 p.m. until dusk throughout the year. As with other sites, it is always best to check in advance, as closures do occur. The college's website is www.magd.ox.ac.uk/discover-magdalen/visiting-magdalen/.

The buildings that are still in existence from Richard's visit are the old kitchen, the Longwall, the chapel, the cloisters and the library. Not all rooms are open to the public, so watch for the signs that mark areas as private.

The old kitchen of the college is one of the oldest areas of the building. The only surviving building of St John's hospital, it was not originally a kitchen. It was converted to a kitchen after the college was founded. Today, you can walk through the area on your way to a tasty bite in the college café.

Standing in the cloisters, look at the Founder's Tower in the middle of the west range. The smoking room is on the first floor to the tower's right. This may have been the former location of the smaller, separate dining area where the president entertained guests.

If driving to Oxford, I recommend you park at one of the park-and-ride locations. Oxford is a true university town and the streets are also packed with tourists. For information about which park and ride would be best for you, visit the website at www.oxford.gov.uk/PageRender/decTS/ParkandRideLocations. htm. Alternatively, two bus companies offer services from London to Oxford. Make your decision by visiting both pages. The first, Oxford Tube, is operated by Stagecoach. Its website is www. oxfordtube.com/. The second, X90, is operated by Oxford Bus Company. Its website is x90.oxfordbus.co.uk/. If neither option appeals to you, there is a regular train service from London to Oxford. For more information, visit First Great Western's website at tickets.firstgreatwestern.co.uk/gw/en/JourneyPlanning/MixingDeck.

Woodstock Manor, Oxfordshire

About nine miles north-west of Oxford, situated on a rise above the banks of the River Glyme, once stood the palace of Woodstock, a favourite residence of the Plantagenet dynasty. It appears there was a hunting lodge at Woodstock as early as the reign of Ethelred II, when a Witan was held here. Henry I had a large park enclosed here and often visited for a hunt. The area became so popular with the royal family that a palace was constructed in the twelfth century. Woodstock's best known story is that of Henry II and his fair Rosamund, who supposedly had a bower at Woodstock where Henry would visit.

By 1163 Woodstock was one of Henry's favourite haunts. He was at Woodstock in July when Malcolm, King of Scotland, Rhys ap Gruffydd, Prince of South Wales and Owain Gwynedd, Prince of North Wales, did homage to him. A grand wedding celebration was held here in September 1186, when Ermengarde de Beaumont, a great-granddaughter of Henry I, married William, King of Scotland. Some sources have erroneously suggested that Ermengarde was Henry's granddaughter, and one even has proposed that she was Henry's great-great granddaughter. However, her father's mother was Constance, Henry I's daughter.

Henry III had enlarged the palace by the time his daughter

Margaret and her husband Alexander III visited him here. There were so many guests from both Scotland and England that tents had to be put up in the meadows for their accommodations. Royal visits continued throughout the years, and several members of the royal family were born here, including Thomas of Woodstock.

Henry VI granted Woodstock to the Archbishop of York, George Neville. Neville was the son of Richard Neville, Earl of Salisbury. In 1479, Edward IV and Elizabeth stopped at the palace for a visit before going on to Oxford.

While on his progress, Richard visited Magdalen College for a few days before retiring to Woodstock, probably for a few days of hunting. At Woodstock, Richard heard the pleas of people who had been harmed when Edward IV incorporated a great portion of the land into his forest at Wychwood. Richard disafforested the area, helping those who had been adversely affected by Edward's actions.

The palace was damaged in the Civil War and destroyed in the eighteenth century. There are no ruins to visit, as the site of the palace is within the grounds of Blenheim Palace. However, there is a plinth that memorialises the location of the old palace.

The Old Palace

While there is nothing left to help us picture how the palace once looked, it is possible to get an idea of its size and features through descriptions of the ruins before they were destroyed. The palace was situated on a hill and reached through a gatehouse, which marked the entrance to the inner courtyard. The palace was positioned around two courtyards. The hall was entered from the courtyard on wide steps of fine freestone. Once inside, a visitor would have been struck by the brightly coloured room, split into two aisles by six large stone pillars. The circular windows in the gable ends of the hall would have allowed for extra light. From the upper end of the hall, Richard would have dominated the room. Here, seated in an intricately painted chair, he would have heard the petitioners asking for the return of public lands.

On the left-hand side of the hall was the entrance to one of the palace's chapels. Richard probably spent some time here observing Mass, with the light streaming in through the windows above the seven arches. There were several chapels at Woodstock, including a round one built to resemble the Holy Sepulchre in Jerusalem. After leaving the chapel, Richard would have seen a staircase which led to the first floor. The privy chamber, queen's chamber and presence chamber were all on the first floor.

If she had been with Richard at Woodstock, Anne would have stayed in the queen's chamber, which was painted green and bordered with red. A fire would have blazed in her inner wardrobe as she walked on tiles decorated with intricate patterns. When she went to her private chapel to worship, she would have noticed that it was also paved with colourful tiles and contained an image of St Mary.

A passage ran between the stairway of the king's chamber and the queen's low chamber. In Richard's chamber, more colourful tiles adorned the floor. His chamber would have been brightly coloured as well. The king's chapel, also paved, contained a chalice.

The king's chamber had gardens on both sides. On one side the garden was laid with turf, and the other side probably held a herb garden. The queen's garden was enclosed by high walls to prevent intruders, and had a walkway through the herb garden beside the king's fishpond. After a long day hunting and receiving petitioners, it is likely Richard took advantage of the relative solitude offered by the garden walk.

Nearby, Rosamund's bower offered a retreat away from the palace. By Richard's time, the bower had chambers for the king and queen, as well as a chapel. Perhaps the legend of Henry and Rosamund would not have appealed to pious Richard, but the beautiful pools nearby would have been pleasing to experience. Everswell, as Rosamund's bower was known, was built round a spring which flowed into a series of pools set within peaceful, cloistered courts.

With his love of hunting, Richard would have enjoyed Woodstock. Its great park was enclosed by a high wall and stocked with a variety of animals. At one point, during the reign of Henry I, a menagerie was supposedly kept in the park. In Richard's time, the leopards and other exotic animals would have gone, but the hunting of deer and other wildlife would have provided both food and entertainment.

Visiting Woodstock Today

Sadly there is nothing left of the palace of Woodstock. It was already in disrepair by Elizabeth I's reign, and after being held a prisoner there in her sister's reign, Elizabeth had little love for the place. Later monarchs repaired it, but it suffered some damage during the Civil War. By the late seventeenth century very little remained. Sarah, the Duchess of Marlborough, had the ruins of the palace destroyed in 1720. Every last stone was removed, leaving nothing to visit. A stone plinth marks the location of the once grand hunting lodge turned palace, but it can only be visited by purchasing a ticket to see Blenheim Palace. Visit Blenheim Palace's website at www.blenheimpalace.com/. Blenheim Palace postcode: OX20 1PP.

While you are in the area, visit nearby Minster Lovell, which was the home of Francis Lovell. It is a short drive from Woodstock and well worth a visit. Minster Lovell postcode: OX29 0RR.

Gloucester, Gloucestershire

When Richard visited Gloucester in 1483 while on his first progress, he was likely met by the leading citizens of the town as well as a procession of clergy from the abbey. Unlike later kings he would not have been met by the mayor and sheriffs dressed in scarlet, as Gloucester did not yet have the privilege of having a mayor. It was Richard who granted the town the notable privilege of incorporating the borough and making it into a county. This privilege allowed Gloucester to have its own mayor, sheriffs and twelve aldermen.

As Richard was arriving from Minster Lovell, he likely entered through the Northgate, which was the primary entrance into town from the London road. No records survive detailing his arrival, but as king he would have been received much like he was at York. The roads had been newly paved during his brother's reign, so his entourage would have been able to traverse them with no trouble.

During his visit, Richard so impressed the citizens of Gloucester that they made him an offering of money. He declined their offer, thanking them and telling him he would rather have their love than money. As Richard was trying to gain popular support in the south, this refusal, along with the charter, probably helped his cause.

Unfortunately there are no records as to where Richard passed this night. The castle was still in existence and had been repaired in his brother's reign. Tradition holds that the castle became a gaol during Richard's reign. It is more likely that since his stay was of such short duration he stayed at the monastery.

Gloucester Castle

Gloucester had been a favourite place of William the Conqueror, who often held his Christmas court here. He likely held his court in an old Anglo-Saxon hall, as the castle's keep was built by his son, Henry I. The castle was approached by two bridges – one crossed the River Severn on the west and the other crossed the moat between the castle and the town on the north-east. Both bridges were of timber, but seem to have been highly fortified. A third bridge was built in the middle of the thirteenth century on the south side of the castle.

One notable resident, albeit prisoner, of the keep was Eleanor of Brittany. Her uncle, King John, kept her here in confinement. The daughter of Geoffrey of Brittany, she was a valuable pawn for her uncle. Rumours swirled that John had killed her brother, Arthur, so perhaps Eleanor was not all that unlucky in her confinement.

The inner bailey, with the keep, also held the king's chapel and royal apartments. The castle was surrounded by high walls, with towers placed at intervals. The castle came under attack several times and had to be repaired. Under Henry IV the keep received a new roof and was repaired. More repairs followed until the reign of Edward IV. It is believed that the castle was in disrepair by the time Richard visited, so he would not have stayed there. Perhaps he intended to strengthen and repair the castle at some point, but no plans were made during his reign. Passing by the castle, he would have seen the tower of the keep with its embattled parapets, as it would have dominated the area around it.

The Abbey of St Peter

The Abbey of St Peter was a Benedictine monastery dedicated to St Peter. Its Anglo-Saxon foundation was largely rebuilt by Serlo, a monk from Mont St Michel. The abbey was consecrated in July 1100. According to T. Francis Bumpus in his work *The*

Cathedrals of England and Wales, Serlo's work consisted of a large nave with arches on pillars soaring thirty feet and measuring six feet in diameter. The transepts were short and both consisted of a polygonal chapel on their east sides.

As Richard entered the grounds of the monastery, the abbot would have welcomed him. Most likely, Richard spent the night in the abbot's lodge. The great hall of the lodge was built of stone, while most of its other buildings were of timber. According to the records of Gloucester Cathedral, the most opulent guest accommodations were to the west of the abbot's great hall. The one surviving part of the original building, the long gallery with its large oriel window, was added many years after Richard's visit.

Although Richard's visit was short, he probably took time to visit the abbey, which contained the tomb of his ancestor, Edward II. He would also have heard Mass before the altar. Before retiring to his great chamber, he might have taken time for a stroll in the abbot's garden. After his visit to Gloucester, Richard would head toward Tewkesbury along the same route that Margaret of Anjou's troops had trod after being turned away from Gloucester.

Visiting the Abbey Today

The Abbey of St Peter is no more, but thankfully, the church building survives. Gloucester was one of the abbeys refounded as a cathedral under King Henry VIII, so the former Benedictine monastery escaped much of the destruction of the Dissolution.

Visitors today enter the through the fifteenth-century south porch with its statues and canopies, which were restored in the nineteenth century. Once inside you are standing in the nave that Serlo built. Here you can see the huge pillars supporting narrow arches. Above the arches is the triforium and clerestory. The rib vaults of the ceiling spring from clusters of columns along the triforium. Traces of colour and gilding have been found on the pillars and arches, suggesting that the features were highly decorated.

It was here in the abbey that Henry III had his first coronation. A Victorian window on the south aisle depicts the event. The south ambulatory was extant when Richard visited the abbey. Perhaps he saw the effigy of Robert, Duke of Normandy, which lies in this area. This part of the church underwent renovations during the anniversary celebrations in the last part of the twentieth century, so the painted stained glass in its windows is fairly new.

Within the north ambulatory lies one of Richard's ancestors. Edward II's tomb, with its alabaster effigy, is made of Purbeck marble, with a canopy of two tiers of delicately carved arches. Edward II's tomb became a place of pilgrimage during medieval times. Perhaps Richard visited the tomb while at the abbey to further underscore his ties with royal ancestry.

The east end of the choir holds an expansive collection of medieval stained glass. Richard would have seen this window, with its colourful stained glass, on his visit. Within the choir are also some wonderful examples of medieval misericords.

Before leaving the building, make sure to see the cloisters. Coming from the abbot's lodge, Richard would have walked through the cloisters to enter the abbey church. It is impossible to stand within these cloisters and not be amazed by the elaborate fan vaulting. On a sunny day the area seems to shimmer. The cloisters as we see them today were finished in the early part of the fifteenth century. Today you can still see the carrels where the monks used to study and the lavatorium where they washed their hands. Gloucester's chapter house is often closed to visitors, but if you are lucky enough to get to visit do take the opportunity.

Unfortunately, the abbot's lodge was destroyed and rebuilt. Today, the King's School occupies the area where the abbot's lodge, later known as the bishop's palace, once stood, fronting what is today Pitt Street. The King's School senior school occupies most of the area of the former building.

For more information on visiting the cathedral, see its website at www.gloucestercathedral.org.uk/index.php?page=visits-events. Gloucester is easily accessible with a car and contains several public car parks, although the cathedral does not have parking available. Trains also leave London Paddington bound for Gloucester. For more information regarding rail service see www.nationalrail.co.uk/.

Warwick Castle, Warwickshire

Built on a rocky cliff overlooking the River Avon, Warwick Castle was an impressive and historic building even in Richard's day. As the patrimony of successive men of brilliance and power, the castle had expanded under most of them.

During the time Richard was under the tutelage of Warwick, he likely visited the castle, which was one of his cousin's many holdings. Having grown up around magnificent buildings, Richard may have still been awed by the castle's grandeur.

As he came across the drawbridge over the dry moat, perhaps Richard's eye was caught by machicolated Caesar's Tower, which was connected to Guy's Tower by an embattled wall. Once inside the castle, he certainly would have noticed where the original timber castle had stood high on the motte. He may have enjoyed dinner in the magnificent Great Hall with the earl and his retainers. It probably never crossed his mind that one day this commanding fortification would have implications for each of the York brothers, passing through George's hands before coming to him. Nor did he imagine that, in just a few years, his brother Edward would be held prisoner here by his cousin.

Edward IV and Warwick

Edward's throne was never more insecure than it was from 1469 until 1471. Hearing of the rebellion of Robin of Redesdale, Edward slowly made his way north. After learning how many men Redesdale had recruited to his side, Edward tried to muster more men to his cause. This did not happen in time, and upon hearing of the defeat of Pembroke and Devon, Edward's men apparently deserted him. At Olney, Edward came under the control of Archbishop Neville and was taken to Warwick Castle. Edward suddenly found himself in the position that Henry VI had once been in – he was king in name only. While at Warwick Castle, he would have been given comfortable lodgings, but he was Warwick's prisoner. Edward was not at the castle long before he was moved to Middleham.

In 1471, after arriving in England from his exile in the Low Countries, Edward made his way south, gathering men as he went. He reached Warwick and made it his base. When it became evident that the Duke of Clarence was headed his way, he went to meet him. Polydore Vergil explains, meane whyle woord was browght that the duke himself was at hand with an huge army; which when king Edward understoode, he raisyd his camp and went to mete the duke. Howbeyt, because yt showld not seme soome suttle practyse concludyd betwixt them two, he marchid in good order of battaylle, as one that myndyd to fight. The duke dyd the lyke. But whan they came within view thone of thother, Richerd duke of Glocestre, as thowghe he had bene apoyntyd arbyter of all controversy, first conferryd secretly with the duke; than he returnyd to king Edward, and dyd the very George same with him. Fynally, not warre but peace was in every man's mouth; than, armor and weapon layd apart uppon both sydes, the meete and broothers gladly embracyd one another.

For the moment, Clarence was back in the family fold, having been pardoned by Edward. Leaving Warwick, the group headed back to London, where they would regroup before heading out to meet the Earl of Warwick at Barnet.

George, Duke of Clarence, and Warwick Castle

After the death of Warwick at Barnet, George came into possession of Warwick castle. This place likely held bad memories for him by the time he was executed. His wife, Isabel, died at Warwick, following the birth of a son, who likewise perished.

George did not take Isabel's death well. He began acting erratically and making accusations that eventually would end with his execution. Following this event, Warwick Castle came under the control of the Crown.

Richard III and Warwick Castle

As Richard and his retinue approached Warwick in August 1483, perhaps these events tumbled through his mind. He was now king, and the castle was under his control. As he crossed the drawbridge and rode into the still-impressive fortification, he was no longer a young boy under the care of his formidable cousin but a powerful man in his own right.

According to Rous, Richard received an ambassador from the Queen of Castile at Warwick. Apparently the queen wanted to pursue a marriage between an infanta of Castile and Richard's son, Edward. The ambassador was received in style, but Richard's response to the marriage proposal has been lost to history.

As he did with many of his castles, Richard embarked on an impressive building scheme at Warwick. He began to build two towers, the Bear and Clarence towers. These two octagonal towers project from the wall, and were meant to be self-contained, with a well. The towers, while still impressive, are not at the height Richard intended. The shape and outline of Warwick Castle would have been greatly changed had Richard not fallen at Bosworth Field. His death ended the building scheme.

Visiting Warwick Castle Today

Be forewarned. While the castle is an interesting place to visit, it is definitely a tourist attraction. The castle is child-friendly and many exhibitions are designed with children in mind, including one on Richard Neville. The Bear Tower is open to the public and is billed as a tower with a bear pit.

Another building of interest is the Great Hall, which, while having been reconstructed twice, stands on the same location as in Richard's time. The inside of most of the rooms will look nothing like they would have appeared back then, but are worth a visit on their own merit.

If you are interested in staying overnight at the castle, accommodation is available. For more information on visiting the castle today, see its website at www.warwick-castle.com/plan/plan-a-visit.aspx. Depending on where you park, Warwick Castle has several postcodes. Stratford Road Car Park: CV34 6AH. Field Car Park: CV34 6AH. Stables Car Park: CV34 4QU.

St Mary's Church, Warwick

A church was likely founded here before the conquest. By the twelfth century, the Collegiate church of St Mary was an important church in Warwick. According to Josephine Wilkinson in her book *Richard: The Young King to Be*, Richard visited here and gave offerings to the church. While here, he probably visited the Beauchamp chapel.

While the nave, transepts and tower had to be rebuilt due to a terrible fire that raged through the centre of town and destroyed many buildings, the Beauchamp Chapel, chancel and vestry survived the mass destruction.

The Beauchamp Chantry, or the Chapel of our Lady, was built in the mid-fifteenth century. Built in imitation Gothic style, the chapel is a testament to its builder, Richard Beauchamp. His altar tomb is built of Purbeck marble and contains an effigy of the earl decked out in full armour, looking up to the image of the Virgin Mary in the ceiling. Some of the 'weepers' around the tomb are familiar names, including Richard Neville, Earl of Salisbury; Edmund Beaufort, Duke of Somerset; and Humphrey Stafford, Duke of Buckingham.

The chapel also has fragments of medieval stained glass in its windows. At more than thirty feet high, the ornate vaulted ceiling is meant to impress. According to the church, the wall painting of the Last Judgment was begun in 1449, but restored in the seventeenth century. Other tombs in the room are from later periods.

Before the high altar stands the tomb of Earl Thomas Beauchamp and his wife Katherine Mortimer, a couple whose names Richard would have recognised. The tomb is intricately designed, with Thomas in armour, his feet resting on a bear. The effigy of his wife lies beside him, holding his hand.

Visiting St Mary's Today
The church is generally open every day. For more information about opening hours, check the church's website at www.stmaryswarwick. org.uk/index.php?/stmarys/visiting or call the church office at +44 (0)1926 403940. St Mary's church postcode: CV34 4RA.

Nottingham Castle, Nottinghamshire

In its day, Nottingham Castle would have been a splendid sight, towering over the surrounding area from its perch on the sandstone ridge. Built soon after the conquest by William the Conqueror, the castle was in a strategic location to command the crossing over the River Trent. The castle consisted of an outer bailey, a dry moat, an inner ward and a middle bailey. Large caves were carved into the sandstone cliffs under the castle, leading to the tradition that it was through one of these caves that Edward III and his men captured

Roger Mortimer as Isabella pleaded with her son for mercy on 'poor Mortimer'.

Up until Edward IV, the kings and queens who lodged here did so within the royal apartments of the inner ward. These chambers were over the Great Hall, which had large dormer windows. When Edward IV came to the throne, these chambers were either not large enough or in a dilapidated state, as he began building new royal apartments within the middle ward.

Once Richard was king he completed Edward's renovations. Antiquarian James Orange said that '... this building did not receive its final touches of embellishments until the time of Richard III when it united the splendid magnificence of a palace with the secure impregnability of a castle'. Edward had begun a great tower at the north-west corner of the yard, which Richard completed. The ashlar-faced tower, later known as Richard's tower, was four storeys with a winding spiral staircase. The royal apartments were built in a crescent against the wall. These elaborate rooms with their large bay windows overlooking the courtyard were begun by Edward and finished by Richard, who added a second storey complete with its own set of bay windows. These apartments were sizable and flooded with light. In the winter a roaring fire in one of the fireplaces would have provided warmth in the draughty chambers.

Richard and Nottingham

Nottingham was one of Richard's most visited castles during his short reign. He spent considerable time here within its walls. Arriving at the castle with a large retinue of horses, wagons and men, Richard, often accompanied by Anne, would have crossed the bridge over the dry moat and entered through the immense door, passing under the raised portcullis of the two-storey gatehouse with its battlements. The castle would have appeared like a fortress with its thick, impregnable walls stretching completely around it. Making their way into the bailey, he and Anne would have retired to their chambers, tired after a long journey.

Richard was at Nottingham in August of 1483 on his way to York. His secretary wrote to York from here advising them to have several festivals and to hang the streets with cloths of arras and tapestry works so that the southern lords would see the city's love for the new king. On this particular trip, Richard stayed less than a week. He was probably excited to get to York where his son Edward was to be invested as the Prince of Wales.

Richard passed through Nottingham after hearing of Buckingham's rebellion, but did not linger long, staying only a night. He was back in Nottingham by March 1484. Such was Richard's affection for the castle that a tradition grew up that when he was in Nottingham he often retreated to a turret in the tower. Whether this was true or not, he certainly stayed at the castle often.

Richard and Anne were at Nottingham when they received the news that no parent wants to hear. Their son, Edward, had died at Middleham. Perhaps the tragic news was received in the Great Hall, as their response was recorded by the *Croyland Chronicle*:

> In the following April ... this only son, on whom, through so many solemn oaths, all hope of the royal succession rested, died in Middleham castle after a short illness ... in the first year of King Richard's reign. You might have seen the father and mother, after hearing the news at Nottingham where they were then staying, almost out of their minds for a long time when faced with the sudden grief.

Richard's marriage appears to have been a close one, as Anne was often with him. Behind closed doors they probably consoled one another, both knowing it was unlikely they would have another child. Only one child had been born to them throughout their entire marriage, and it was not likely they would conceive another. Making their way to the chapel, they probably grieved together. Perhaps they found some solace in the peace of the room with its picture of St Katherine painted in front of the altar and the mural of her story painted above it.

Unfortunately a king cannot grieve overlong, and soon Richard was busy with the running of the government. The threat of another uprising was strong and Henry Tudor was busy making plans overseas. War with Scotland was not going well, either, and Richard may have realised he needed to focus his efforts on maintaining control of the situation with Tudor.

James Gairdner says that Richard sent his ambassadors to the King of Scotland, James III, to offer a peace agreement. Among the men James III appointed to meet with Richard and his ambassadors were the Earl of Argyll, the Bishop of Aberdeen and the Archdeacon of Lothian. Richard sent them safe passage in August and in September the men arrived in Nottingham.

The Scottish delegation entered the Great Hall where Richard was sitting under his cloth of estate, surrounded by his own delegation and members of his household. The Archdeacon of Lothian, Archibald Whitelaw, opened the meeting by delivering an oration in Latin. The terms of the peace were mutually beneficial, with the promise of a marriage between James IV and Anne de la Pole, Richard's niece. This marriage never took place, and after the death of Richard, James IV would go on to marry Henry VII's daughter, Margaret Tudor. However, at the time it was a success, and one can imagine Richard standing at one of the large bay windows at dusk, looking out on to his courtyard, pleased with his triumph.

Richard's next visit to Nottingham was in June 1485. Here he made his base, while rumours swirled around the country of an imminent invasion by Henry Tudor. Nottingham was a central location from which to counter any invasion attempt. Richard acknowledged the threat, saying that 'oure Rebelles and traytors ... entende hastely to invade this oure Royaulme purporting the distruccion of us ...' He notified his commissioners of array that they should review the soldiers and put them on alert to be ready at an hour's warning whenever they were commanded.

The waiting game ended when, near the end of July, Richard's spies brought word that Henry was making preparations to leave for England. Henry landed at Milford Haven in Wales and began his march toward ultimate victory in the Battle of Bosworth. Receiving word of Henry's landing, Richard left Nottingham on his march to Leicester and his ultimate defeat and death. As he rode under the gatehouse of Nottingham for the last time, perhaps he pictured the joyous moment when he and Anne rode into the great courtyard for the first time as king and queen, with their dreams of a splendid future.

Visiting Nottingham Today

Nothing substantial remains of Richard's palatial residence at Nottingham. Following the Civil War, the castle was ordered to be destroyed. The gatehouse and parts of the wall are medieval, but they have been greatly restored. Fragments of the middle bailey's north-east tower remain, but not enough to get an accurate picture of the entire structure. One of the best places to get an idea of the extent of Nottingham is right after you enter through the gatehouse. Standing and looking up at the inner and middle baileys, you can get an idea of how large the complex once was.

Entering the middle bailey, walk to the centre of the grass. Here you are standing in what was the courtyard of the royal apartments. See if you can recreate the two-storey chambers that once surrounded it in your mind.

In the *History and Antiquities of Nottingham*, James Orange discusses a strange legend involving Richard planting a tree at the castle:

> ... not a tree grew in the park ... except one which grew at the foot of the rock on which the castle stood, and, according to tradition, had been planted there by Richard III, nick-named 'Crook Backed Dick,' and says, certainly the form of the tree was in unison with the form of its planter, for it had not a straight inch in its whole composition.

The current castle, which is located in what was the inner ward, was not built until well after Richard's time. Today it serves as a museum and art gallery. The museum has a model of the castle as it was in the year 1500, which gives an idea of the layout and proportions of the complex. After spending time wandering around the grounds, visit the castle's museum, which provides a great deal of history about Nottingham and the castle's role in England.

If you have time and are not claustrophobic, take a tour of Mortimer's Hole. The caves and tunnels are fascinating. The art gallery is worth a visit as well. You can easily spend a full day at the castle if you explore all it has to offer. Before you leave you might want to visit the castle café. Sitting on a terrace with an incredible view while sipping coffee and eating a scone smothered with clotted cream and strawberry jam is an experience that cannot be missed. From the terrace you can see almost all of Nottingham and much of the surrounding countryside.

For more information on visiting the castle, visit the castle's website at www.nottinghamcity.gov.uk/Castle. If you are driving to Nottingham, take advantage of its park-and-ride scheme. For more information, visit www.nottinghamcity.gov.uk/parkandride or call the city council at +44 (0) 115 915 5555.

High-speed trains from London St Pancras can make the journey in under two hours. For more information visit www.eastmidlandstrains.co.uk/travelling-with-us/our-network/trains-to-nottingham. There is also a coach service via National Express, which makes the journey in under three hours from London's Victoria bus station. The website for National Express is www.nationalexpress.com/home.aspx.

Gainsborough Old Hall, Lincolnshire

After leaving Pontefract in October 1483, Richard headed toward Lincoln. On his way he paused to spend some time with one of his supporters, Sir Thomas Burgh. Burgh had been present in York for Edward's investiture as Prince of Wales, and he likely invited Richard to stay with him there on his return south.

Burgh had been Edward IV's Master of the Horse and had transferred his loyalty to Richard III upon his taking the crown. Not only did Burgh keep his offices under Richard, he was also elected to the Order of the Garter, and had received the honour of holding the coronation canopy over Richard's head, along with a gift of black satin from the newly crowned king.

Burgh's Old Hall lies in Gainsborough, which is a market town situated on the eastern bank of the Trent River. The Old Hall is an oak-framed building, which was built on three sides of a quadrangle, probably in the mid-fifteenth century. A section of the home was destroyed in a Lancastrian attack between 1469 and 1470. This was probably the west range, which had recently been rebuilt just in time for Richard's visit. Burgh would have understandably been proud of this section and probably made this area of his home available to the king.

One can imagine the bustle of Thomas Burgh's household as they prepared for a visit from the king. The mayhem and madness that a king's visit caused then would be an interesting sight to see. In Gainsborough Old Hall, the staff would be scurrying about readying the Great Hall for the king's reception, preparing a chamber and storing food.

Richard was likely received by the family in the Great Hall. The evening meal would have been served here, with King Richard taking the dais as the honoured guest. A pantler and butler would attend to Richard, with the pantler placing wrapped bread in front of him and the butler giving him an expensive goblet from which to drink. An illustration transcribed from *The Black Book of the household of Edward IV* sets out the space between the king and the other guests.

With the king present, Burgh would have ensured that proper entertainment was provided. Jugglers or jesters would have entertained the guests as the wine flowed and meats were served. A screen at the end of the hall probably blocked the sight of the servants coming in and out of the kitchen and pantry areas.

With no fireplace, a fire would have roared in the centre of the room, providing warmth for the occupants of the hall. As in other medieval buildings, a louvre would have been above the fire to pull the smoke from the room.

After the final course, fruits and spices would likely have been served. After the meal Richard probably retired to his chamber. The next day he would ride on to Lincoln.

Visiting Gainsborough Old Hall Today
Gainsborough Old Hall is one of the best surviving examples of a medieval manor hall. Once you step through the door it is like stepping back in time. One of the first rooms on the self-guided tour is the Great Hall. According to the visitor guidebook, the tiled floor is from a later period; the original floor would have been of packed earth.

Look above you to see the oak-framed ceiling. The arches are free standing, without cross-beams to pull the eye downward, making the ceiling appear even higher than it is.

If you stand with your back towards the dais, you will see three doorways at the end of the room. The central doorway leads into the kitchen area, where an interesting display of medieval cookery flourishes. The door to the right is the buttery, and the one to the left is to the pantry.

Enter into the kitchen area to see the display. A sample menu on display gives you an idea of what may have been served during Richard's visit. The first course probably had items such as pottage or broth and a whole side of roast beef. The second course may have had such foods as white pudding of hog's liver and baked sparrow. You can almost feel the servants jostling about you as they prepared the courses for the king's feast.

Wander around the rest of the hall to your heart's content. The west wing can be reached by going through the pantry. One feature not to miss is the squint in the solar. This looks out on to the Great Hall. It had once been removed, so the squint today is a more recent addition, but you get an excellent view from there.

The chimney stacks on the outside of the building likely date from Tudor times, so the building doesn't look quite like it did on Richard's visit. However, he would recognise much of what can be seen today.

For information about opening times, visit Gainsborough Old Hall's website at www.gainsboroughholdhall.com/visiting-us. Gainsborough Old Hall postcode: DN21 2NB.

Lincoln, Lincolnshire

Lincoln has been an important city since before Roman times. The city was well placed upon a hill where the surrounding countryside can be viewed for miles. First occupied by the Celts, the city was later used by the Romans. After the Romans left, the city declined. It was not destined to stay in decline, however. With its strategic location near a river, the Danes also chose to occupy Lincoln. After the coming of William the Conqueror, the city was further fortified by a castle.

In medieval times, it was an important area of trade and commerce, and was called one of the top three cities in Britain. Kings and queens visited, sometimes while at war. It was here that Empress Matilda (also known as Maud), daughter of Henry I, captured the usurper, King Stephen. Edward I held a parliament in Lincoln, as did his son, Edward II.

Before the coming of the Industrial Revolution, the city was even more magnificent than it is today. Poets wrote verses about the beauty of this city on a hill. Poet Michael Drayton wrote:

> By this to Lincolne com'n, upon whose lofty site,
> Whilst wistly Wyiham looks with wonderful delight,
> Enamoured of the state, and beauty of the place,
> That her of all the rest especially doth grace.

Richard and Lincoln

As king, Richard visited Lincoln in October of 1483. He had just come from Pontefract, via Gainsborough Old Hall, and was making his way to Nottingham. He learned of Buckingham's rebellion and sent a letter to his chancellor, Bishop John Russell, requesting that his seal be sent to him at Lincoln. His emotional reaction to Buckingham's treachery can be seen in the letter's postscript, where he added that he was:

> well and truly determined, and for to resist the malice of him that had best cause to be true, the Duke of Buckingham, the most untrue creature living; whom with God's grace we shall not be long till that we will be in those parts, and subdue his malice. We assure you there was never false traitor better purveyed for, as this bearer, Gloucester, shall show you.

After leaving Lincoln, Richard was able to put down the uprising and execute Buckingham. For the superstitious soul, an ancient prediction involving kings and Lincoln might have served as a warning to Richard. The prediction says, 'The crowned head that enters Lincoln's walls; his reign proves stormy and his kingdom falls.' As several kings with long rules spent time in Lincoln, the veracity of the prophecy is in doubt.

There are several sites in Lincoln that Richard would have visited while here. Lincoln still has a medieval feel and this greatly adds to the atmosphere for any Richard III enthusiast.

Visiting Lincoln Today

There are several car parks around Lincoln. The visitor information centre has a map of the parking areas available for download at their website: www.visitlincoln.com/things-to-do/visitor-information-centre. The centre is located in the cathedral quarter. If you are planning on spending the night or visiting any other local sights, the centre's staff can assist you.

After you visit the Richard III sites, I recommend that you walk around the city and take in the other medieval sites. The city has quite a bit to offer, and it is worth a trek down and up Steep Hill to see the buildings along the way.

Visitor information centre postcode: LN1 3AA.

Bishops' Palace

The Bishops' Palace is most likely where Richard, as king, would have lodged while in Lincoln. Several other monarchs stayed in the comfortable ecclesiastical palace instead of the castle, and it is probable that Richard would have done the same.

The Bishops' Palace was built on a grand scale. Bishop Hugh, later St Hugh, began a large hall to the building that was later finished by another Hugh, Hugh of Wells. Under Bishop Henry Burghersh, in the fourteenth century, the palace was crenellated and turrets and battlements were added. At this time the garden along the south side of the building was extended.

One of the most prolific builders was Bishop Alnwick in the early fifteenth century. He added a chapel to the palace and a square stone tower with a turret. The tower contained large chambers, perhaps for guests of the bishop. It may have been here that Richard stayed, or perhaps he took over the bishop's own chamber. According to Edward James Wilson, writing in 1848, a large stained-glass bay window with pictures of the kings of England and coats of arms was placed above the doorway to Alnwick's tower. The tower's door was elaborately carved. Above the door's pointed arch was a carving of Bishop Alnwick's coat of arms; below it were little arches with capitals.

From surveys and early descriptions, we know that the hall, eighty-four feet by fifty-eight feet, was open and airy. Divided by eight marble columns and arches into one large centre aisle with two outlying aisles, the room resembled a church with large windows. The upper portions of the windows were likely glazed, and the lower portions boarded up by shutters.

Like many medieval buildings, the fire was in the middle of the room under a timber roof covered with lead. Here is where Richard would have conducted business while he was in Lincoln. His secretary would have been seated at the table while Richard dictated letters. Imagine Richard pacing back and forth until his frustration with Buckingham grew into such a fury that he added his postscript to the bottom of the letter. His close followers would have joined him here for meals. The wine would have flowed as the men discussed the days ahead. Servants moving back and forth between this room and the kitchen beyond would have brought tasty dishes for the bishop's guests. Someone would be tending the fire, keeping it burning steadily on the cold October nights.

The view from the palace would have been beautiful, the majestic cathedral towering over the palace in the front, and a view of the surrounding countryside from the back. Preoccupied with news of the rebellion in the South, perhaps Richard took an evening stroll to clear his mind by enjoying the view of the countryside, cloaked in the breathtaking colours of a Lincolnshire autumn. As he watched the sun set in a mix of brilliant hues, it is possible his worries eased a bit.

There were other buildings in the palace complex. Another hall, often called the 'little hall', as well as a brewhouse, outside kitchen, and more apartments, were spread throughout. The palace also had a vineyard.

Visiting the Palace Today

Today the ruins of the palace are overseen by English Heritage and located near the cathedral. Visiting information may be found at English Heritage's website: www.english-heritage.org.uk/daysout/properties/lincoln-medieval-bishops-palace/. Postcode: LN2 1PU.

Lincoln Cathedral

As he was in Lincoln during the feast of St Edward, it is likely that Richard would have visited the massive cathedral. Even for a king used to luxury, it is easy to believe that Lincoln Cathedral would have filled him with a sense of awe. At that time each of the towers had tall spires of timber, covered with lead. One of these blew down and the others were later removed.

The cathedral church, known today as the Cathedral church of the Blessed Virgin Mary of Lincoln, was started soon after the Normans arrived. While several architectural styles can be detected in the building, most of the cathedral is Gothic, mainly Early English and Decorated. As with most cathedrals, the church was built in the form of a cross. The cathedral has three towers, each one elaborately decorated with pillars, tracery and carvings. It is possible to see the church from miles around, as it rests high on the hill above the surrounding land.

The western front of the cathedral is immense. The large door in the centre is covered by a stone archway, exquisitely decorated. Four carved columns stand on either side, some carved with grotesques. Above the door are carved figures of kings, originally painted and gilded, each with a stone canopy. Above them is the great western window, and above that is a smaller, circular window. At the top of the building is a pointed arch. Flanking the door on each side are two further statues. The other two arches are also recessed.

On the south side of the cathedral is the Galilee Porch. This porch was the entrance for the bishop, whose palace was to the south. The porch is arcaded with elaborate slender arches. Two huge doors, decorated with foliage, open into the transept. This gem of architecture is one of the highlights of a tour of the cathedral. This is the way Richard would have entered the church, coming from the Bishops' Palace.

The chapter house is in the shape of a decagon, with the roof supported by a single pillar. Twenty ribs issue out of the foliated capitals at the top of the pillar. Windows with pointed arches grace each part of the interior. Recesses for seats where the cathedral chapter would sit adorn the walls, and decorated grotesques abound in the room. If the room looks familiar, it might be because you recognise it from the film *The Da Vinci Code*.

As the cathedral was never part of a monastery, this room was never used by monks for daily meetings. Instead, it would have been used by the cathedral chapter. The chapter house also served as a parliament on at least one occasion.

The inside of the cathedral as we see it today has vastly changed from Richard's time. Very few of the many chantries that filled the cathedral remain. During the Reformation, the chantries were dissolved and St Hugh's shrine was stripped of all its jewels.

To the right of the altar is one of the chantries that did survive the Reformation. It is the chantry of Katherine Swynford, first mistress and later wife of John of Gaunt. It was John of Gaunt's legitimate son who seized the throne from Richard II and reigned as Henry IV. In addition to his legitimate children, Gaunt, with Katherine, produced illegitimate children who had the surname Beaufort. This family, later legitimised, would become powerful in England. It was from this branch that Henry Tudor would come; his mother was Margaret Beaufort.

Near the shrine of St Hugh lies Eleanor of Castile's visceral tomb. As she died near Lincoln, Edward I had her entrails interred in the cathedral here before moving her body to London.

Visiting Lincoln Cathedral Today

I recommend that you enter the minster yard through the Exchequer Gate. Before coming into the yard, take some time to admire the gate. Several stories tall, it has numerous windows. Three archways in the gate allowed pedestrian access to the minster yard, while the archway in the centre is slightly larger to permit access by horse and carriage. This gate was where tenants came to pay the church their rents. Offices for the men who kept the accounts would have been inside the gate. In Richard's time, the cathedral would have been protected by a large wall, embattled with turrets and housing several gateways.

Entering into the minster yard, you will approach the west front of the cathedral. Before you enter, it is well worth your time to simply enjoy this side of the building. If you brought binoculars, now would be a great time to pull them out and focus in on each carving. Take the time to walk around the cathedral before going inside. Lincoln Cathedral postcode: LN2 1PX.

My Favourite Place

I have visited Lincoln in the pouring rain and in the sparkling sun of a gorgeous June afternoon. No matter when I visit, one thing I always do is enter the minster yard. Standing outside of Lincoln Cathedral and just staring up at it is one of my favourite parts of a visit to the city. No description of its magnificence can prepare you for the first awe-inspiring glimpse. When the sun hits the stone, it seems to glow. Everywhere you look, there is an architectural gem to be found. No detail was overlooked in the construction of this building, which Victorian art critic John Ruskin called 'the most precious piece of architecture in the British Isles'.

I like to walk completely around the exterior, spending time at each section absorbing all the minute details. From the elegant tracery to the mouldings and canopies, each design is unique. Today, it is an immense structure. In the fifteenth century, it would have appeared even larger, as skyscrapers were unknown. At one time it was the largest building in England.

Lincoln Castle

As Lincoln Castle served as a gaol, it would not have provided as comfortable accommodation as the palace did, so it is unlikely that Richard would have visited the castle while in Lincoln. However, the castle was nearby, and he would definitely have been aware of it and the role it held in the city.

The castle was built during Norman times, high above the city on a steep hill. It was probably built on the site of an existing fortification. The keep was a typical shell keep, which was erected on a tall mound. It was most likely wooden at first, but was later rebuilt with stone. The castle walls are Norman, standing about twenty feet tall and measuring about ten feet thick. Inside the walls is an area of about six and a half acres.

The castle was unusual in that it had two tall mounds, each with a tower resting on it. The Norman castle consisted of the gateways, the keep, known as Lucy Tower, and the tower that later became known as the Observatory Tower. Much of the Observatory Tower was added in later years, although the base is Norman.

All that is left today of the medieval structure is the west gate, remnants of Lucy Tower, the Observatory Tower and parts of the walls. The east gate has been rebuilt several times. Visitors today can see a visual representation of where the barbican would have been, as it is marked with red granite.

Visiting Lincoln Castle Today

The castle is presently undergoing a considerable renovation and construction project that is due to be completed in the spring of 2015. The plan is ambitious, and includes restoring the towers and finishing a complete wall walk. There are also plans for an underground vault for the Magna Carta, as well as a new café and gift shop. This construction means that the keep and the Observatory Tower are closed to visitors. The prison is also closed, but most of the castle grounds and other buildings are still open. Postcode: LN1 3AA.

Salisbury, Wiltshire

Salisbury has its roots in nearby Old Sarum. The first Norman cathedral was established there and finished in 1092. For two centuries, the clergy and soldiers had to live in close proximity to one another, prompting Peter of Blois to say, 'Sarum is a place exposed to the wind, barren, dry, and solitary ... the church of Sarum is a captive on a hill; let us therefore in God's name, go down ... where the valleys will yield plenty of corn ... fields are of rich soil.' It would be some time before his vision was achieved.

Finally the cathedral was moved to the valley and through a charter of the king, a new town was established there. In 1220 the new site for the cathedral was consecrated and the first stones were laid. Soon the town of New Salisbury was a bustling centre of trade and commerce, surpassing many other previously established towns.

Richard and Salisbury

Richard's first recorded experience with Salisbury came in 1469 when he, as Duke of Gloucester, headed a special commission of oyer and terminer in the city. Henry Courtney and Thomas Hungerford were accused of plotting with Margaret of Anjou for the death and destruction of Edward IV. Even though other conspirators went free, these two were found guilty and executed.

By the time Richard was king, New Salisbury was the one of the largest towns in England. Its markets were busy with the wool trade, making it a prosperous place. In the autumn of 1483 it would become embroiled in the aftermath of an uprising against King Richard III.

While Richard was in the North to celebrate the investiture of his son Edward as Prince of Wales, an uprising was brewing in the South. Although it was known as Buckingham's rebellion, Henry Stafford was only part of the rebellion. The fact that Richard had showered Buckingham with offices made his defection all the more unbelievable and treacherous. Many of the rebels were local gentry. According to the Croyland chronicler, the gentry were alarmed by rumours of the death of Richard's nephews in the Tower and asked Henry, Earl of Richmond, to come to England and marry Edward's eldest daughter and heir.

Richard, hearing the news, made his way from Lincoln towards Pontefract and then to Salisbury. The Duke of Norfolk had quickly controlled the uprising in Kent, and Richard moved to deal with the rebels in Wiltshire. Buckingham, who was not popular in Wales, was having a difficult time raising troops. One calamity after another befell the duke, including flooded rivers which effectively trapped him. Slipping away from his men, he tried to escape, but he was betrayed and captured. Henry Tudor, arriving off the coast of England, learned of Buckingham's failure and fled, as did many of the rebel leaders.

Arriving in Salisbury, Richard's eye would have been caught by the sheer height of the spire adorning the cathedral church. The cathedral was built in the form of a cross. Running 473 feet from west to east and 229 feet from north to south, it was an immense structure. Built within one generation, the style kept mainly to Early English Gothic.

The west front was the main entrance during medieval times and was one of the most elaborately decorated sections of the cathedral. It still is today. Several layers of niches and pedestals dominate the front with the statues and canopies covered in delicate stonework. Two square towers rest on either side of the front and are covered with intricate designs. Upon entering through one of the three ornamented pointed archways, Richard would have stepped into the nave.

Today, as in Richard's time, giant stone pillars with slender columns of Purbeck marble on each side support the vaulted ceiling. Richard's view would have been blocked by a decorated screen but today a visitor can see all the way down the nave and through the choir. Finely detailed wall paintings would have adorned the nave, with a painted ceiling above those who entered the edifice.

Possibly Richard observed Mass here on the day of Buckingham's execution. He, with his mind troubled by the defection of someone he'd flooded with favours, would have enjoyed the peace and tranquillity offered here.

Richard would also have visited the shrine of St Osmund in the Trinity Chapel. While not as well known as Our Lady of Walsingham or St Edward the Confessor, St Osmund's was a site for pilgrimages as well. After Richard entered the chapel with its slender clusters of shafts supporting delicate rib vaulting, he would have made an offering at the shrine of the saint. Perhaps he even made an offering for the soul of Henry Stafford, whose execution was imminent.

Buckingham's execution was carried out in Salisbury's market square on Sunday 2 November. No one knows for sure where Buckingham was buried, although a tomb in Britford church has been attributed to him. An interesting story claims he was hurriedly buried nearby. In the nineteenth century a body was uncovered during renovations at the local inn. Missing both its head and one arm, the remains were thought by some to be Buckingham. Whether or not this was the case will probably never be ascertained, as the remains were destroyed.

News that Buckingham's execution had been carried out would have been rushed to Richard at his lodgings in Sherborne House, known today as King's House. Richard continued conducting state business and making plans for dealing with the other rebels now that Henry Stafford was no more.

Salisbury Cathedral

Today tourists enter the nave through the visitor's entrance to the side of the West Front. There is no admission fee but a donation is requested. Once inside the nave, take a minute to absorb its different features. Today you can see all the way to the high altar, which gives the cathedral an open feel. This tour will take you through the portions particular to Richard, but take some time to visit the other areas, particularly the choir with its painted ceiling.

Make your way to the north nave aisle. Richard would not have seen the elaborate tomb resting here as its occupant died years after Richard. Sir John Cheyne lies in this tomb, its effigy showing a man with long, flowing locks of hair, his hands pressed together in prayer. Cheyne had defected to Henry and fought against Richard at Bosworth. Rumoured to have been as tall as six feet, eight inches, Cheyne was a veritable giant in the medieval period.

Move on towards the back of the cathedral. Here is the Trinity Chapel. In the fifteenth century a shrine to St Osmund stood in the centre of the chapel. Today look for the shrine tomb of St Osmund located on the floor near the centre of the room. The shrine would have been much more sumptuous when Richard visited than it is today, but the chapel is still an architectural wonder. The vaulted ceiling rests delicately on slender shafts of Purbeck marble. The beautiful stained-glass window you see is modern, but there would have been painted or stained glass in the window during Richard's time as well.

On leaving the Trinity Chapel, make your way to the chapter house. Today the room is more famous for its Magna Carta exhibit than for the gorgeous medieval frieze that spans the wall. One pillar in the centre of the octagonal room supports the ceiling. After you look at the Magna Carta, take some time to walk around the room and examine the stone frieze with its biblical stories.

After you have experienced the wonders of the Cathedral church of the Blessed Virgin Mary, stay within the grounds of the cathedral close. This beautiful expanse was one entirely enclosed by walls. Parts of the walls, with their battlements, are believed to have been built with stone from the first cathedral church at Old Sarum.

Salisbury Cathedral is open daily for visitors. For more information on times and costs, see its website at www.salisburycathedral.org. uk/ or call +44 (0) 1722 555120.

King's House

From the cathedral, make your way straight across the green to the gateway and turn left. After a short walk, the King's House will be on your right. The history of the house dates back to the thirteenth century. At that time it was the home of the Abbot of Sherborne. The house was largely renovated in the early fifteenth century and much of its main core is still visible. At the time of Richard's visit the house was still known as Sherborne House. It was here he received the news that Buckingham had been executed, and it was here he finalised plans to deal with the rest of the uprising.

The house was further enlarged during the seventeenth century by then owner Sir Thomas Sadler. It was during Sadler's tenure that the home would receive the name 'King's House', as James I stayed in the home several times.

Visiting the King's House Today

Now home to the Salisbury Museum, the home still retains much of its stately look. Standing in the car park facing the building, look to your left. The vaulted stone porch you are looking at is part of the thirteenth-century home and would have been here when Richard visited. Step inside the porch and look up to see the intricate designs on the ceiling. While you are here take some time to visit the museum and step inside the house itself. The museum has interesting collections, including an exhibit on medieval Salisbury. From the pilgrim badge to the preserved medieval rodent, there are several interesting artefacts. Once back outside, take a moment to look at the exterior to see the fifteenth-century stonework. For more information on visiting the museum, see the website at www. salisburymuseum.org.uk/your-visit or call + 44 (0) 1722 332151. King's House postcode: SP1 2EN.

Buckingham Marker

Head back toward the market. Standing in the middle of the open area, find Debenhams department store. Here on the wall of the department store is a plaque that commemorates the death of Buckingham. The store stands on the site of the former Blue Boar Inn and the Saracen's Head Inn. Buckingham's execution was carried out near here.

Standing here today with the sound of buses going past and crowds of people rushing by with shopping bags filled to the brim, it is difficult to picture the grim scene. It was near this spot that the remains of a body missing a head and arm were supposedly uncovered. Today his ghost is said to haunt the department store.

Visiting Salisbury Today

Salisbury has several sites associated with Richard and the Wars of the Roses. The cathedral church will take the longest to visit. All of the sites could be visited within half a day if you rushed, but by taking your time you can absorb some of the ambience of the area. If you are driving in for a day trip, I suggest you use the park-and-ride scheme offered by the Wiltshire Council. For more information, see www.wiltshire.gov.uk/parkingtransportandstreets/carparking/parkandride.htm. If you are inclined to drive to the city itself, follow the signs for city centre. Trains are available from London Waterloo. See www.nationalrail.co.uk/. Salisbury Cathedral postcode: SP1 2EJ.

Exeter, Devon

People have been living in Exeter for thousands of years. The city was occupied by both the Romans and the Saxons, before giving way to the Normans. The city was bustling with trade throughout the medieval period and was a commercial centre for the region. The city was also home to several parish churches as well as a large cathedral.

Richard and Exeter

After leaving Salisbury, Richard quickly headed west. After a brief stay in Bridport, Richard approached Exeter. Richard Izacke, in his book *Remarkable Antiquities of the City of Exeter*, gives an account of Richard's reception. Richard was met at the east gate, the principal entrance of the city, by the mayor and 'his brethren' clothed in sumptuous robes. After a warm greeting, the recorder, dressed in a scarlet gown, offered Richard a congratulatory oration. The mayor then presented Richard with the maces and the keys to the city. Richard 'graciously' accepted the purse of money offered by the city before giving the maces and keys back to the mayor.

He was then led in a grand procession through the city to

the cathedral quarter. The cathedral close was surrounded by a twelve-foot wall and could be entered only through several gates. Richard would have entered through the three-storey Broad Gate from the High Street. Here he would have been met by the ecclesiastics at the brightly painted west front of the cathedral before retiring to the elegant comfort of the Bishop's Palace. John Hooker, Chamberlain of Exeter, records his visit in his *Commonplace Book*, now found in the Exeter city archives. Hooker says that Richard was '... conducted to the bishopys palace where he was lodged'. Richard's men were lodged throughout the town and entertainments were planned for them.

Despite the entertainments, Richard would have been busy dealing with the aftermath of Buckingham's rebellion. While in Exeter he issued a commission to the Earl of Surrey, among others, to summon men to the counties of Kent and Sussex. He also issued commissions to arrest and imprison any rebels captured.

While the palace had its own chapel where Richard would have heard Mass, he would also have likely visited the cathedral church of St Peter at least once during his stay. After making his way through the nave with its clustered columns of Purbeck marble and elaborate Gothic vaulting with gilded bosses, he would have observed the service. At some point, his eye would have been drawn to the east window with its beautiful fourteenth-century stained glass. Perhaps he found a bit of peace here from the turmoil of the previous month.

Visiting Exeter Today
Exeter is a city proud of its medieval heritage. Several self-guided heritage trails are available to walk. Most of the locations related to Richard are no longer extant. During the reign of Henry VII the great East Gate was attacked by Perkin Warbeck and eventually fell to its ruin. It was rebuilt but was once again destroyed. None of Exeter's gates remain but a great deal of its walls do.

The Bishop's Palace was largely redone throughout the years. In the nineteenth century, massive rebuilding occurred, so little remains of the crenellated palace where Richard stayed. The great hall of the palace has been converted into smaller offices. The chapel is still attached to the palace but appears quite different than it did in Richard's reign. The Bishop's Palace is closed to visitors although the grounds may be visited with a town tour. The gatehouse of Bishop's Palace still remains, although it has also been greatly changed.

The Cathedral church of St Peter is open for visitors daily. Be sure to visit the bishop's throne, the medieval clock and the east window. For more information about current hours see www.exeter-cathedral.org.uk/visiting/visitorsinformation.ashx. The cathedral offers armchair visitors a virtual tour of the cathedral which can be found at www.exeter-cathedral.org.uk/visiting/virtual-tour-.ashx. Sometimes the cathedral may be closed for special events, so call ahead at +44 (0) 1392 285983. Exeter Cathedral postcode: EX1 1HS.

Exeter also offers a park-and-ride scheme for drivers. For more information, see www.exeter.gov.uk/index.aspx?articleid=9924. Trains run from London Paddington to Exeter. Check the National Rail website at www.nationalrail.co.uk/.

Cambridge, Cambridgeshire

A settlement existed in Cambridge long before the Norman invasion. By the time the area became a haven for scholars it was already quite large. A centre for commercial activity due to its proximity to the river, the town attracted clergy as well as merchants. By the time Richard and Anne visited in March 1484, Cambridge was well known as a place of learning.

King's College
The history of King's College dates back to the 1440s when Henry VI founded a college dedicated to St Nicholas. Stones from nearby Cambridge Castle were used in the building works, and soon afterwards, Henry further enlarged his foundation. The buildings already completed became known as the Old Court. Henry issued specific directions for how he wanted the buildings of his college to look. The chapel would occupy the entire north side of the large courtyard. On the east and south side of the court would be chambers with the hall and library on the west.

Work was interrupted by the Wars of the Roses. *The History of the King's Works* quotes Provost Wodelarke's memorandum as saying:

> When Henry the Sixth ... was taken prisoner by the Earls of Salisbury and Warwick, they pledged their word to him ... that they would hasten the completion of his church and royal building operations in Cambridge ... before long, however, fresh disturbances broke out in the kingdom ... royal letters were sent under the signet to all receivers of the duchy ... to forward all the money they had collected to the king and his council at London.

The work on the college continued slowly during the subsequent years, but little was done during the 1460s. Richard III contributed greatly to the work on the college. In 1484 he directed that building should go on in haste. He was responsible for building quite a bit of the chapel, as well as providing his glazier to see that the windows were properly finished. According to *The History of the King's Works*, by Richard's death two of the side chapels had been both vaulted and glazed and five bays in the chapel were complete.

Queens' College
Originally founded by Andrew Dokett as St Bernard's College, the college was renamed 'The Queen's College of St Margaret and St Bernard' after Margaret of Anjou received permission to refound it. Building was started immediately, but as with King's College, the breakout of hostilities stopped it. During the reign of Edward IV, his wife, Elizabeth Woodville, became the college's supporter. When Richard III came to the throne, Queen Anne continued the tradition as its patroness.

Richard and Cambridge
As king and queen, Richard and Anne's reception in Cambridge would have been similar to that of Richard's in Oxford. He and Anne would have been met at the outskirts of the town by the leading citizens, the regents and the non-regents. A cross would have been carried before the king in the procession which would take Richard and Anne to their lodgings.

Richard granted money both to the university and to King's College. He planned to re-establish the building works at King's and granted funds to do so. Richard and Anne both granted extensive endowments, including land grants, to Queens' College as well. Unfortunately for the college, most of the grants were taken away during Henry VII's reign. After their visit to the university, it established an annual Mass of Salus Populi in their honour to be held on 2 May until after Richard's death. At that time, a requiem Mass would be said for him.

Visiting Cambridge Today

Regrettably, no record survives to tell where Richard and Anne spent the night while in Cambridge. Perhaps they stayed at either King's or Queens' colleges, or even at nearby Barnwell Priory. While we do not know where they passed their nights, we can be assured that they would have visited both King's and Queens' colleges.

When visiting King's College, step inside the college grounds, then turn and face the chapel. Looking to the right of the building, you can make out the portion that Henry VI started and that Richard commissioned to be completed. If he had not died at Bosworth, this building would likely have been completed much earlier than it was. I recommend that you attend the evensong service at King's College as the acoustics are incredible.

For armchair travellers, King's College offers a virtual tour of the chapel at www.kings.cam.ac.uk/chapel/virtual-tour/index.html. From this site you can also experience a virtual tour of the grounds and library.

Both King's and Queens' colleges are open for guests at certain times of the year. It is always best to check ahead to avoid disappointment. For more information on visiting King's College, see www.kings.cam.ac.uk/visit/admission.html. For Queens' College visitor information, see www.queens.cam.ac.uk/general-information/tourist-information.

If arriving by car, park in one of Cambridge's park-and-ride lots, as the town is difficult to manoeuvre. For more information on the park-and-ride scheme, visit www.cambridgeshire.gov.uk/transport/around/park-ride/. There are frequent rail services from London King's Cross or London Liverpool Street. If arriving by train, you can either walk into town or take the city's bus service. If you prefer arriving by coach, National Express runs a service from London. See www.nationalexpress.com for more information.

King's College postcode: CB2 1ST and Queens' College postcode: CB3 9ET.

Durham Cathedral, Durham

Perched high on a rock above the River Wear, Durham Cathedral appears to rise out of the land surrounding it. Begun in the late eleventh century, the cathedral has its roots on the Holy Isle of Lindisfarne. After the death of Cuthbert, a bishop at Lindisfarne, miracles were said to have occurred at his tomb and he was canonised. The body was first moved during the invasion of the Danes, and after a period of several moves, finally came to rest in Durham.

The Saxon church that was built to house the saint's body no longer exists as it was replaced by the Normans. The priory established here was Benedictine, and the Norman foundation stone of the cathedral was laid in 1093. Said to represent Noah's Ark in its proportions, most of the church as Richard would have known it had been completed by the fourteenth century.

Richard and Durham

Richard was often generous to religious establishments, and his experience with Durham was no exception. Both he and Anne were admitted into the fraternity of St Cuthbert. According to Josephine Wilkinson, this was a rare privilege for those with a strong devotion to the saint. As Richard and Anne made several pilgrimages to the shrine, this devotion is obvious. Perhaps, as Wilkinson suggests, Richard felt a connection to the saint who had once served as a soldier.

Durham historian James Raine described the procession that Richard and Anne would have witnessed on St Cuthbert's day. He said the banner was carried in a procession, and 'whenever it [the banner of St Cuthbert] was carried in procession, it was the Clerk's office to attend it, with his surplice on, with a fine red painted staff, having a fork or cleft ... which cleft was lined with soft silk. Four men went along with the banner. The banner cloth was fringed and made of red velvet and wrought with flowers of green silk and gold.' If Richard and Anne were present for the procession, they would have been able to see the banner cloth. After watching the procession, it may be that Richard and Anne were invited to the feast that the bishop and monks partook of on their saint's day. As nobles had been invited before, it was likely that they would have been, too.

On one particular visit in 1484, King Richard III presented the monks at the altar of St Cuthbert with his parliament robe of blue velvet richly wrought with great lions of pure gold. Even with the other rich gifts that royalty had given the church, this gift was specifically noted.

As Anne and Richard had family connections at Durham, this cathedral may have been one of their favourites. Members of the Neville family had been buried there, and Richard Neville, Earl of Salisbury, had also been admitted into the fraternity of St Cuthbert.

Visiting Durham Cathedral Today

It is hard not to be impressed by the enormous scope of Durham Cathedral as one crosses the Palace Green. At 469 feet long, the cathedral almost takes up the entire area in front of you as you approach. Before entering the cathedral, look at the replica of the Sanctuary Knocker on the north door. Tradition states that those grabbing the Sanctuary Knocker were entitled to sanctuary in the cathedral.

As one enters the nave, the sacred space seems to soar endlessly upwards. The large columns along the nave are twins and each set is different, with every column having elaborately carved detail. Brilliant today in its stonework, one can imagine the bright colours that would have graced the room dazzling all who entered into the cathedral.

The tomb of John, Lord Neville, can be found in the south arcade. Ralph Neville's monument can be found nearby. Today both tombs are damaged, but it is possible to picture them the way they once appeared. Pause here for a moment and imagine Anne and Richard looking at the tombs and monuments to members of the Neville family.

The screen behind the high altar was a gift from John Neville to the cathedral. Stunning today, it was even more splendid in Richard and Anne's time. In the fifteenth century, both the screen and its more than 100 alabaster statues would have been brightly painted. Unfortunately, these medieval statues were removed and hidden so well after the Reformation that they have never been found. The screen itself was divided into three parts, with the second and third open so that the statues could be seen in the canopies. The Neville coat of arms could be found above the doorways.

As you make your way into the Shrine of St Cuthbert, realise that it would have appeared much different to Richard and Anne. They would have seen the shrine elaborately decorated with precious stones and silver, and gilded. Today a black slab marks the place where the saint's body rests, the shrine having been destroyed in the Dissolution.

The cathedral is open daily and is free to visit, although donations are suggested. It is always wise to phone or email before visiting to ensure the cathedral will be open during your visit. For more information regarding the cathedral, visit its website at www. durhamcathedral.co.uk/visit/opening-times or call +44 (0) 191 386 4266.

Scarborough, North Yorkshire

The death of Richard III probably affected Scarborough more than most towns. The town had recently been granted a charter by Richard, which provided that the town would have a mayor, sheriff and twelve aldermen. In addition, the town and surrounding area would be its own county, separated from York. It must have been with sad hearts that the citizens learned of the king's death. This would be especially true after Henry VII did not recognise the charter, leaving Scarborough in the same state as it had been in previously.

Richard had a long association with Scarborough. In 1474 he exchanged Anne's lands in Derbyshire and Hertfordshire for the manor of Cottingham and the castle and lordship of Scarborough. The great royal castle of Scarborough was now in the hands of the Duke of Gloucester. His ties with the town would last until his death.

The port of Scarborough held importance as it was a safe harbour for a navy. Its natural defences were strengthened by the addition of a jetty and quay. The pier had to be repaired often, but the harbour was considered a safe place for ships to rest.

Richard spent two weeks in Scarborough in the June and July of 1484. At the time, he was still considering war with Scotland. Some successes had been made, leading the *Croyland Chronicle* to say that 'in the same maritime theatre he had remarkable success against the Scots'. Eventually, Richard would give up the idea of war with Scotland in favour of preparing for an invasion by Henry Tudor. To that end, he met with ambassadors from Scotland at his castle in Nottingham to secure peace with the Scots.

Scarborough Castle

Scarborough Castle was begun by William, Count of Aumale, during the reign of Stephen. Eventually it fell into the hands of Henry II and would remain a royal castle, with the exception of its ownership by Richard while Duke of Gloucester, until James I. It was Henry II who was responsible for building the great stone keep.

Situated on rocky headland, the castle had a prime defensive location overlooking the harbour. Protected on three sides by cliffs nearly 300 feet high and by the sea, it could only be reached from the town via a great drawbridge over the double ditch.

Richard and Anne, along with their retinue, would have crossed the drawbridge and entered the outer area of the castle. Making their way past the Barbican Tower, which had been built during the reign of Henry III, they would have continued up the hill towards the inner bailey, with the keep dominating the view on their right.

The keep, with each of its four walls measuring more than fifty feet across and rising more than ninety feet high, was both a majestic and formidable sight. With its turrets and embattlement walks, combined with the thickness of the walls at twelve feet thick, it was a strong defensive structure. Described in the nineteenth century as having three storeys, each vaulted and containing strong arches, it would have also had an elegant interior.

Tradition holds that Anne stayed in what was known as the

Queen's Chamber along the curtain wall. In the survey of 1538, this building was described as being four storeys high and six yards long. Records indicate that the chamber had its own porch. Anne would have been used to staying in luxurious surroundings and she would have brought some items with her as well as made use of those available. Richard likely stayed in the keep or in another part of the Queen's Chamber. There is a tradition that Richard lodged in a house within the town, now known as the King Richard III house, but no evidence remains to prove this claim.

Following in Richard and Anne's Footsteps

Entering the castle today, you will follow in Richard and Anne's footsteps as you leave the visitor centre and head towards the inner bailey. Even in its ruined condition, the keep still presents a formidable view as you make your way up the hill. Richard and Anne would not recognise the Master Gunner's House as it was not built until the eighteenth century. Wander into the large green expanse and head towards the ruined shell of the keep. The entrance is up a stairway, as it likely would have been in Richard's time. According to the Scarborough Castle guidebook, three sides of the keep had a 'buttress-like projection down its centre'. On the west side of the keep, a spiral staircase ran upwards, forming a projecting turret.

The east side of the building is almost intact. From here you can see one of the two pairs of rounded windows that lit the third floor. The second floor contains two sets of windows, each separated by pairs of slender columns with capitals. This floor was probably for the king's chambers. Large archways which may have contained windows adorn the first floor.

After taking time to visit the keep, make your way over to the curtain wall to see the chamber block. All that is left of the beautiful 'Queen's Chamber', which attached to King John's chamber block, is the basement of the building. By 1538, the building was ruined, so it may have already been in a state of disrepair when Anne lodged there.

The views from the headland are incredible. Take some time to wander around, passing the ruins of the king's hall, the Roman Signal Station and Chapel of Our Lady, before heading to the viewing platform to take advantage of the views out over the sea and the town below.

Visiting Scarborough Castle Today
The castle is under the care of English Heritage. For more information about opening times, see www.english-heritage.org.uk/daysout/ properties/scarborough-castle/prices-and-opening-times, or call the property at +44 (0) 1723 372451. Parking is available within the town. Scarborough Castle postcode: YO11 1HY.

Part VII

Richard's Final Days

Richard travelled a great deal throughout his kingdom during his short reign. Even while on progress, he was worried about the threat of Henry Tudor. He was also busy quelling rumours that he planned to marry his niece, Elizabeth. Having lost both his wife and his son in a short time, he was still in the process of grieving.

Hospital of the Knights of St John of Jerusalem in Clerkenwell, London

The order of St John has its roots in Jerusalem, where a group of monks established a hospice for Christians on pilgrimage. This later became a hospital and members of the order became known as the Knights Hospitallers or as the Hospitallers of St John. The order came to England and established a priory church at Clerkenwell in the twelfth century.

The order had a long history of entertaining royalty. King John stayed here for a month, King Edward I and Eleanor stayed here soon after their marriage and King Henry IV also spent time with the Knights Hospitallers. Richard would come to the priory for another reason, however.

After rumours swirled through London claiming that Richard was planning to marry his niece, Elizabeth, he felt he had to publicly deny this. At a council of civic authorities in the priory's hall, Richard appeared to denounce the rumours as false and scandalous. He forbade anyone to say anything further regarding the matter.

Visiting the Museum Today

The museum of the Order tells the story of the history of the Knights Hospitallers, and includes many relics, such as paintings and armour. Unfortunately, due to the Dissolution, very little remains of the medieval priory. The Tudor gate, where the museum is housed, and the priory's twelfth-century crypt are all that remains. Richard would never have seen the Tudor gate as it was built after his death. To get to the museum, get off at the Farringdon tube stop. The museum is a short walk. For more about visiting the museum, see the museum's website: www.museumstjohn.org.uk/index.html. Postcode: EC1M 4DA.

Kenilworth Castle, Warwickshire

The red sandstone of Kenilworth Castle exudes a rosy hue in the warmth of the summer sun. One of the most picturesque ruins in all of England, Kenilworth was begun in 1120 by Geoffrey de Clinton and eventually fell into royal hands. Through the years, Kenilworth has seen major rebuilding works. Henry III built the outer wall on the south side of the castle and repaired the chapel, adding a royal seat for himself and his queen. John of Gaunt was responsible for the construction of the magnificent great hall. Henry V built a manor house, which was called 'Pleasance in the marsh', at Kenilworth and spent much time there. With just one look at the castle, it is easy to understand why it was a favourite.

Richard and Kenilworth

Richard was at Kenilworth in May and June of 1485. Records indicate that he used it as a base from which to visit other areas nearby, as he was at Coventry for a few days in June before coming back to Kenilworth. He would leave Kenilworth and head to Nottingham, where he would spend most of his last days.

While at Kenilworth, Richard probably took time to hunt in

its park and perhaps even visited the Pleasance on the edge of the mere. The mere at Kenilworth was large, and the Pleasance could be reached by boat from the castle. The Pleasance was a timber-framed building with towers on the north, south, and east corners.

Visit of 1485

Journeying from Berkhamsted and a visit with his mother, Richard and his retinue would have entered Kenilworth through the Mortimer Tower. Today there is little left of the two towers of the embattled gatehouse. The king would have entered the outer court as the portcullis was raised. Trees would not have eclipsed his view of the magnificent group of buildings which made up the inner court.

Although the chambers of the impressive keep were still in good condition during his visit, he would have lodged in the state apartments. However, some of the nobility accompanying him may have made the chambers in the keep their lodging. Turning slightly left across the green expanse, he would have made his way to the richly ornamented state apartments. The building as Richard would have seen it is hard to pick out as much of it has been lost through the centuries. Thanks to surveys from the sixteenth century, we can reconstruct some of its layout.

Facing the octagonal porch, you can make out the entrance from the inner court. Richard would have entered through the door and made his way up a spiral staircase to the first-floor lobby, which was lit by elegant windows with fine tracery. He would have entered into the great chamber, which is believed to have served as an audience chamber. Here, under a great cloth of estate, he would have received visitors or discussed matters of state. With an imminent invasion by Henry Tudor threatening, he had much to consider. His private dining chamber would have been the next room, and beyond that was his bedchamber. While the audience chamber possibly served as a dining area for his important staff, it is likely that Richard would have dined most of the time in his private dining area.

Retracing your steps back outside, turn and face the porch. The building to your right once was John of Gaunt's splendid great hall. An enormous building with large windows under pointed arches, the hall was a symbol of Gaunt's status, both as a prince of England and as the self-titled King of Castile and León through his marriage to the Spanish heiress, Constanza. One of the sons of Edward III, Gaunt served his nephew Richard II loyally, but his son, Henry Bolingbroke, would usurp his cousin's crown to become Henry IV. This decision would have long-lasting consequences for his descendants, as his grandson's crown would also be usurped by Richard's elder brother, Edward IV.

We do not know if Richard used the great hall during his visit as it was usually reserved for great occasions. It is possible that he did have a grand meal here. When you enter today, you are directly below the hall, which was on the first floor. Look up to make out the details. The grandeur of the room is still obvious today, even in its ruined state. It is easy to picture the scene: Richard sitting at the dais, his cloth of estate above him. Roaring fires blazed in each of the six fireplaces, as the chill of a May evening rolled in. Tapestries adorned each of the walls, laughter pealed and wine flowed. Servants moved from the kitchen and down the stairs to the wine cellar to fetch more wine for the feast.

After the meal, the guests could wander over to the deeply recessed windows with their stone seats to observe the view. Perhaps some form of entertainment would have passed the time. Richard may have enjoyed the view out of the oriel with its three large windows. Whether his thoughts turned to his family or whether he waved melancholia aside to enjoy an evening we will never know. It would be Richard's last May.

Visiting Kenilworth Castle Today

There is so much to see at Kenilworth that you should allot at least a half day for your visit. Besides the rooms already discussed, you will need some time to visit Leicester's buildings, the stables and the grounds. Only the earthworks of the Pleasance remain today, and these are on private grounds.

The castle is managed by English Heritage. For more information, visit the website at www.english-heritage.org.uk/daysout/properties/kenilworth-castle/ or call +44 (0) 1926 852078.

Leicester, Leicestershire

As the final place he visited before his army clashed with that of Henry, Earl of Richmond, Leicester has always had an association with Richard. However, after the discovery of his bones under a car park in 2012, Leicester experienced a boom in Richard-related tourism and in 2015 the king was reinterred in Leicester Cathedral.

There has been major controversy regarding Richard's reburial in Leicester. Many Ricardians advocated for reburial in York, saying that Richard wanted to be buried there. Others felt that Westminster, where Richard's wife was buried, was a better choice. Still others declared the St George's Chapel at Windsor, where both Edward IV and Henry VI are buried, was the best location. In addition, there was disagreement regarding the service that was used during his reburial. This king, who has stirred controversy throughout centuries, is continuing to inspire heated debate even today. One could even say he is inspiring the most debate since he was placed in his grave in Leicester. One thing, however, cannot be disputed. Richard was initially buried in Leicester, whether he wanted to be or not, and he is now, once again, buried under the soil of the city where he rested for more than 500 years.

The days leading up to the fateful battle were not Richard's first time in Leicester. The king had visited the city before, having stayed in Leicester Castle near the start of his reign. The two visits, both in August, were polar opposites of each other. The first would have seen Richard full of optimism about the future of his family and his reign; the second would have seen a Richard who had lost both his wife and legitimate son, facing a foe who was trying to usurp his throne. His final visit would be post mortem and was an inglorious end to a promising reign.

Richard's re-entry to the city was very different from his exit. As one chronicle said,

And Richard, late king, as gloriously as he by the morning departed from that town, so as irreverently was he that afternoon brought into that town, for his body despoiled to the skin ... with ... filth was brought to a church in Leicester for all men to wonder upon ... [translated into a modern version]

Leicester Castle

Situated near the River Soar, a fortification has rested on this hill since at least the eleventh century. The first castle built upon this spot was of motte-and-bailey construction. A stone edifice would replace it in the twelfth century, with the Great Hall being built soon after. The castle was home to the earls of Lancaster and Leicester.

Robert de Beaumont is believed to have been responsible for restructuring the castle in stone, and his son, Robert le Bossu, is given credit for the construction of the Great Hall. After the death of Simon de Montfort, Henry III gave the castle to his son, Edmund. The earls of Lancaster probably spared no expense in turning the castle into an opulent home. As in most castles, the walls would have been plastered and either painted or hung with tapestries.

Although parliaments had previously been held in the Great Hall of Leicester Castle, the one that was called in 1426 earned a unique moniker, 'The Parliament of Bats'. Growing tensions between Henry Beaufort, the Bishop of Winchester, and Humphrey, Duke of Gloucester, led to fears of an outbreak of violence. Warned to leave weapons at home, the lords' retainers had armed themselves with cudgels, leading to the nickname. Another parliament held here in 1450 was interrupted by the king rushing back to London due to Jack Cade's rebellion in Kent.

Not only did Leicester host parliaments, but it also received other marks of royal favour. Edward IV granted the city the right to a fair. The grant, which allowed for a fair to be held yearly for seven days, was witnessed by both Richard and George. Richard granted the city an annuity in November of 1484. The *Records of the Borough of Leicester* say that Richard 'in consideration of the true and faithful service which our well-beloved Mayor and burgesses of our town of Leicester have rendered to us, as also in relief of their costs had and borne in this behalf, as also of the great ruin and decay in which the aforesaid town now is grants to them a certain annuity of 20 for twenty years ...'

The Great Hall underwent substantial renovations in the centuries following Richard's death. The roof was replaced in the early part of the sixteenth century, and years later a brick face was added to the building. Despite the rebuilding, we can reconstruct how it might have looked by checking various accounts. With walls built of sandstone, it was a wide open space, consisting of large wooden columns supporting the roof and dividing the nave, forming side aisles. The entire room was lit with round-arched narrow windows. Richard would have taken his place on the dais at the top of the room, resting under his cloth of estate. The excitement would have been almost palpable as Richard and his trusted councillors continued the difficult business of running the country. One of his concerns while at the castle was the protection of English merchants as they traded in France.

We know Richard visited the castle in August 1483, as he wrote a letter to the King of France from here, replying to a short letter from Louis XI regarding Richard's elevation to king. Richard's reply was much more eloquent than Louis' letter and was written to enquire about what protection France would offer English merchants in the country:

> My lord, my cousin, I have seen the letters you have sent me by Buckingham herald, whereby I understand that you wish to have my amity, of which I am very glad, in good form and manner, for I do not mean to break such truces as have hitherto been concluded between the late king of most noble memory, my brother deceased, and you, for the term of the same ... Upon which matter, in order that my said subjects and merchants be not deceived under the shadow of the same, I pray you that by my servant, this bearer, one of the grooms of my stable, you will let me know by writing your full intention, and at the same time if you desire anything that I can do for you, that I may do it with good will. And farewell, my lord my cousin. Written in my castle of Leicester, the 18th day of August.

Louis did not reply to the letter as he died on 30 August that year. He was succeeded by his young son, Charles VIII, with his aunt Anne acting as regent. Had Richard lived it is interesting to wonder what the relations would have been between the two countries. Would Richard have pressed the advantage when the great lords of France rebelled against Anne?

The castle was already in a sad state of decay during the reign of

Henry VIII. It may have already been in a state of disrepair upon Richard's visit in 1483, which may explain why he is believed to have stayed at the Blue Boar Inn on his last visit to Leicester.

The area around the castle consisted of several buildings within and right outside the inner bailey. One of these buildings, St Mary de Castro, served as the castle's chapel. Few of the buildings which once surrounded the mighty castle remain today.

The Rebellion of 1483 and Leicester Castle

Shortly after his coronation, Richard went on progress. While he was in the North, mutterings and murmurings turned into outright rebellion. As Richard proudly watched the investiture of his young son, Edward, as Prince of Wales, rebels in Kent and the South were starting to organise to secure the release of the princes from the Tower.

Richard learned of the rebellion while in Lincoln, and his letter (a part of which is shared in the Lincoln section) shows his torment at the betrayal of Buckingham. The uprising is best known as Buckingham's rebellion. This is a misnomer, as Buckingham was only a part of the rebellion. Buckingham had been highly favoured by Richard, receiving among other offices those of the Constable of England, Chief Justice and Chamberlain in North and South Wales, and Constable and Steward of the King's Castles in Salop and Hereford. Why Buckingham chose to throw away the favour of a king who had rewarded him high above all others is still a subject of contention among historians. Perhaps he held a belief that he might be offered the throne, but that does not explain why he began to support Henry Tudor. Historian Charles Ross offered a plausible reason for Buckingham's defection: fear. As Richard grew increasingly unpopular, Buckingham may have believed that he would be the target of men's hatred. Without some sort of primary source, perhaps a letter from Buckingham, it is likely we will never know his reasons.

The rebellion included a large number of gentry. The Croyland chronicler says that once rumours began spreading about the death of the princes in the Tower, those involved in the uprising realised that they needed someone new at the head of the rebellion and sent for Henry, Earl of Richmond. The chronicler also says that it was the Duke of Buckingham who dispatched the message to Henry, on the advice of Bishop Morton, who was prisoner in Brecknock Castle. Historians have suggested that it was the influence of Bishop Morton that convinced Buckingham to turn on Richard. Regardless, Henry was asked to come to England and marry Edward's eldest daughter, and with the princes' alleged death, his heir, Elizabeth.

Richard had learned of Buckingham's defection while in Lincoln and he was soon mustering troops. He stopped at Leicester Castle on his way from Lincoln to stay for a few days, probably awaiting the men he had summoned. From Leicester he headed to Coventry.

The rebellion seemed flawed from its beginning. The Kentish rising occurred prematurely and the Duke of Norfolk learned of it quickly and protected London. Buckingham was not liked in Wales, and had a difficult time raising troops. Some of his retainers rose up and captured the duke's castle in Brecon. Another subject, Sir Humphrey Stafford, blocked the exits across the upper Severn by destroying the bridges. Then the capricious weather struck, flooding the rivers and keeping Buckingham and his men trapped. He was betrayed by one of his servants and captured. Once the news of Buckingham's capture and the news of Richard's army advancing south reached them, many of the other rebel leaders fled to France. Thomas St Leger, Richard's former brother-in-law, was one of the few caught and executed. His memorial is in St George's Chapel in Windsor. Buckingham was executed in Salisbury on 2 November 1483. A few of the leaders received pardons from Richard.

Visiting Leicester Castle Today

Very little remains of the castle or its outbuildings today. The best place to experience the castle atmosphere is in the Castle Gardens. Within this serene setting stand the remains of the medieval castle walls. Surrounded by dense vegetation, the cleared top of the motte is fairly flat today, as it has been lowered several feet since Richard's day. A photograph from 1888 shows the motte with few trees surrounding it dominated by the towering spire of St Mary de Castro.

The Great Hall is open for special events and for private groups. For more information, contact the Guildhall on +44 (0) 116 253 2569. Great Hall of Leicester Castle postcode: LE1 5FQ.

St Mary de Castro

St Mary de Castro means St Mary of the Castle. A college consisting of a dean and twelve secular canons was established here in the twelfth century by Robert de Beaumont. Through the years the church saw a number of royal guests, including Henry VI. On Whitsunday in 1426, Henry's uncle Bedford knighted him as part of the closing ceremonies of the 'Parliament of Bats'. There is some confusion as to whether the knighting ceremony happened here or in the Great Hall of Leicester Castle, but the fact it was a religious day gives support to the theory that the ceremony occurred in the chapel. Supposedly, after he was conferred with knighthood, Henry knighted the other men present, beginning with an adolescent Richard, Duke of York. It is hard to believe that Henry, only four years old, was able to wield the heavy sword. Instead, it is more likely the knighting was done in the king's name.

Richard was at the castle in 1483, and given his reputation as a pious man, he probably visited the chapel. Even though he presumably did not stay at the castle on his other visits, he may have taken solace within the chapel's comforting, familiar walls. One feature he would have noticed on his visit is the fine example of an elaborate Norman sedilia in the chancel. He would not have rested on the pews that are in the church today, as pews in chapels were a much later addition.

Church lore says that his body rested here briefly after Bosworth before being buried in Leicester. It is possible, but in all likelihood Richard's body was taken straight to the Annunciation of St Mary in the Newarke.

Visiting St Mary de Castro Today

St Mary de Castro closed for several months in 2014 due to safety issues, but reopened in August 2014. Its great spire was removed due to safety concerns. Check the church's website for more information at www.stmarydecastro.org.uk/.

The Church of the Annunciation of the Blessed Virgin Mary in the Newarke

In 1330, Henry, Earl of Lancaster, received a royal licence to establish a hospital at Leicester, which was founded in honour of the Annunciation of Virgin Mary. In the middle of the fourteenth century, the hospital became a college, with a dean, several canons and vicars. It continued in its care of the poor and infirm.

One of the patrons of the college was John of Gaunt, who granted money to help with the completion of the college church. Gaunt left instructions for a chantry chapel with two chaplains in his will. Another patron of the church seems to have been William, Lord Hastings, who helped the church secure lands.

It is possible that during one of his visits to Leicester Richard passed by this church, which had been built in the mid-fourteenth century. One wonders if he felt the proverbial ghost walk across his grave as he gazed upon the church. It would be here in August 1485 that Richard's bloody body would be displayed after Bosworth, resting among the tombs of prominent Lancastrians.

Visiting the Church Today

During the reign of Edward VI, the college was suppressed and fell to ruin. All that is left today is the remains of two arches. These arches are in the basement of the Hawthorn Building of the De Montfort University and are not usually open to the public.

Turret and Magazine Gateways

Richard's body would have been brought to the church through one of two gateways – either the Turret Gateway or the Magazine Gateway. The Turret Gate separated the castle precincts from the Newarke, and was built with defence in mind as the grooves for a portcullis were found. When it was built, it was probably also embattled, but the upper storey was destroyed in the nineteenth century. The remains of this structure, built in 1422, can still be seen today.

The Magazine Gateway is much more imposing with its height and vaulted passageway. Two arches cut through its massive shape. Carriages and horses entered through the larger arch with its vaulted stone ceiling, while pedestrian traffic came through the narrower arch. Probably placed in a wagon, Richard's body would have passed through here on its way to Greyfriars.

The Blue Boar Inn

Richard arrived in Leicester on 20 August 1485. After travelling from Nottingham Castle to Beskwood, he stayed there for a few days before leaving for Leicester. Polydore Vergil said that Richard arrived in Leicester slightly before the sun set on the town. Tradition says that on this occasion, he decided to stay at the Blue Boar Inn. Legend has it that he brought his own bed, which, according to Amy Licence in her book *Richard III: The Road to Leicester*, was not an unusual practice for the time. Historian John Ashdown-Hill points out that he can find no mention of the inn prior to 1570. While this casts doubt on the fact that Richard stayed here, many historians accept that he did, so the location has been included. Whether Richard was here or not, this location is deeply engrained in the accepted tradition of Richard's story, and many people want to visit it.

The Blue Boar had been built in the fifteenth century, and as a large coaching inn was used to wealthy travellers staying within its walls. Richard's welcome would have been effusive, as the innkeeper did his best to make the king's stay a pleasant one. Depending on the weather, a large fire might have been blazing in the fireplace with its decorative moulding as Richard and his closest advisors made their way into the room for a meal before Richard retired. The best room would have been reserved for Richard. If he did bring his bed with him, it would have been carried in and assembled before he retired.

After awakening and breaking his fast, Richard would have left the inn early the next day to ride out to Bosworth. Perhaps he turned his head for a look at the town as he rode out, seeing the spires of St Mary de Castro and the other churches. It would be his last glimpse of Leicester.

Legends and the Blue Boar Inn

One legend that sprung up after Richard's death is that the inn was formerly called the White Boar, after Richard's emblem. Upon hearing of Richard's death, the innkeeper scurried outside and hastily repainted the sign, renaming the inn the Blue Boar after the emblem of the Earl of Oxford, who had supported Henry.

A competing version of the legend says that the townspeople, incensed by the fact Richard III had stayed there, began to vandalise the inn. The innkeeper agreed to change its name to placate the unruly crowd.

Another legend is that of gold within Richard's bed. According to the story, during the reign of Elizabeth I, the innkeeper was a man named Clarke. One day as his wife prepared the bed for new guests she knocked loose a gold coin, which led to her discovery of a cache of coins. She and her husband were suddenly wealthy, which eventually led to her murder by thieves. Richard's bed was supposedly purchased from the inn and came into the possession of a manor house. However, the bed's decorative features appear to be from later than the fifteenth-century.

Description of the Blue Boar Inn

The Blue Boar was demolished in 1836 to make way for other buildings. All that is left to describe the inn is engravings of the time and a written description by Mr Goddard, an architect who examined the inn before it was destroyed.

The inn was two storeys and was half timbered with oak and plaster. Two large windows allowed in enough light to illuminate the rooms. On the second storey, there was another window, which projected out, having five panels. It was Perpendicular in style, with moulded mullions and delicate tracery. The wooden beams in the inn were decorated with painted scroll work. The beam in what is believed to have been Richard's room was adorned with a vine painted in vermillion.

Mr Goddard believed that the inn had been larger in the fifteenth century than it was in 1836, surmising that it probably consisted of two wings and a centre. Open galleries may have connected to rooms from outside staircases. The rooms in the inn were spacious and beautifully decorated.

Visiting the Inn Site Today

The Blue Boar Inn no longer exists. Today, the location is a Travelodge, where history enthusiasts can stay for a night on the same spot Richard did. The Travelodge is located on Highcross Street, which was the medieval high street. A memorial plaque is nearby.

The Bow Bridge

Perhaps no other site in Leicester is as well-known for its association with Richard as the Bow Bridge. Unfortunately, the bridge that is seen today is not the one that Richard would have ridden across, since the latter was demolished in the mid-nineteenth century. The bridge, famous as it is for two myths about Richard, was rebuilt by the city of Leicester. When it was rebuilt, it was designed as a quasi-memorial to Richard III. Adorning the ironwork of the bridge are emblems of the Tudor rose, the white rose of York, Richard's white boar and his motto, 'Loyaulte me Lie'.

Legend recounts that as Richard rode out of Leicester, his spur hit a rock on Bow Bridge, leading a woman in the crowd to call out that where his foot had hit, there would his head hit, too. After the Battle of Bosworth, Richard's corpse was slung across a horse, leaving his head to dangle over the side. The legend says that his head hit the exact stone, making the soothsayer's prediction come true.

Another myth regarding Richard is that after the Dissolution, his body was chucked into the River Soar. The exact foundation of this myth is hard to trace, but it seems to have its roots in the Dissolution. When Greyfriars Priory was dissolved, a group of citizens supposedly defaced Richard's tomb, flung his body under the Bow Bridge and used his coffin as a water trough. This theory was still being bandied about in December 1878, despite a lack of evidence from earlier chronicles, when Henry Irving wrote about it for an issue of *The Theatre*. He claimed,

The abhorrence in which Richard's memory was held by the nation had not sensibly diminished with lapse of time, and the publication of Sir Thomas More's famous book served in many quarters to add fuel to the flame. The Church of St. Mary having been destroyed, the populace of Leicester, actuated at once by their detestation of Richard's character and a belief that their conduct would win the approval of the powers that were, took the remains from the coffin, dragged them through the streets to the spot where the old woman uttered the prophecy, dashed them against the historic battlement, and finally cast them ignominiously into the Soar. A few spectators of the outrage, thinking that the body of a King of England ought to have been treated with at least a show of respect, hastily collected the bones and reinterred them in the burying-place of the Augustine Friars, on the west side of Bow Bridge, without a coffin.

Much of the blame for this myth can be laid at the feet of John Speed, a cartographer in the early seventeenth century. Speed wrote that Richard's monument had been defaced during the Dissolution, that grass and weeds now covered its previous location, that the coffin was being used as a water trough, and that Richard's body had been put under the Bow Bridge. Even though Speed discounted the rumours as hearsay, they were picked up and embellished by later writers. Even today, some people still believe the myth, even though the earlier chroniclers make no mention of it in the years following the Dissolution.

Visiting the Site of Bow Bridge Today

The site of the former Bow Bridge is located near Castle Gardens. It is about a five-minute walk from Leicester Cathedral. Watch for traffic as the area is quite busy.

Leicester Cathedral

In Richard's time, Leicester Cathedral was the parish church of St Martin. Begun by the Normans in the twelfth century, the original church was built in a cruciform shape with narrow aisles. Through the next few centuries the church was renovated and rebuilt. Richard probably never visited the interior of the church of St Martin, but he would have been familiar with the outside.

The 220-foot spire was not added until the nineteenth century, when a new tower was built. The church was renovated around the same time and magnificently restored. In 1927, the Diocese of Leicester was reinstated, and St Martin's was chosen to become the cathedral church, probably due to the church having strong ties to the Guildhall.

Leicester Cathedral's association with Richard is that it is the final resting place for this controversial king. On 26 March 2015, Richard was reinterred in this cathedral. The ceremonies were a week-long. On 22 March, the University of Leicester placed the remains into a coffin and travelled from Leicester to Bosworth, stopping at the same villages that Richard did. Returning to Leicester, his body was accompanied by a cortege and was treated with honour and respect. His entry back into the city ended at Leicester Cathedral, where his body was transferred to the church.

For three days, Richard's coffin remained in Leicester Cathedral for those who wanted to pay their respects. The service itself was not open to the general public but was broadcast live on 26 March 2015, when Richard was reburied in the presence of the Archbishop of Canterbury and senior members of other Christian denominations. On 27 March, the tomb was revealed to the public.

The tomb is made of Swaledale fossil stone and sits on a plinth of dark Kilkenny marble. A cross shape is cut deep into the stonework. Tilted slightly to incorporate the Christian belief of rising to meet the risen Jesus, the stone is adorned with an inlaid coat of arms. The coffin itself is in a brick vault underneath the tomb.

The cathedral underwent a renovation process, overseen by van Heyningen and Haward Architects, in order to prepare the space for the body of the former king. The tomb sits within the ambulatory between the Chapel of Christ the King and the sanctuary. The Nicholson Screen has been relocated to shield the tomb from the main area of worship.

Visiting Leicester Cathedral Today
Since the tomb was unveiled, Leicester Cathedral has become a busy place, as Ricardians and others interested in this medieval king file through to visit his final resting place. For information about current opening times and visits, see the cathedral's website at leicestercathedral.org/visit-us/visitor-information-faq/. At the current time, admission is free, but donations are requested.

King Richard III Visitor Centre, Leicester
The King Richard III Visitor Centre stands on the site of the medieval priory of the Greyfriars, which was where Richard was buried. The name of the centre is 'Dynasty, Death and Discovery'. Iain Gordon, the visitor centre director, said its aim is to tell the story of Richard and to 'steer the line between myth and man'. Basically, the centre hopes to help visitors learn more than just the

Shakespearean version of the king without taking sides. The story of Richard's life and his death are the 'Dynasty' and 'Death' part of the theme, while the 'Discovery' part of the attraction is the actual science behind the discovery and identification of Richard. Visitors are able to visit the actual grave site itself and view the area through the glass floor. The exhibition also explains how the discovery of Richard's body is the first genome sequencing of ancient DNA, as well as telling the story of the dig itself, through the 'Dig Diary' exhibit.

The Greyfriars Priory, Leicester

As the King Richard III Visitor Centre sits atop part of the site of the priory, it is easy to guess that nothing else remains. However, now that the centre exists to show visitors where Richard was buried, it is possible to 'visit' a bit of its history.

The priory is said to have been founded by Simon de Montfort the second in the thirteenth century. The monks – Franciscans – followed the rule of the order of St Francis of Assisi. Known as the Greyfriars after the grey habit they wore, the friars were charged with preaching to the people. After Richard's death, his body was displayed at the Church of the Annunciation of the Blessed Virgin Mary in the Newarke for several days. As this was a Lancastrian stronghold, it is likely that Henry did not want Richard buried among the tombs of his relatives. Vergil said Richard was brought to the Franciscans and was 'buryed ... without any pompe or solemne funerall'. From the pictures of his body in the grave, it appears Richard was buried in a too-small grave with his hands still tied.

The priory was dissolved during the Dissolution and sold in 1536. Through the next few centuries it was sold again and its building materials were used to create new buildings elsewhere, until finally nothing remained of this priory that once housed the body of the last Plantagenet king.

Visiting the King Richard III Visitor Centre Today

It is expected that most visitors will take about ninety minutes to get around the centre. Included in the exhibition are a full and partial facial reconstruction completed after the discovery of the body. Another feature of the exhibition is a 3D print of a replica of Richard's skeleton that illustrates the spine curvature. A temporary exhibition space will be available to explore other parts of Richard's story.

The centre also has a café and a courtyard for visitors. After visiting each part of the exhibit, it is nice to have a place to sit and reflect on what you've seen. Despite the initial controversy regarding the centre, it is currently a hotspot for tourists, so if you are planning to visit be sure to book your tickets in advance.

For more information about tickets and admission, see the centre's webpage at www.kriii.com/.

Bosworth, Leicestershire

> Give me my battle-axe in my hand,
> Set the crown of England on my head so high!
> For by Him that shope [shaped] both sea and land,
> King of England this day will I die!
>
> *The Ballad of Bosworth Field*

In 2005 a grant was awarded for a battlefield survey of Bosworth Field, and after several years of hard work the battlefield site was discovered in 2009. With the discovery of this new site for Bosworth, scholarship was turned on its head. Previously accepted facts are being re-examined in the light of archaeological evidence. It may be years before a completely accurate account of troop deployments may be deduced.

At the beginning of August, Henry Tudor set sail either from Honfleur or Harfleur bound for England. Surrounded by a group of displaced Lancastrians, he came ashore near Milford Haven in Pembrokeshire. According to Fabyan, once Henry made it ashore he dropped down and kissed the soil of England. On 11 August Richard, learning of Tudor's arrival in England, began ordering men to meet him in Leicester. After organising his troops, Richard rode out of Leicester with 'great pomp, wearing his diadem on his head'.

As Henry and his men were marching south on Watling Street towards London, Richard was heading to intercept them. He marched from Leicester and made his camp near the battlefield, either near Sutton Cheney or on Ambion Hill, as suggested by Glenn Foard and Anne Curry in *Bosworth 1485: Battlefield Rediscovered*. Vergil says Richard encouraged his troops the night before the battle and 'with many woords exhortyd them to the fyght to coome'.

As the morning of 22 August dawned, Richard awoke to face his last day. The *Croyland Chronicle* says that Richard's chaplains were not ready to celebrate Mass. Tradition has it that Richard may have taken Mass at Sutton Cheney church. It is hard to believe that a man as pious as Richard would have skipped Mass, especially on such an important day.

Henry is believed to have camped near Merevale Abbey. Later records indicate that he paid the surrounding villages for damages to their land. The next morning he moved towards Richard's army. The two armies would meet on Fenn Lane between Dadlington, Stoke Golding and Shenton. This location is about three kilometres away from Ambion Hill.

According to Vergil, after Richard assembled his men, his line was of 'wonderful length so full replenished both with footmen and horsemen that to the beholders afar it gave a terror for the multitude'. Accounts differ as to how many men each army had amassed, but Richard had the larger army.

As the two armies clashed, Richard's scouts noticed that Henry and a small group of men were moving away from the main army. Richard probably decided that killing Henry would make for a quick end to the battle and charged across the battlefield directly at Henry. Making his way into the thick of the fray, Richard managed to kill William Brandon, Henry's standard bearer, as he tried desperately to reach Henry.

At this moment, Stanley reached a decision and his troops headed for Richard, pushing him back into the marsh and forcing him to fight on foot. Richard fought valiantly but he was struck down. He fell 'like a spirited and most courageous prince … in battle on the field and not in flight'. After the discovery of his body, scientists determined that Richard had a number of injuries to his skull. The exact location where Richard was struck down is not known, although Henry issued a proclamation saying that it was at a place known as 'Sandeford'. Recent archaeological work in a field unearthed a boar badge near what was part of the medieval marsh. This fascinating find may mean that this was the location where Richard met his end.

With Richard's death, the cause was lost, and many of his men surrendered or fled. Vergil says that after his victory Henry made for the nearest rising ground. Here he gave the nobility and gentlemen 'immortal thanks' while the soldiers cried out 'God save King Henry!' It was here that Stanley took Richard's crown, which had been found in the field, and placed it on Henry's head. Today the accepted location for this event is Crown Hill. Henry then proceeded towards Leicester.

Richard's body, stripped of clothing, was slung across a horse's back. Examination of his bones shows that he was subject to many wounds. These would have been exposed for all eyes to see as he was taken back to Leicester. The *Croyland Chronicle* says that many insults had been offered to the body and it was carried to Leicester with 'insufficient humanity'. The reign of the last Plantagenet king of England was over, and the reign of the Tudors had begun.

Sutton Cheney Church

The church of St James at Sutton Cheney has stood here since the thirteenth century. It is so peaceful that it seems frozen in time. The church embraces the tradition that Richard heard Mass for the last time within its walls and has allowed the Richard III Foundation to erect memorials to the fallen king. Each kneeler in the church has an emblem of Richard III and was provided by the foundation. Also provided by the foundation is the memorial plaque on the wall. Each August there is a memorial service held on the Sunday that falls closest to 22 August.

The exterior of the church is largely the same as it was in the fifteenth century. The addition to the tower was done afterwards. Visitors to the church are welcome. For more information about visiting the church, see the website at suttoncheneyvillagehall. yolasite.com/the-battlefield-church.php. Postcode: CV13 0AG.

Bosworth Battlefield Heritage Centre, Leicestershire

The Bosworth Battlefield Heritage Centre is one of the best interactive museums I have had the privilege of visiting. The centre was the country's first battlefield interpretation site, and its dedication to educating people about the battle shines through. The material is presented in such a way that both adults and children get a clear idea of this confusing battle.

Four characters lead you through each exhibit, telling the story of the battle from different viewpoints. An exhibition of weaponry will fascinate adults and children and helps one make sense of what type of weapons the soldiers were facing.

One area not to be missed is the exhibition of the artefacts found around the battle area. The Bosworth Boar badge and other artefacts are on display in the museum. The exhibit also tells the story of how the battle site was located.

After you leave the museum area, walk to the top of the hill. Here a memorial sundial commemorates the battle and all the men who died. There are three chairs at the sundial. The two larger chairs are for Henry and Richard, while the smaller chair is for Stanley. From atop the hill you will also have excellent views of the surrounding countryside and the battlefield. Two-kilometre guided tours of the Battlefield Trail are available every weekend. For the fit, special twelve-kilometre walks of the battlefield are available to be pre-booked in the summer and autumn months. The Tithe Barn restaurant is on-site for refreshments after either of the hikes.

The area where the boar badge was found is on private land and is not accessible, although a public footpath is nearby. The best way to see the locations of the new battle sites is to take one of the walks. Once you have explored the area, the nearby St James's church at Dadlington is another good place to visit, as it is where many of the dead at Bosworth were buried.

For more information about the centre's opening times and prices, see the website at www.bosworthbattlefield.com/welcome/visit or call +44 (0) 1455290429. Postcode: CV13 0AD.

List of Illustrations

York family tree. (© Amy Licence and Amberley Publishing)
Map of England. (© Kristie Dean and Amberley Publishing, design by Thomas Bohm, User design)

1. Richard III, King of England. (Courtesy of Ripon Cathedral)
2. Edward IV. (Courtesy of Ripon Cathedral)
3. Anne Neville with her husband Richard III. (Courtesy of Yale University Art Gallery, Edwin Austin Abbey collection)
4. Fotheringhay. (© Kristie Dean)
5. Church of St Mary the Virgin and All Saints, Fotheringhay. (© Kristie Dean)
6. Ludlow. (© Kristie Dean, by permission of Ludlow Castle)
7. Ludlow Castle plan. (With permission of Brian Byron and Logaston Press from *Ludlow Castle: Its History and Buildings*; eds Ron Shoesmith and Andy Johnson)
8. Richard, Duke of York, stained glass at St Laurence's church, Ludlow. (© Shaun Ward)
9. Wijk bij Duurstede castle. (Arch, Wikimedia Commons, http://commons.wikimedia.org/wiki/File:Kasteel_Duurstede_pano.JPG)
10. Sluis Belfry. (© Kristie Dean)
11. Gruuthuse Museum. (© Kristie Dean)
12. Bruges Belfry. (© Kristie Dean)
13. Église Notre Dame de Calais. (© Kristie Dean)
14. Canterbury Cathedral. (© Adrian Fletcher, www.paradoxplace.com)
15. Greenwich. (© Kristie Dean)

16. Chichele's Tower exterior. (© Kristie Dean)
17. Chichele's Tower interior. (© Kristie Dean, with permission of Lambeth Palace)
18. Middleham Castle. (© Studio 8)
19. The Church of St Mary and St Alkelda, Middleham. (© Kristie Dean)
20. Pontefract Castle. (© Kristie Dean, by permission of Wakefield Council)
21. Walmgate Bar. (© Kristie Dean)
22. Micklegate Bar. (© Kristie Dean)
23. Holy Trinity Church, Micklegate. (© Kristie Dean)
24. York Minster. (© Kristie Dean)
25. Cawood Castle. (© Kristie Dean, with permission of National Trust)
26. Relic from Abbey of Stratford Langthorne. (© Kristie Dean, courtesy of West Ham Parish Church)
27. Margate. (© Kristie Dean)
28. Bury St Edmunds Great Gate. (© Kristie Dean)
29. Bury St Edmunds Norman Tower. (© Kristie Dean)
30. Walsingham Abbey entrance. (© Kristie Dean)
31. Norwich Halls. (© Kristie Dean, with permission of Norwich City Council)
32. Blackfriars' Hall, Norwich. (© Autumn Speegle, with permission of Norwich City Council)
33. Alnwick Gate, Norwich. (© George Plunkett)
34. Castle Rising, Norfolk. (Wikimedia Commons, User PawelMM)
35. Crowland Abbey. (© Kristie Dean)
36. Sudeley Castle. (© Kristie Dean, with permission of Sudeley Castle)
37. King's Lynn quay. (© Kristie Dean)
38. Veere. (© Kristie Dean)
39. Vlissingen. (© Kristie Dean)
40. Sandal Castle *c.* 1150. (Courtesy of Wakefield Council)
41. Sandal Castle. (© Kristie Dean)
42. West side of Spon Gate, Coventry, 1817. Engraving. (With permission of Rob Orland, Historic Coventry)
43. St Mary's Priory, Coventry. (© Kristie Dean)
44. Tapestry from St Mary's Guildhall, Coventry. (© St Mary's Guildhall, Coventry)
45. Tredington Church. (© Kristie Dean)
46. Tewkesbury Abbey. (Image taken by Kristie Dean, © Vicar and Churchwardens of Tewkesbury Abbey and used with permission)
47. Tewkesbury Abbey. (© Kristie Dean)
48. Lower Lode Lane, Tewkesbury. (© Kristie Dean)
49. Bloody Meadow, Tewkesbury. (© Kristie Dean)
50. Barnard Castle. (© Kristie Dean)

73. Reading Abbey. (© Kristie Dean, with permission of Reading Borough Council)

74. Magdalen College, Oxford. (© Kristie Dean, used with permission of Magdalen College)

75. Map of Gloucester, 1500. (*A History of the County of Gloucester: Volume 4: The City of Gloucester*, ed. N. M. Herbert. Accessed with permission of Victoria County History via British History Online)

76. Gloucester Cathedral cloisters. (© Kristie Dean, with permission of Gloucester Cathedral)

77. Warwick Castle. (© Kristie Dean)

78. Nottingham Castle Gatehouse. (© Kristie Dean)

79. Nottingham Castle middle bailey. (© Kristie Dean)

80. Gainsborough Old Hall. (© Kristie Dean)

81. Lincoln Medieval Bishop's Palace. (© Kristie Dean)

82. Exchequer Gate and Lincoln Cathedral. (Wikimedia Commons, user Poliphilo)

83. King's House, Salisbury. (© Kristie Dean)

84. Salisbury Cathedral. (© Kristie Dean)

85. Salisbury Cathedral plan. (© Salisbury Cathedral, with kind permission)

86. Salisbury Cathedral, Sir John Cheyne. (© Kristie Dean)

87. Entrance to Bishop's Palace, Exeter. (© Mike Smith)

88. King's College, Cambridge. (© Kristie Dean)

89. Durham Cathedral. (Wikimedia Commons, Alexbouditsky, http://commons.wikimedia.org/wiki/File:Durham_Cathedral_2011.jpg)

90. Scarborough Castle. (© Kristie Dean)

91. Plan of Leicester Castle and surrounding areas. (Used with permission of University of Leicester and My Leicestershire History, www.myleicestershire.org.uk)

92. Crypt of former priory church. (© Kristie Dean, used with courtesy of Museum of the Order of St John, London)

93. Magazine Gate, Leicester. (© Kristie Dean)

94. Remains of the church of the Annunciation of the Blessed Virgin Mary in the Newarke, Leicester. (© De Montfort University)

95. Leicester ambulatory. (© van Heyningen and Haward Architects)

96. Leicester tomb. (© van Heyningen and Haward Architects)

97. Sutton Cheney church. (© Kristie Dean)

98. Location where the boar badge was found. (© Kristie Dean, used with permission of the landowners through the Battle Centre)

Further Reading

A Collection of Ordinances and Regulations for the Government of the Royal Household (London: Society of Antiquaries, 1790)

Armstrong, C. A. J. (ed.), *The Usurpation of Richard III: Dominic Mancini* (Oxford: Clarendon Press, 1969)

Ashdown-Hill, J., *The Last Days of Richard III and the Fate of His DNA* (Stroud: The History Press, 2013)

Ashdown-Hill, J., *The Third Plantagenet: George, Duke of Clarence, Richard III's Brother* (Stroud: The History Press, 2014)

Attreed, L. C., *The York House Books: 1461–1490, Volume One: House Books One and Two/Four* (Alan Sutton for Richard III and Yorkist History Trust, 1991)

Baldwin, D., *Richard III* (Stroud: Amberley, 2013)

Binns, J., *Scarborough's Heroes, Rogues and Eccentrics: A Biographical Journey Through Scarborough's Past* (Pickering: Blackthorn Press, 2010)

Blatherwick, S. and Richard Bluer, *Great Houses, Moats and Mills on the South Bank of the Thames: Medieval and Tudor Southwark and Totherhithe* (London: Museum of London Archaeology, 2009)

Bruce, J. (ed.), *History of the Arrival of Edward the Fourth in England and the Final Recovery of His Kingdom from Henry the Sixth, AD 1471* (London: Camden Society, 1838)

Bumpus, T. F., *The Cathedrals of England and Wales* (London: T. Werner Laurie Ltd., 1929)

Burke, T., *The Streets of London* (London: B. T. Batsford Ltd., 1940)

Burley, P., Michael Elliot and Harvey Watson, *The Battles of St Albans* (Barnsley: Pen and Sword Books Ltd., 2007)

Burne, A. H., *The Battlefields of England* (London: Greenhill Books, 1950)

Butler, L., *Sandal Castle, Wakefield: The History and Archaeology of a Medieval Castle* (Wakefield Historical Publications, 1991)

Calendar of the Patent Rolls, Preserved in the Public Records Office: Edward IV, Edward V, Richard III, AD 1476–1485 (London: His Majesty's Stationery Office, 1901)

Caley, J., Sir Henry Ellis and Bulkeley Bandinel (eds) (William Dugdale) *Monasticon Anglicanum: A New Edition: Volume the Sixth, Part One* (London: T. G. March, 1849)

Castor, H., *Blood and Roses: One Family's Struggle and Triumph During the Tumultuous Wars of the Roses* (New York: HarperCollins, 2006)

Cheetham, A., *The Life and Times of Richard III* (New York: Welcome Rain, 1998)

Clark, D., *Barnet –1471: Death of a Kingmaker* (Barnsley: Pen and Sword Books Ltd., 2007)

Colvin, H. M. (ed.), *The History of the King's Works: Volume I, The Middle Ages* (London: Her Majesty's Stationery Office, 1963)

Colvin, H. M. (ed.), *The History of the King's Works: Volume II, The Middle Ages* (London: Her Majesty's Stationery Office, 1963)

Cosman, M. P., *Medieval Holidays and Festivals: A Calendar of Celebrations* (New York: Charles Scribner's Sons, 1981)

Coss, P., *The Lady in Medieval England 1000–1500* (Stroud: Sutton Publishing, 1998)

Crawford, A. (ed.), *Letters of the Queens of England* (Stroud: Sutton Publishing, 1994)

Crawford, A., *The Yorkists: The History of a Dynasty* (London: Continuum, 2007)

Davies, J. (ed.), *An English Chronicle of the Reigns of Richard II, Henry IV, Henry V, and Henry VI: Written Before the Year 1471* (Oxford: Camden Society, 1856)

Davies, R. (ed.), *Extracts from the Municipal Records of the City of York, During the Reigns of Edward IV, Edward V, and Richard III: With Notes and an Appendix, Containing Some Accounts of the Celebration of Corpus Christi Festival at York* (London: J. B. Nichols and Son, 1843)

Dean, G., *Medieval York* (Stroud: The History Press, 2008)

Dickens, A. G. (ed.), *The Courts of Europe: Politics, Patronage and Royalty, 1400–1800* (New York: Greenwich House, 1977)

Dockray, K. and Peter Hammond, *Richard III: From Contemporary Chronicles, Letters and Records* (Fonthill Media, 2013)

Edwards, R., *The Itinerary of King Richard III: 1483–1485* (London: Alan Sutton Publishing for The Richard III Society, 1983)

Ellis, H. (ed.), *The New Chronicles of England and France in Two Parts: By Robert Fabyan* (London: for F. C. and J. Rivington, et al., 1811)

Ellis, H. (ed.), *Three Books of Polydore Vergil's English History: Comprising the Reigns of Henry VI, Edward IV, and Richard III* (London: Camden Society, 1844)

Evans, M., *The Death of Kings: Royal Deaths in Medieval England* (New York: Hambledon Continuum, 2003)

Foard, G. and Anne Curry, *Bosworth 1485: A Battlefield Rediscovered* (Oxford: Oxbow Books, 2013)

Gairdner, J., *History of the Life and reign of Richard III of England* (London: Longmans, Green and Co., 1879)

Gairdner, J. (ed.), *Letters and Papers Illustrative of the Reigns of Richard III and Henry VII: Volume 1* (London: Longman et al., 1861)

Gairdner, J. (ed.), *Three Fifteenth-Century Chronicles* (London: Camden Society, 1880)

Gairdner, J. (ed.), *The Paston Letters, A.D. 1422–1509: Volume II* (London: Chatto and Windus, 1904)

Giles, J. (ed.), *The Chronicles of the White Rose of York* (London: James Bohn, 1864)

Gillingham, J. (ed.), *Richard III: A Medieval Kingship* (London: Collins and Brown Limited, 1993)

Goodchild, S., *Tewkesbury: Eclipse of the House of Lancaster – 1471* (Barnsley: Pen and Sword Books Ltd., 2005)

Gristwood, S., *Blood Sisters: The Women Behind the Wars of the Roses* (London: HarperPress, 2012)

Hall, E., *Hall's Chronicle: The History of England During the Reign of Henry the Fourth and the Succeeding Monarchs, to the End of the Reign of Henry the Eighth* (London: Johnson et al., 1809)

Halsted, C. A., *Richard III as Duke of Gloucester and King of England: Vol I* (London: Longman et al., 1844)

Halsted, C. A., *Richard III as Duke of Gloucester and King of England: Vol II* (London: Longman et al., 1844)

Hammond, P. W., Anne F. Sutton and Livia Visser-Fuchs, *The Reburial of Richard, Duke of York, 21–30 July 1476* (Richard III Society, 1996)

Harris, M. D., *The Coventry Leet Book* (London: Kegan Paul, Trench, Trübner, 1907)

Hastings, J. M., *St Stephen's Chapel* (Cambridge: Cambridge University Press, 1955)

Hearne, T. (ed.), *The Itinerary of John Leland the Antiquary, in Nine Volumes* (Oxford: for James Fletcher and Joseph Pote, 1744)

Hicks, M., *The Wars of the Roses: 1455–1485* (Oxford: Osprey, 2003)

Higginbotham, S., *The Woodvilles* (Stroud: The History Press, 2012)

Hilton, L., *Queens Consort: England's Medieval Queens* (London: Weidenfeld and Nicolson, 2008)

Hindson, A. B. (ed.), *Calendar of State Papers and Manuscripts in the Archives and Collections of Milan: 1385–1618* (London: His Majesty's Stationery Office, 1912)

Holinshed, R., *Holinshed's Chronicles of England, Scotland and Ireland in Six Volumes: Vol. 3* (London: J. Johnson et al., 1808)

Horrox, R. and P. W. Hammond (eds) *British Library Harleian Manuscript 433: Volume One* (Gloucester: Alan Sutton for Richard III Society, 1979)

Horrox, R. and P. W. Hammond (eds) *British Library Harleian Manuscript 433: Volume Two* (Gloucester: Alan Sutton for Richard III Society, 1980)

Hull, L., *Britain's Medieval Castles* (Westport, Connecticut: Praeger, 2006)

Ingram, M., *Battle Story: Bosworth 1485* (Stroud: The History Press, 2012)

Jones, M. and Malcolm G. Underwood, *The King's Mother: Lady Margaret Beaufort: Countess of Richmond and Derby* (Cambridge: Cambridge University Press, 1992)

Jones, N., *Tower: An Epic History of the Tower of London* (London: Hutchinson, 2011)

Kelsall, J., *Humphrey, Duke of Gloucester, 1391–1447* (St Albans: The Fraternity of the Friends of St Albans Abbey, 2013)

Kendall, P. M. and Vincent Ilardi, *Dispatches of Milanese Ambassadors in France and Burgundy: Vol I: 1450–1460* (Athens, Ohio: Ohio University Press, 1970)

Kendall, P. M. and Vincent Ilardi, *Dispatches of Milanese Ambassadors in France and Burgundy: Vol II: 1460–1461* (Athens, Ohio: Ohio University Press, 1970)

Kendall, P. M., *Richard the Third* (Garden City: Anchor Books, 1965)

Kendall, P. M., *The Yorkist Age: Daily Life During the Wars of the Roses* (New York: W. W. Norton and Company, Inc., 1962)

Kingsford, C. L., *Chronicles of London* (Oxford: Clarendon Press, 1905)

Kingsford, C. L., *The Stonor Letters and Papers; ed. for the Royal Historical Society, from the Original Documents in the Public Records Office* (Ann Arbor: University of Michigan Library, 2006)

Kirby, J. L. (ed.), *Calendar of Signet Letters of Henry IV and Henry V (1399–1422)* (London: Her Majesty's Stationery Office, 1978)

Langley, P. and Michael Jones, *The King's Grave: The Search for Richard III* (Great Britain: John Murray, 2013)

Legg, L. G. W. (ed.), *English Coronation Records* (Westminster: Archibald Constable and Company Ltd., 1901)

Leyser, H., *Medieval Women: A Social History of Women in England 450–1500* (London: Weidenfeld and Nicholson, 2002)

Licence, A., *Cecily Neville: Mother of Kings* (Stroud: Amberley Publishing, 2014)

Licence, A., *Richard III: The Road to Leicester* (Stroud: Amberley Publishing, 2014)

Lulofs, M., 'King Edward in Exile', *The Ricardian* (March 1974)

Madden, H. E. (ed.), *The Cely Papers: Selections from the Correspondence and Memoranda of the Cely Family, AD 1475–1488* (New York: Longmans, Green and Company, 1900)

More, T., ed. J. R. Lumby, *The History of King Richard III* (Cambridge: Cambridge University Press, 1883)

Morris, M., *Castle: A History of the Buildings that Shaped Medieval Britain* (London: Windmill Books, 2003)

Mortimer, I., *The Time Traveller's Guide to Medieval England: A Handbook for Visitors to the Fourteenth Century* (London: The Bodley Head, 2008)

Mount, T., *Everyday Life in Medieval London: From the Anglo-Saxons to the Tudors* (Stroud: Amberley Publishing, 2014)

Myers, A. R. (ed.) and David C. Douglas (general ed.), *English Historical Documents, Volume IV: 1327–1485* (New York: New York Press, 1969)

Myers, A. R. (ed.), *The Household of Edward IV* (Manchester: University of Manchester, 1959)

Newman, P. B., *Daily Life in the Middle Ages* (Jefferson, N. C.: McFarland and Company, 2001)

Nicolas, N. H. and Edward Tyrrell (eds), *A Chronicle of London, From 1089 to 1483; Written in the Fifteenth Century* (London: Longman et al.)

Nicolas, N. H. (ed.), *Privy Purse Expenses of Elizabeth of York: Wardrobe Accounts of Edward IV* (London: William Pickering, 1830)

Norton, Elizabeth, *Margaret Beaufort: Mother of the Tudor Dynasty* (Stroud: Amberley, 2011)

O'Regan, M., 'Richard III and the Monks of Durham', *The Ricardian* (March 1978)

Pollard, A. J. (ed.), *The North of England in the Age of Richard III* (New York: St Martin's Press, 1996)

Pollard, A. J., *Richard III and the Princes in the Tower* (Godalming: Bramley Books, 1997)

Pronay, N. and John Cox (eds), *The Crowland Chronicle Continuations: 1459–1486* (London: Richard III and Yorkist History Trust, 1986)

Pryor, F., *Britain in the Middle Ages: An Archaeological History* (London: HarperCollins, 2006)

Reeves, C., *Pleasures and Pastimes in Medieval England* (Oxford: Oxford University Press, 1998)

Ross, C., *Edward IV* (Berkeley and Los Angeles: University of California Press, 1974)

Ross, C., *Richard III* (Berleley and Los Angeles: University of California Press, 1981)

Rous, J., *This Rol Was Laburd and Finished by Master John Rows of Warrewyk* (London: William Pickering, 1845)

Santiuste, D., *Edward IV and the Wars of the Roses* (Barnsley: Pen and Sword Military, 2010)

Schama, S., *A History of Britain 1: 3000 BC – AD 1603, At the Edge of the World?* (BBC Worldwide Ltd., 2003)

Scoble, A. R. (ed.), *The Memoirs of Philip De Commines, Lord of Argenton: Containing the Histories of Louis XI and Charles VIII, King of France and Charles the Bold, Duke of Burgundy, Volume I* (London: Henry G. Bohn, 1855)

Scofield, C. L., *The Life and Reign of Edward the Fourth: King of England and of France and Lord of Ireland: Volumes One and Two* (Frank Cass and Co. Ltd., 1967)

Seward, Desmond, *The Wars of the Roses: Through the Lives of Five Men and Women of the Fifteenth Century* (New York: Penguin Books, 1995)

Seymour, R., *A Survey of the Cities of London and Westminster, Borough of Southwark and Parts Adjacent, Volume II* (London: J. Read, 1735)

Singman, J. L., *The Middle Ages: Everyday Life in Medieval Europe* (New York: Sterling, 1999)

Steane, J., *The Archaeology of the Medieval English Monarchy* (London: B. T. Batsford Ltd., 1993)

Stevenson, W. H., *Calendar of the Records of the Corporation of Gloucester* (Gloucester: John Bellows, 1893)

Sutton, A. and P. W. Hammond, *The Coronation of Richard III: The Extant Documents* (Gloucester: Alan Sutton, 1983)

Tames, R., *A Traveller's History of Oxford* (New York: Interlink Books, 2003)

Tatton-Brown, T., *Great Cathedrals of Britain* (London: BBC Books, 1989)

Thomas, A. H., *The Great Chronicle of London* (Alan Sutton Publishing, 1983)

Visser-Fuchs, L., 'Richard Was Late', *The Ricardian* (December 1999)

Wilkinson, J., *Richard: The Young King To Be* (Stroud: Amberley Publishing, 2008)

Wolffe, B., *Henry VI* (New Haven and London: Yale University Press, 1981)

Woolgar, C. M., *The Great Household in Late Medieval England* (New Haven and London: Yale University Press, 1999)

Young, P. and John Adair, *Hastings to Culloden: Battles of Britain* (Stroud: Sutton Publishing Limited, 1996)

Guidebooks

Barnard Castle
Castle Rising
Coventry Cathedral and Priory
Durham Cathedral
Exeter Cathedral
Gainsborough Old Hall
Lincoln Cathedral: The Story So Far
Medieval Bishops' Palace, Lincoln
Nottingham Castle
Pontefract Castle: Key to the North
Scarborough Castle
St George's Chapel: Windsor Castle
Tewkesbury Abbey
The Palace of Westminster: Official Guide
Walsingham Abbey
Westminster Abbey
York Minster Guidebook

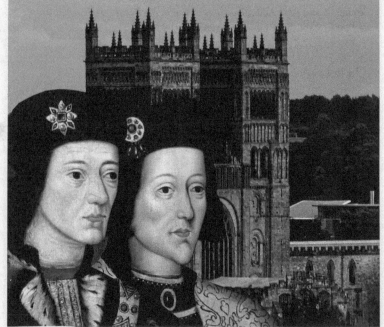